Tenth International Workshop on Natural Language Processing for Social Media (SocialNLP 2022)

Online
14 - 15 July 2022

ISBN: 978-1-7138-5640-5

Printed from e-media with permission by:

Curran Associates, Inc.
57 Morehouse Lane
Red Hook, NY 12571

CURRAN ASSOCIATES INC. proceedings.com

Some format issues inherent in the e-media version may also appear in this print version.

Printed with permission by Curran Associates, Inc. (2022)

For permission requests, please contact the Association for Computational Linguistics at the address below.

Association for Computational Linguistics
209 N. Eighth Street
Stroudsburg, Pennsylvania 18360

Phone: 1-570-476-8006
Fax: 1-570-476-0860

acl@aclweb.org

Additional copies of this publication are available from:

Curran Associates, Inc.
57 Morehouse Lane
Red Hook, NY 12571 USA
Phone: 845-758-0400
Fax: 845-758-2633
Email: curran@proceedings.com
Web: www.proceedings.com

SocialNLP 2022

The Tenth International Workshop on Natural Language Processing for Social Media

Proceedings of the Workshop

July 14-15, 2022

Order copies of this and other ACL proceedings from:

Association for Computational Linguistics (ACL)
209 N. Eighth Street
Stroudsburg, PA 18360
USA
Tel: +1-570-476-8006
Fax: +1-570-476-0860
acl@aclweb.org

SocialNLP 2022@NAACL Chairs' Welcome

Happy 10th Anniversary to SocialNLP!

It is our great pleasure to welcome you to the Tenth Workshop on Natural Language Processing for Social Media-SocialNLP 2022, associated with NAACL 2022. SocialNLP is an inter-disciplinary area of natural language processing (NLP) and social computing. We hold SocialNLP twice a year: one in the NLP venue, the other in the associated venue such as those for web technology or artificial intelligence. This year the other version has been successfully held in conjunction with TheWebConf 2022 (formerly WWW), and we are very happily looking forward to the NLP version in NAACL 2022. We are very glad that the number of submissions to this year's workshop keeps increasing, and the submissions themselves were still of high quality with the accepted threshold of 3.33 (maximum 5), which again leads to a competitive selection process. We received submissions from Asia, Europe, and the United States. Considering the review process is rigorous and we want to encourage authors to participate in the workshop, we accepted 8 oral papers. These exciting papers include novel and practical topics for researchers working on NLP for social media, such as bias mitigation, domain transfer, and dataset constructed for the newly emerged research problems. We believe they will benefit our research community.

On this 10th anniversary, we would like to share our happiness and celebrate the success together with our community members with the special speaker reunion event. Most of our previous invited speakers, including Prof. Saif Muhammad from National Research Council Canada, Prof. Yohei Seki from University of Tsukuba, Prof. Tim Weninger and Mr. Nicholas Botzer from University of Notre Dame, Prof. Sonjanya Poria from Singapore University of Technology and Design, Prof. Cristian Danescu-Niculescu-Mizil from Cornell University, Prof. Dan Goldwasser from Purdue University, Dr. Ian Stewart from University of Michigan, and Prof. Thamar Solorio from University of Houston will participate in this event and give an insightful talk. We deeply appreciate their support. Their talk should reveal the past and the future of related research topics to participants in the hope of encouraging more researchers to join us. We couple each invited talk with one oral paper presentation to encourage attendees to (virtually) attend both sessions to have more discussions with outstanding researchers.

Putting together SocialNLP 2022 was a team effort. We first thank the authors for providing the quality content of the program. We are grateful to the program committee members, who worked very hard in reviewing papers and providing feedback to authors. Finally, we especially thank the NAACL Workshop chairs Prof. Dan Goldwasser, Dr. Yunyao Li, and Dr. Ashish Sabharwal for helping us with all the complicated logistics for this year's online version.

We hope you enjoy the workshop and keep supporting us!

Organizers

Lun-Wei Ku, Academia Sincia, Taiwan
Cheng-Te Li, National Cheng Kung University, Taiwan
Yu-Che Tsai, National Taiwan University, Taiwan
Wei-Yao Wang, National Yang Ming Chiao Tung University, Taiwan

Organizing Committee

Organizers

Lun-Wei Ku, Academia Sinica
Cheng-Te Li, National Cheng Kung University
Yu-Che Tsai, National Taiwan University
Wei-Yao Wang, National Yang Ming Chiao Tung University

Program Committee

Program Committee

Silvio Amir, CCIS, Northeastern University
Yung-Chun Chang, Graduate Institute of Data Science, Taipei Medical University
Zhiyu Chen, University of California, Santa Barbara
Monojit Choudhury, Microsoft Research
Min-Yuh Day, Tamkang University
David Jurgens, University of Michigan
Tsung-Ting Kuo, University of California San Diego
Chuan-Jie Lin, National Taiwan Ocean University
Manuel Montes, INAOE
Derek Ruths, McGill University
Saurav Sahay, Intel Labs
Yohei Seki, University of Tsukuba
Steven Wilson, Oakland University
Shih-Hung Wu, Chaoyang University of Technology
Liang-Chih Yu, Yuan Ze University
Zhe Zhang, Meta AI
Huaping Zhang, Beijing Institute of Technology

Keynote Talk: Facilitating Citizens' Voices on Social Media to Address Regional Issues

Yohei Seki
University of Tsukuba

Abstract: I will talk about our research on extracting issues and evaluations for the administrative aspects of local governments from the analysis of citizens' voices on social media. Specifically, I will explain our method of collecting and analyzing citizens' voices from Twitter on a city-by-city basis and analyze how the actions of local governments in Japan changed citizens' voices. As an applied case study, I will also present our work on understanding the mood of citizens' interest for the region and our analysis of citizens' opinions on childcare and restaurant take-out services in the COVID-19 disaster.

Bio: Dr. Yohei Seki is currently an associate professor, Faculty of Library, Information and Media Science, University of Tsukuba, Japan. He received his Ph.D. degree in Informatics from the Graduate University for Advanced Studies (SOKENDAI) in 2005. He was visiting scholars at Columbia University in 2008 and at National University of Singapore in 2018, respectively. His main research interests are natural language processing, sentiment analysis, and information access. He leads sentiment analysis work as one of co-organizers in NTCIR multilingual opinion analysis task from 2006 to 2010. He received best paper award at CEA 2014 and nominated best paper award runner-up at ICADL 2020. He recently published international standards for smart cities ISO/IEC 30146 in 2019 and ISO/IEC 30145-3 in 2020 as co-editor.

Keynote Talk: Conversational Flow and Moral Judgment on Reddit

Tim Weninger and Nicholas Botzer
University of Notre Dame

Abstract: The focus of this talk will revolve around two works that both leverage the large amount of conversational data that is available on Reddit. In the first work we will look at how conversations flow across entities in discussions threads on Reddit. In the study of social networks the typical perspective is to view users as nodes and concepts as flowing through user-nodes within the social network. In this work we take the opposite perspective: we extract and organize group discussion into a concept space we call an entity graph where concepts and entities are static and human communicators move about the concept space via their conversations.In the second work, we will look at how users cast moral judgements of each other by extracting and analyzing self-contained labels from the subreddit /r/AmITheAsshole. These labels allow us to train a BERT classifier to determine when someone is casting a moral judgment on another.

Bio: Tim Weninger is the Frank M. Freimann Collegiate Associate Professor of Engineering in the Department of Computer Science and Engineering in the College of Engineering at the University of Notre Dame. His research is at the intersection of machine learning, network science and social media. Generally speaking, his work is to uncover how humans consume and curate information.
Nicholas Botzer is a 5th year PhD student at the University of Notre Dame advised by Tim Weninger. His interests are focused in computational social science, natural language processing, and machine learning. His current research focuses on how conversations form online and how people make moral judgements of others.

Keynote Talk: Ethics Sheets for Social NLP: Task-Specific Guides to Responsible Research

Saif Mohammad
National Research Council Canada

Abstract: Several high-profile events, such as the mass testing of emotion recognition systems on vulnerable sub-populations and using question answering systems to make moral judgments, have highlighted how technology will often lead to more adverse outcomes for those that are already marginalized. At issue here are not just individual systems and datasets, but also the AI tasks themselves. In this talk, I make a case for thinking about ethical considerations not just at the level of individual models and datasets, but also at the level of AI tasks. I will present a new form of such an effort, Ethics Sheets for AI Tasks, dedicated to fleshing out the assumptions and ethical considerations hidden in how a task is commonly framed and in the choices we make regarding the data, method, and evaluation. I will also present a template for ethics sheets with 50 ethical considerations, using the task of emotion recognition as a running example. Ethics sheets are a mechanism to engage with and document ethical considerations before building datasets and systems. Similar to survey articles, a small number of ethics sheets can serve numerous researchers and developers. I will wrap things up with concrete steps for students and early researchers.

Bio: Dr. Saif M. Mohammad is a Senior Research Scientist at the National Research Council Canada (NRC). He received his Ph.D. in Computer Science from the University of Toronto. Before joining NRC, Saif was a Research Associate at the Institute of Advanced Computer Studies at the University of Maryland, College Park. His research interests are in Computational Linguistics and Natural Language Processing (NLP), especially Lexical Semantics, Emotions in Language, Sentiment Analysis, Computational Creativity, Fairness in NLP, Psycholinguistics, and Information Visualization. He has published over 100 scientific articles (journal articles, book chapters, and conference papers). He has served in various capacities at prominent journals and conferences, including: action editor for Computational Linguistics, senior action editor for ACL Rolling review, chair of the Canada–UK symposium on Ethics in AI, co-chair of SemEval 2017-19 (the largest platform for semantic evaluations), workshops co-chair for ACL 2020, co-organizer of WASSA 2017 and 2018 (a sentiment analysis workshop), and area chair for ACL, NAACL, and EMNLP (in the areas of sentiment analysis, lexical semantics, and fairness in NLP). His team developed a sentiment analysis system which ranked first in shared task competitions. His word–emotion resources, such as the NRC Emotion Lexicon, are used for analyzing affect in text. His work has garnered media attention, including articles in Time, SlashDot, LiveScience, io9, The Physics arXiv Blog, PC World, and Popular Science.

Keynote Talk: Linguistic Bias as a Window into Social Attitudes

Ian Stewart
University of Michigan

Abstract: When considering the presence of bias in language models, NLP researchers have generally treated it as a problem to be solved, e.g. removing the association between nurse and woman in word embeddings. Alternately, researchers can use the bias in language models as a window into social attitudes expressed through user-generated text. While promising, such bias as a window work should be careful to define the appropriate task and construct for the research question at hand. I present work from three studies that address linguistic bias in user-generated text written in everyday settings, including a controlled experiment, online blog posts, and college course reviews. Using supervised classification, word embeddings, and domain-specific lexicons, we identify specific stereotypes (e.g. associating Black people with basketball) and general attitudes (describing female professors as generally nicer) that are directed toward minority groups. Such analyses of social attitudes demonstrate the wealth of information that exists in "biased" language models, as well as a reminder of the social inequality that is constructed through everyday communication.

Bio: Ian is interested in building natural language processing models that incorporate social information to improve the writing experience for system users. Ian is also interested in computational social science to better understand the benefits and limitations of discussions on social media platforms such as Twitter and Reddit.

Keynote Talk: New Avenues in Dialogue Systems

Soujanya Poria
Singapore University of Technology and Design

Abstract: Lately, the topic of dialogue systems has witnessed a significant surge in research interest due to the vast availability of conversational data on the Web and elsewhere. Dialogue systems also have wide applications in healthcare, e-commerce, and many other sectors. However, the progress in this research area has mostly been limited to the tasks of — (a) dialogue generation using seq2seq frameworks; (b) dialogue act classification, (c) slot filling, and (d) dialogue state tracking. While these tasks are of prime importance when creating a dialogue system, one should not overlook the other aspects of natural language such as emotions, and causal and commonsense reasoning as they are equally vital to attain a superior dialogue understanding. To this end, in this talk, I will explain some of the emerging and challenging dialogue-level tasks related to the above-mentioned aspects — (a) (multimodal) emotion recognition in conversations, (b) empathetic dialogue generation, and (c) recognizing emotion cause in conversations, and (d) commonsense inference in dialogues. Further, I will present strong baselines to address these tasks and shed light on the numerous associated challenges when you attempt to solve these tasks using today's Language Models.

Bio: Soujanya Poria is an assistant professor of Computer Science at the Singapore University of Technology and Design (SUTD), Singapore. He holds a Ph.D. degree in Computer Science from the University of Stirling, UK. Soujanya was a recipient of the prestigious early career research award called 'NTU Presidential Postdoctoral Fellowship' in 2018. Before taking up the presidential fellowship position at the NTU, he was a scientist at the A*STAR and the Temasek Laboratory, NTU. He is also PI of multiple academic and industrial grants with the amount totaling US$2,500,000. Hehasco$

$authoredmorethan 100 papers, publishedintop-tierconferencesandjournalssuchasACL, EMNLP, AAAI, NAACL, Neurocomputing$
$STAR, Singaporeasaseniorscientist. Hewasanareaco-chairatseveralACL, NAACL, andEMNLPconferences, andapublicity$
$SEM2019. HeservedasaseniorPCmemberatseveralAAAI, andIJCAIconferences, andoftenserveasaPCmemberinreputedconf$
$indexis58. Soujanyaisarecipientofseveralacademicawardssuchasthe IEEECIMoutstandingpaperaward, andtheACMICM$

Keynote Talk: TBD

Cristian Danescu-Niculescu-Mizil
Cornell University

Bio: Online communication is gaining a central role in our society and the opportunities for more and more people to interact online in potentially fruitful ways continue to grow. Sadly, online interactions have also acquired a reputation for not going well: this extends all the way from unproductive and inefficient online collaboration to outright antagonism and harassment in online discussions. During his fellowship, Cristian Danescu-Niculescu-Mizil will take a mixed-methods approach to explore the benefits and potential risks of using novel computational tools to increase the quality of online discussions.
Danescu-Niculescu-Mizil is an associate professor in the information science department at Cornell University. His research aims at developing computational methods that can lead to a better understanding of our conversational practices, supporting tools that can improve the way we communicate with each other. He is the recipient of several awards – including an NSF CAREER Award, the WWW 2013 Best Paper Award, a CSCW 2017 Best Paper Award, and two Google Faculty Research Awards – and his work has been featured in popular media outlets such as The Wall Street Journal, NBC's The Today Show, NPR and The New York Times.

Keynote Talk: TBD

Dan Goldwasser
Purdue University

Bio: I am an associate professor at the department of computer science at Purdue university. I am broadly interested in connecting natural language with real world scenarios, and using them to guide natural language understanding. Before starting at Purdue I was a postdoctoral researcher at the University of Maryland in College Park. I completed my Ph.D. studies at the University of Illinois at Urbana-Champaign in the department of Computer Science.

Keynote Talk: Code-switching and social media data: an overview of common challenges and recent developments

Thamar Solorio
University of Houston

Abstract: In this talk I will aim to expose the audience to major developments in the brief history of research in NLP for code-switching data. Starting from the first non-empirical paper in a *CL venue on the topic, to the more recent, transformer based papers. I will then discuss how addressing challenges in code-switching data can help advance NLP for social media and vice versa. To conclude, I will point to the outstanding questions in processing this type of data.

Bio: Thamar Solorio is a Professor of Computer Science at the University of Houston (UH) and she is also a visiting scientist at Bloomberg LP. She holds graduate degrees in Computer Science from the Instituto Nacional de Astrofísica, Óptica y Electrónica, in Puebla, Mexico. Her research interests include information extraction from social media data, enabling technology for code-switched data, stylistic modeling of text, and more recently multimodal approaches for online content understanding. She is the director and founder of the Research in Text Understanding and Language Analysis Lab at UH. She is the recipient of an NSF CAREER award for her work on authorship attribution, and recipient of the 2014 Emerging Leader ABIE Award in Honor of Denice Denton. She is currently serving a second term as an elected board member of the North American Chapter of the Association of Computational Linguistics.

Table of Contents

Program

Thursday, July 14, 2022

08:30 - 08:40 *Opening Remarks*

08:40 - 09:40 *Day-1 Keynote Speech 1 by Prof. Saif Muhammad (National Research Council Canada)*

09:40 - 10:00 *Towards Toxic Positivity Detection*

Towards Toxic Positivity Detection
Ishan Sanjeev Upadhyay, KV Aditya Srivatsa and Radhika Mamidi

10:00 - 10:30 *Day-1 Coffee Break*

10:30 - 11:30 *Day-1 Keynote Speech 2 by Prof. Yohei Seki (University of Tsukuba)*

11:30 - 11:50 *Mask and Regenerate: A Classifier-based Approach for Unpaired Sentiment Transformation of Reviews for Electronic Commerce Websites*

Mask and Regenerate: A Classifier-based Approach for Unpaired Sentiment Transformation of Reviews for Electronic Commerce Websites.
Shuo Yang

11:50 - 13:30 *Day-1 Lunch Break*

13:30 - 14:30 *Day-1 Keynote Speech 3 by Prof. Tim Weninger (University of Notre Dame)*

14:30 - 14:50 *Detecting Rumor Veracity with Only Textual Information by Double-Channel Structure*

Detecting Rumor Veracity with Only Textual Information by Double-Channel Structure
Alex Gunwoo Kim and Sangwon Yoon

14:50 - 15:30 *Day-1 Coffee Break*

15:30 - 16:30 *Day-1 Keynote Speech 4 by Prof. Sonjanya Poria (Singapore University of Technology and Design)*

16:30 - 16:50 *OK Boomer: Probing the socio-demographic Divide in Echo Chambers*

Thursday, July 14, 2022 (continued)

Friday, July 15, 2022

08:40 - 09:40	*Day-2 Keynote Speech 1 by Prof. Cristian Danescu-Niculescu-Mizil (Cornell University)*
09:40 - 10:00	*Exploiting Social Media Content for Self-Supervised Style Transfer*
	Exploiting Social Media Content for Self-Supervised Style Transfer Dana Ruiter, Thomas Kleinbauer, Cristina España-Bonet, Josef van Genabith and Dietrich Klakow
10:00 - 10:30	*Day-2 Coffee Break*
10:30 - 11:30	*Day-2 Keynote Speech 2 by Prof. Dan Goldwasser (Purdue University)*
11:30 - 11:50	*Identifying Human Needs through Social Media: A study on Indian cities during COVID-19*
	Identifying Human Needs through Social Media: A study on Indian cities during COVID-19 Sunny Rai, Rohan Joseph, Prakruti Singh Thakur and Mohammed Abdul Khaliq
11:50 - 13:30	*Day-2 Lunch Break*
13:30 - 14:30	*Day-2 Keynote Speech 3 by Dr. Ian Stewart (University of Michigan)*
14:30 - 14:50	*A Comparative Study on Word Embeddings and Social NLP Tasks*
	A Comparative Study on Word Embeddings and Social NLP Tasks Fatma Elsafoury, Steven R. Wilson and Naeem Ramzan
14:50 - 15:30	*Day-2 Coffee Break*
15:30 - 16:30	*Day-2 Keynote Speech 4 by Prof. Thamar Solorio (University of Houston)*
16:30 - 16:50	*Leveraging Dependency Grammar for Fine-Grained Offensive Language Detection using Graph Convolutional Networks*
	Leveraging Dependency Grammar for Fine-Grained Offensive Language Detection using Graph Convolutional Networks Divyam Goel and Raksha Sharma

Friday, July 15, 2022 (continued)

16:50 - 17:00 *Day-2 Closing Remarks*

Mask and Regenerate: A Classifier-based Approach for Unpaired Sentiment Transformation of Reviews for Electronic Commerce Websites

Shuo Yang
yangshuo@toki.waseda.jp

Abstract

Style transfer is the task of transferring a sentence into the target style while keeping its content. The major challenge is that parallel corpora are not available for various domains. In this paper, we propose a Mask-And-Regenerate approach (MAR). It learns from unpaired sentences by modifying the word-level style attributes. We cautiously integrate the deletion, insertion and substitution operations into our model. This enables our model to automatically apply different edit operations for different sentences. Specifically, we train a multi-layer perceptron (MLP) as a style classifier to find out and mask style-characteristic words in the source inputs. Then we learn a language model on non-parallel data sets to score sentences and remove unnecessary masks. Finally, the masked source sentences are input to a Transformer to perform style transfer. The final results show that our proposed model exceeds baselines by about 2 per cent of accuracy for both sentiment and style transfer tasks with comparable or better content retention.

1 Introduction

A text style is a feature that specifies text. The objective of style transfer is to rewrite a given sentence into a target-style domain with the preservation of semantic content. In this paper, we follow the opinion (Fu et al., 2018; Prabhumoye et al., 2018) that textual sentiment should also be treated as styles and conduct experiments to transfer sentiments of sentences collected from three electronic commerce websites. E.g. "*The food here is delicious.*" (Positive) → "*The food here is gross.*" (Negative)

A key issue is that the lack of available parallel data has a considerable impact on the use of supervised learning. It results in the majority of recent studies concentrating on unpaired text transfer approaches (Shen et al., 2017; Luo et al., 2019; Krishna et al., 2020). Compare with related work,

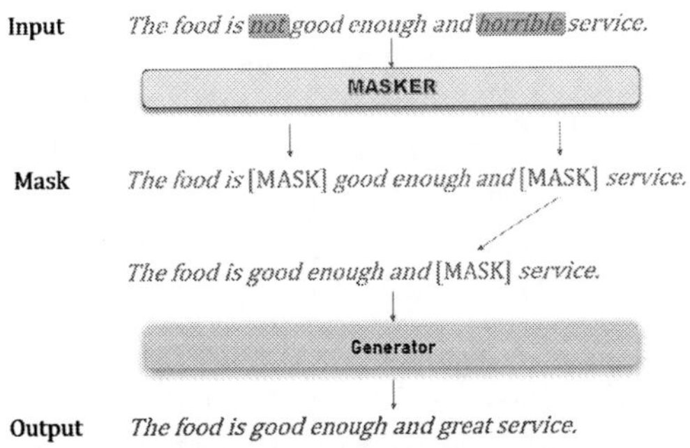

Figure 1: The proposed Mask-and-Regenerate approach. In this example, we transfer a negative sentence to a positive one. The [MASK] of the word 'not' has been removed by a language model.

methods based on word-level operations (Li et al., 2018; Wu et al., 2019a) have become one of the most frequently used approaches because they ensure high content preservation.

The approach we introduce in this paper mainly follows two works, the Delete-Retrieval-Generate (DRG) model (Li et al., 2018) and the Tag-and-Generate model (TAG) (Madaan et al., 2020). The motivation behind the DRG model is to delete style-characteristic words by computing the frequency of occurrence of words, retrieve one similar sentence in the target style corpus and generate a new sentence which is the result of crossing the two sentences. By following the idea of DRG, the TAG model is proposed. The TAG model calculates tf · idf scores (Ramos et al., 2003) to determine style-characteristic words and it includes a Tagger to insert a special symbol '[TAG]' into the input sentences, that will be filled by target-style-characteristic phrases. We identify the following weak points in these models:

1. The hypothesis that the frequency of a word is indicative of style is not always true.

2. Edit operations are not considered equally for all input sentences. Even in the same data set,

Proceedings of the Tenth International Workshop on Natural Language Processing for Social Media (SocialNLP 2022), pages 1 - 10
July 14-15, 2022 ©2022 Association for Computational Linguistics

for parts of sentences, deletion may be the best option to apply, whereas insertion or substitution may be the best for others. For example, we can transfer a sentence from negative to positive by inserting the word 'never' under certain conditions, e.g. "*I will give it up.*" $\rightarrow$ "*I will never give it up.*" while deletion can also realize a negative to positive transformation, e.g. "*The dipping sauce is too sweet.*" $\rightarrow$ "*The dipping sauce is sweet.*"

3. Retrieval module might not find suitable sentences. This may result in poor semantic content preservation. The results reported in this paper demonstrate this problem.

To tackle the above problems, we suggest that:

1. We use neural networks instead of statistical methods for the recognition of style-characteristic words. More precisely, we train a style classifier on the two data sets. For each source sentence, we mask each word in it and input it into the classifier. Masks that cause larger variations in the classifier logits correspond to words with higher style contributions. This is based on the fact that if a word is relevant to the style, then masking this word will increase the probability that the source sentence be classified into the wrong style domain. By masking these words, we arguably get a representation of content that is independent of the source style.

2. When multiple possible solutions exist for an input sentence, we propose that the selection of the optimal solution depends on their semantic fluency. For that, we learn a language model (LM) to validate the masks. If a mask-independent content representation already tends to get a low perplexity on the target data set, it means that deletion is a better choice for this sentence than substitution. In this situation, the masks are removed directly.

3. We generate a new sentence without retrieving similar sentences. We do not use any templates that have been summarised from retrieved sentences. As an improvement approach, extracted content representations are input to a Transformer (Vaswani et al., 2017) to rewrite sentences with the target style. The Transformer is designed to fill in the masks with style-characteristic phrases, insert words or retain the original version.

Our main contributions are as follows:

- We propose a novel approach to recognize style-characteristic words. For that, we rely on a neural classifier. To our best knowledge, previous studies of style transfer have not dealt with word recognition using masking models.
- We propose to use an LM to select edit operations (insertion, substitution and deletion) for different inputs. In such a mode, all possible situations for the transformation are covered.
- The results show that our approach outperforms baselines in terms of accuracy with comparable or higher BLEU scores.

2 Related Work

2.1 Style Transfer in Latent Space

Disentangling the style and content is a general idea in unpaired text transfer. Shen et al. (2017) proposed a cross-aligned auto-encoder training method to align transferred samples with target style samples at a shared latent content distribution level across different corpora. Fu et al. (2018) proposed techniques to use adversarial approaches to extract pure content representations and decode them into sentences. Models based on manipulating representations in the latent space (Hu et al., 2017; Prabhumoye et al., 2018) were proposed in the same period. Nevertheless, it is reported that the extraction of style information in a latent space can be very difficult (Elazar and Goldberg, 2018).

2.2 Style Transfer by Modifying Words

In contrast to operations in latent space, recent representative methods are proposed to extract style-independent content representations (Sudhakar et al., 2019; Zhang et al., 2018). Li et al. (2018) presented that a Delete-Retrieve-Generate pipeline also performs well in sentiment transfer tasks. Nevertheless, the retrieving was reported as an unnecessary step (Madaan et al., 2020). Models based on the edit operations show better results (Wu et al., 2019b; Reid and Zhong, 2021). However, the traditional attribute word recognition methods used only focused on word counting. Furthermore, these studies ignored the basis of selecting edit operations.

In this paper, we mainly follow the second approach which assumes the existence of style-characteristic words. We propose a new style-characteristic word recognition method and use a language model to score sentences to determine specific operations.

3 Methodology

We are given a sentence set $X_A = (x_A^{(1)}, ..., x_A^{(M)})$ with the source style A and another sentence set $X_B = (x_B^{(1)}, ..., x_B^{(N)})$ with the target style B. The sentences in these two sets are non-parallel, i.e., $x_A^{(i)}$ does not correspond to $x_B^{(i)}$. The objective is to generate a new set of sentences $\hat{X} = (\hat{x}^{(1)}, ..., \hat{x}^{(M)})$ in the domain of B, where $\hat{x}^{(i)}$ is the result of transferring $x_A^{(i)}$ into style B.

For an overview, we train two independent modules called the Masker and the Generator respectively. The Masker consists of a text MLP and an LM. For an input sentence $x_A^{(i)}$, the Masker masks or deletes style-characteristic words to generate a content representation sequence z_A. The generator is a standard Transformer which is used to insert style-characteristic words into the sequence z_A and replace masks with attribute words of style B.

3.1 Where to Mask?

We propose to use a trained style classifier f_ϕ and an LM to mask words, which is more effective for retaining plain and less style-indicative words. We train the classifier f_ϕ on the two sets to classify sentences to two different styles. The loss function is shown in the Formula (1).

$$\mathcal{L}_{\text{CLS}}(\phi) = -\sum_j \log P(y_j|x_j;\phi) \tag{1}$$

where x_j is the j-th example in a train set and y_j is the style label for x_j.

Inspired by BERT (Devlin et al., 2019), we select a mask-based approach for its reliability and validity. In particular, for a source sentence with k words, $x_A = (w_1, ..., w_k)$, we replace each of them with a special symbol [MASK] and input the masked sentence to the classifier to compute the probability that the classifier classifies this sentence to the target style. We first calculate a distribution $\eta(w_j)$ on sentence x_A to reflect the style contribution of each word w_j.

$$\eta(w_j) = P(B|x_A^{\text{MASK}(j)};\phi) \tag{2}$$

Here, $x_A^{\text{MASK}(j)}$ stands for the sentence x_A with word w_j replaced with a [MASK].

Our objective of this stage is to get the content representation z_A from the input sentence x_A. For that, we mask the word with the highest style contribution in sentence x_A. We repeat this operation until style A cannot be clearly distinguished from the masked sentence by the classifier. Here, we assume that the masked sentence can be regarded as a content representation of the input sentence.

Notice that, if the masking operation cannot extract z_A from x_A, which indicates that there is no obvious style-characteristic word in x_A, then the words in z_A should not be masked. In such a case, the transformation should mainly be performed by insertion. Similarly, if x_A is already judged in the style domain B, it should also not be masked. In this situation, it is possible that x_A is a mistakenly classified sample in the used corpus.

The second step is to tell whether it is necessary to retain masks in z_A. A widespread acknowledgement is that there is not a consistent one-to-one match between each input sentence and each output sentence. For example, an input negative sentence "*I am not really impressed.*", the content representation "*I am [MASK] really impressed.*" can be transferred to "*I am really impressed.*" or "*I am really really impressed.*". The former sounds more natural than the latter.

To make transferred sentences more fluent, we train a 5-gram language model (Heafield, 2011) and use it to score a generated sentence by its probability. If z_A gets a higher score than x_A, then the mask in z_A should not be held anymore. Since we consider insertion as a reverse operation of deletion, the scores computed by the LM are only used to decide whether deletion or substitution should be performed. For a sentence x_A with j words, we compute the probability of it as its score by using Formula (3).

$$P(x_A) = \prod_j P(w_j|w_{j-4}, ..., w_{j-1}), \tag{3}$$

where $P(w_j|w_{j-4}, ..., w_{j-1})$ is approximated by word frequency counting. Here, the LM used was learned on the target style sentence set X_B.

3.2 How to Transfer?

For an input content representation z_A from the Masker, we purpose to learn a mapping function to transfer it into the target style domain instead of retrieving other sentences.

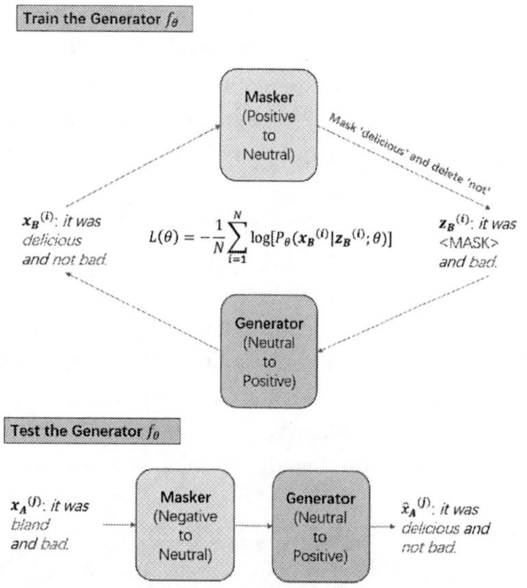

Figure 2: The training and testing stages of the generator. The generator learns to rebuild the original version of x_B from its content representation z_B.

We introduce a reconstruction loss (Luo et al., 2019; Madaan et al., 2020) to train the generator. Specifically, we first generate a content representation z_B of a sampled sentence x_B and treat z_B, x_B as a sentence pair. With the sentence pair, we train a generator f_θ to transfer x_B from its content representation z_B to its original version x_B.

$$\hat{x_B} = f_\theta(z_B), \quad (4)$$

where the generated sentence $\hat{x_B}$ is expected to be the same as x_B.

For a content representation z_A created from sentence x_A, by inference, the trained classifier cannot tell the source style A accurately. Therefore, if we apply f_θ to z_A, the output $\hat{x_A}$ will have the attribute of style B arguably. The loss function of the generator is given in Formula (5).

$$\mathcal{L}(\theta) = -\frac{1}{N}\sum_{i=1}^{N}\log[P(x_B^{(i)}|z_B^{(i)};\theta)] \quad (5)$$

We now give a brief analysis of how these edit operations are respectively used in our model.

The first simple case is when the Masker module does not delete any [MASK] after masking style-characteristic words in every sentence. In this situation, the generator is only trained to fill in the masks. For example, in a sentiment transfer task, the generator learns how to substitute these [MASK] in the content representations z_A with emotional words or phrases. In this case, the transformation is performed by substitution.

For the transfer tasks which are expected to be mainly performed using deletion operations, all of the masks in z_A are deleted. In this case, even if the generator still learns how to fill in the masks, with no masks in the input Z_A, the generator will only learn to copy a sequence to itself. Therefore, the transformation is mainly performed by the Masker.

For the transfer tasks which are expected to be mainly performed by insertion operations, we perform them through an opposite method of the deletion pattern. In training steps, the generator learns how to insert words into z_B to get x_B, with the parallel relation between x_B and z_B. For example, "*That's not bad.*" (x_B) → "*That's [MASK] bad.*" → "*That's bad.*" (z_B) In practice, when the generator encounters a sentence "*That's bad.*", it will insert the word "*not*" to it automatically.

For other tasks which are in a mixed mode, the above three approaches are performed automatically by the model to find the optimal solution. To summarize, the training process of the generator is shown in Figure 2. Note that the top yellow Masker and the bottom one are in reverse order.

4 Experiments

4.1 Data Sets Used

We test our proposed method on 3 data sets for sentiment transfer and 1 data set for formality transfer. Statistics of the used data sets are shown in Table 1.

Yelp The Yelp data set is a collection of reviews from Yelp users. It is provided by the Yelp Data set Challenge. We use this data set to perform sentiment transfer between these positive and negative business remarks.

Amazon Similar to Yelp, the Amazon data set (He and McAuley, 2016) consists of labelled reviews from Amazon users. We used the latest version provided by (Li et al., 2018).

IMDb The IMDb Movie Review (IMDb) contains positive and negative reviews of movies. We use the version provided by Dai et al. (2019), which is created from previous work (Maas et al., 2011).

GYAFC The Grammarly's Yahoo Answers Formality Corpus (GYAFC) (Rao and Tetreault, 2018) is a parallel corpus of informal and formal sentences. To demonstrate the situation of unsuper-

Category	Sentiment transfer						Formality transfer	
Data set	Amazon		Yelp		IMDb		GYAFC	
	Positive	Negative	Positive	Negative	Positive	Negative	Formal	Informal
Train set	266,041	177,218	277,228	277,769	178,869	187,597	51,967	51,967
Dev. set	2,000	2,000	985	1,015	2,000	2,000	2,247	2,788
Test set	500	500	1,000	1,000	1,000	1,000	1,019	1,332

Table 1: Statistics of the used data sets. 'Dev.' denotes 'development'. The Yelp, Amazon and IMDb data sets are used for sentiment transfer. The GYAFC data set is used for formality transfer.

vised learning, we shuffle all of the used sentences in training.

4.2 Baselines

We select 5 style transfer models as baselines for sentiment transfer comparison and 2 additional models for formality transfer comparison. These 7 baselines can be broadly divided into two categories. The first category consists of a Cross-Align model (Shen et al., 2017) a Style-Transformer (Dai et al., 2019) a DualRL (Luo et al., 2019) model and a DGST (Li et al., 2020) model. These models mainly transfer sentences in a latent space. The second category consists of a DRG (Li et al., 2018) model, a TAG model (Madaan et al., 2020) and an LEWIS model (Reid and Zhong, 2021). These models are mainly based on the substitution of words.

4.3 Automated Evaluation Metric

Transfer accuracy and content preservation are currently the most commonly considered aspects in evaluation. Following standard practice, we consider the following metrics.

Transfer Accuracy Accuracy is considered one of the most important evaluation metrics (Cao et al., 2020; Zhou et al., 2020). It stands for the successful transfer rate. We train a self-attention based convolutional Neural Networks (CNN) as the evaluation classifier f_ω to calculate accuracy. The accuracy is the probability that generated sentences $\hat{X}_A$ are judged to carry the target style B by the trained classifier f_ω. The computation of accuracy is shown in (6).

$$\text{Accuracy} = P(B|\hat{X}_A; \omega) \tag{6}$$

Notice that, to avoid an information leakage problem, the evaluation classifier is completely different from the one, i.e., f_ϕ, we used in the training period.

Here, our classifier was able to classify samples with success rates of 83.2%, 98.1%, 97.0% and 84% on the Amazon, Yelp, IMDb and GYAFC datasets, respectively. We understand that the automatic measures via our classifiers may not be convincing enough for the Amazon and GYAFC datasets, whereas quality issues in the two datasets, e.g. misclassification of samples, result that we cannot find a classifier with high accuracy in related work.

Content Preservation BLEU (Papineni et al., 2002) measures the similarity between two sentences at the lexical level. In most recent studies, two BLEU scores are computed: self-BLEU is the BLEU score computed between the input and the output; ref-BLEU is the BLEU score between the output and the human reference sentences (Lample et al., 2019; Sudhakar et al., 2019). We use NLTK (Bird et al., 2009) to calculate them.

4.4 Human Evaluation

Since the use of automatic metrics might be insufficient to evaluate transfer models. To further demonstrate the performance, we select outputs from the two similar models we introduced, i.e., the DAG model and the TAG model, to carry out a human evaluation of the Yelp data set (a popularly used corpus).

We hired 12 paid workers with language knowledge to participate in it. By following (Dai et al., 2019), for each review, we show one input sentence and three transferred samples to a reviewer. Reviewers were asked to separately select the best sentence in terms of three aspects: the degree of the target style, the content preservation and the fluency. We also offer the option "No preference" for concerns about objectivity. Furthermore, we ensure that transferred samples are anonymous to all reviewers in the whole process.

Model	Amazon			Yelp			IMDb	
	ACC.	s-BLEU	r-BLEU	ACC.	s-BLEU	r-BLEU	ACC.	s-BLEU
DRG (Li et al., 2018)	52.2%	57.89 ± 2.19	32.47 ± 12.68	84.1%	32.18 ± 2.05	12.28 ± 1.33	55.8%	55.40 ± 1.79
StyTrans (Dai et al., 2019)	67.8%	82.07 ± 1.56	32.88 ± 2.47	92.1%	52.40 ± 2.14	19.91 ± 2.01	86.6%	66.20 ± 1.55
DGST (Li et al., 2020)	59.2%	83.02 ± 1.25	**42.20 ± 22.37**	88.0%	51.77 ± 2.41	19.05 ± 1.89	70.1%	**70.20** ± 1.42
TAG (Madaan et al., 2020)	79.4%	58.13 ± 1.46	25.95 ± 1.86	88.6%	47.14 ± 2.23	19.76 ± 1.45	N/A	N/A
DIRR (Liu et al., 2021)	62.7%	66.63 ± 2.51	32.68 ± 2.25	91.2%	56.56 ± 1.89	25.60 ± 2.33	83.5%	65.96 ± 1.12
LEWIS (Reid and Zhong, 2021)	71.8%	65.53 ± 1.44	30.61 ± 1.57	89.4%	54.67 ± 1.62	23.85 ± 1.57	N/A	N/A
MAR (Ours)	**80.2%**	**83.42 ± 1.46**	41.21 ± 23.54	**93.9%**	53.32 ± 1.86	22.90 ± 2.01	**87.8%**	66.12 ± 1.33

Table 2: The test results on 3 data sets (sentiment transfer) with 0.95 confidence level. "ACC." stands for Accuracy, "s-BLEU" stands for self-BLEU and "r-BLEU" stands for ref-BLEU. We report the results of baselines by running their official codes or evaluating their official outputs.

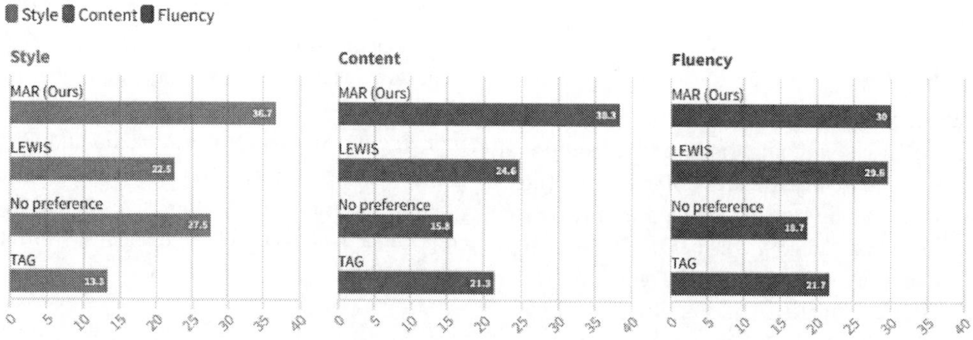

Figure 3: Results of human evaluation of sentences produced by three different models in terms of style, content and fluency. Following standard practice (Dai et al., 2019; Madaan et al., 2020), we randomly selected 100 sentences for evaluation.

4.5 Details

We pre-process the input data to mini-batches with a batch size of 64. All the encoders and decoders in the Transformers used in this paper are made up of a stack of 6 layers. For each layer, it has 8 attention heads and a dimension of 512. The MLP used in training has 4 layers with the same dimension of 512 for each layer. For training steps, the Adam algorithm (Kingma and Ba, 2015) with a learning rate of 0.0001 is employed to update the used models. We use a greedy algorithm to sample words from the probability distribution of the generator logits.

5 Results

5.1 Analysis

Table 2 compares the experimental data obtained on 3 data sets for sentiment transfer. Our proposed model obtains relatively better transfer accuracy than the other 5 models.

For the Amazon data set, our proposed model surpasses the state-of-the-art approach for accuracy and self-BLEU. An interesting aspect is that the DGST model shows a high self-BLEU, but the outputs are far away from the target style domain. We notice that there are no significant differences between the inputs and the outputs with the DGST model. For the Amazon data set, the DGST model merely learns how to copy sentences from inputs to outputs in lots of cases.

For the Yelp data set, our proposed model outperforms the baselines and gets an accuracy of 93.9. In terms of content preservation, our model performs closely to the state-of-the-art model (about 1 per cent) with a self-BLEU of 53.32 and ref-BLEU of 22.90. As all of the models achieved relatively good transfer results on the Yelp data set, we carry out an ablation study and a human evaluation in the next section.

For the IMDb data set, the average sentence length of the IMDb data set is much longer than in the first two data sets, but the number of sentences is much less. In this situation, it is difficult to perfectly train a classifier. This leads to the fact that the Masker in our proposed model tends to mask more words to ensure that the content representation z_A does not contain any emotional words. Theoretically, these operations result in a low self-BLEU. We conclude that our proposed model favours accuracy over self-BLEU scores. Because the IMDb

Yelp	Positive to negative	Negative to positive
Input	it is a cool place , with lots to see and try .	unfortunately , it is the worst .
DRG	it is my waste of time , with lots to try and see .	tender and full of fact that our preference menu is nice and full of flavor .
DGST	it is a sad place , with lots to see and try .	overall , it is the best .
LEWIS	it is a very busy place , with lots to see and try .	cajun food , it is the best !
Ours	it is a horrible place , with nothing to see and try .	wow , it is the best .
Amazon	**Positive to negative**	**Negative to positive**
Input	i won t be buying any more in the future .	because it is definitely not worth full price .
DRG	i won t know how i lived without this in the future .	because it is worth the full price and i am happy with it .
DGST	i won t be buying any more in the future .	because it is definitely not worth full price .
LEWIS	i won t be buying any more in the future . highly recommended .	because it is definitely well made and worth full price .
Ours	i will be buying more in the future .	because it is definitely worth full price .
IMDb	**Positive to negative**	**Negative to positive**
Input	i rate this movie 8/10 .	please , do n't see this movie .
DRG	i rate this movie an admittedly harsh 4/10 .	please , told every one to see this movie .
DGST	i rate this movie 1/10	u , do n't see this "
Ours	i rate this movie 2/10 .	please , you must see this movie .

Table 3: Sentences sampled from sentiment transfer data set. Red text stands for failed style transformation, brown text stands for poor content preservation and blue text stands for suitable transformation.

data set has no human reference, we cannot report a ref-BLEU score in Table 2.

Table 4 shows the result for GYAFC data set. The GYAFC is a formality transfer data set, so it is listed separately. On the GYAFC data set, our proposed model showed strengths in both transfer accuracy and content preservation. However, transfer between formal and informal styles is a very challenging task even for humans. This leads to poor performance of the classifier. Accordingly, all the models we tested in Table 4 do not achieve high accuracy.

Data set	GYAFC		
	ACC.	self-BLEU	ref-BLEU
CrossAlign(Shen et al., 2017)	68.1%	3.77 ± 0.26	2.85 ± 0.20
DualRL(Luo et al., 2019)	72.6%	53.10 ± 1.86	19.27 ± 1.18
StyleTrans(Dai et al., 2019)	74.1%	65.95 ± 1.61	$\mathbf{22.11 \pm 1.35}$
DGST(Li et al., 2020)	60.5%	62.62 ± 1.21	15.72 ± 1.13
MAR (Ours)	74.6%	70.12 ± 2.12	23.25 ± 1.44

Table 4: The test results on the GYAFC (formality transfer). The confidence level of BLEU is 0.95.

In terms of human evaluation, the results are shown in Figure 3. We analyse that our proposed model shows better results in terms of accuracy and content preservation than the two similar models. In terms of fluency, our proposed model and the TAG model are evenly matched with similar proportions. As we mentioned, the relatively poor fluency of the DRG model might stem from its retrieving module. Comparing these three models, we conclude that our model has the strongest overall performance.

5.2 Case Study

To further demonstrate the superiority of our model, We randomly sampled sentences from the outputs of our model and DRG model for comparison. Table 3 shows that, for particular inputs, the retrieval-based method, i.e., DRG, does not always find a suitable counterpart. When this is the case, the output can largely differ from the original semantics of the input sentence. Redundant words are also introduced. The method based on the transformation in latent space, i.e., DGST, always copies sentences without transferring them into correct style domains.

For the transformation of negative to positive on the IMDb data set, we note that the mask for the word 'do' seems to be redundant. We analyse that the training of the classifier is influenced by the quality of the used data set. In this example, the masking module incorrectly masks a content word. It results in the low self-BLEU in Table 2.

5.3 Additional Study

Following previous work (Dai et al., 2019), we make ablation studies on the Yelp data set to confirm the validity of our model. We inspect the following three aspects:

- Is the special symbol [MASK] necessary?
- How will the results be affected in the absence of a language model in the Masker?
- What is the correlation between human and automatic evaluation?

For the first question, we removed all of the [MASK] in z_A and z_B, and we repeated the above experiments. As shown in Figure 4, the performance of our proposed model without masks shows a lower transfer accuracy and self-BLEU score. Besides, the model without masks is more unstable

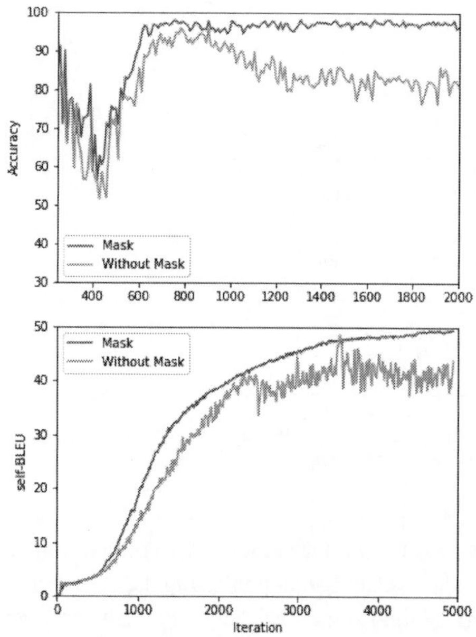

Figure 4: Accuracy and self-BLEU curves of the model during the training phase, with and without masks.

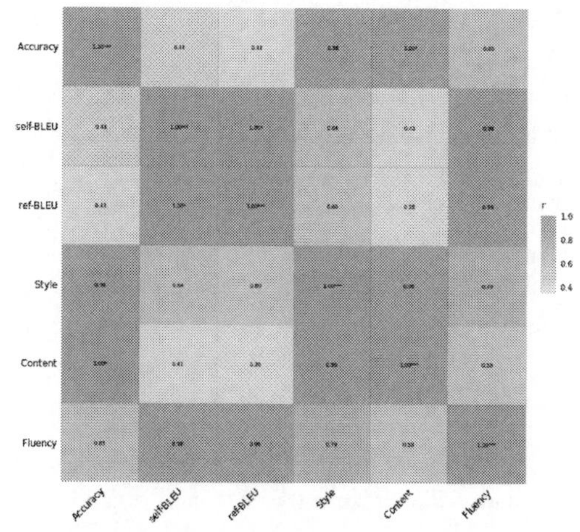

Figure 5: Pearson correlation between different evaluation metrics. Scores marked with * denotes p<0.01.

in performance in the latter stages of training. The mask operation will make the generator easily figure out the positions where the words need to be filled in. Sequences that do not include a mask require the model to make additional judgments about the position, which increases the burden of the model and is likely to lead to text degradation.

For the second question, we removed the used LM and repeated the experiments. It means that the [MASK] will not be removed and the model only learns to do substitution without any insertion or deletion. The results show that the accuracy is not affected (less than one per cent). However, the absence of the LM results in a 4 per cent reduction in BLEU scores. The absence of LM corresponds to the fact that the model cannot perform direct deletion of words. This means that all sentences need to be processed with word substitution, and during word substitution, the generator may insert multiple words for a [MASK], which may be an important cause of the drop in self-BLEU scores.

For the third question, we calculated the Pearson correlation between different evaluation metrics and the results are presented in Figure 5. Overall, positive correlations are observed between all metric combinations. It shows that both automatic evaluation and human evaluation are consistent in sentence evaluation.

Specifically, we observed that: (1) The correlation between "Accuracy" and "Style" is relatively large than the association between "Accuracy" and "Fluency". (2) The BLEU score metrics significantly correlate with the "Content" metric. (3) The "ref-BLEU" and "self-BLEU" metrics show very similar properties. It illustrates that people might have an instinct for copying content words in style transfer tasks.

6 Conclusion

We proposed a novel word substitution based approach called Mask-and-Regenerate for sentiment and style transfer. It can be regarded as a generator in a generative adversarial network to facilitate the training of a detector which can better identify fake comments on electronic commerce platforms.

Due to the lack of available parallel corpora, the original sentences were edited to delete, insert, or substitute words. We carried out a study on the neural-based style-characteristic word recognition and the automatic application of edit operations in the domain of style transfer. For sentiment and formality transfer, the results showed that our proposed model generally outperforms baselines by about 2 per cent in terms of accuracy with comparable or better BLEU scores.

References

Steven Bird, Ewan Klein, and Edward Loper. 2009. *Natural language processing with Python: analyzing text with the natural language toolkit.* " O'Reilly Media, Inc.".

Yixin Cao, Ruihao Shui, Liangming Pan, Min-Yen Kan, Zhiyuan Liu, and Tat-Seng Chua. 2020. Expertise style transfer: A new task towards better communication between experts and laymen. In *Proceedings of the 58th Annual Meeting of the Association for Computational Linguistics*, pages 1061–1071, Online. Association for Computational Linguistics.

Ning Dai, Jianze Liang, Xipeng Qiu, and Xuanjing Huang. 2019. Style transformer: Unpaired text style transfer without disentangled latent representation. In *Proceedings of the 57th Annual Meeting of the Association for Computational Linguistics*, pages 5997–6007, Florence, Italy. Association for Computational Linguistics.

Jacob Devlin, Ming-Wei Chang, Kenton Lee, and Kristina Toutanova. 2019. BERT: Pre-training of deep bidirectional transformers for language understanding. In *Proceedings of the 2019 Conference of the North American Chapter of the Association for Computational Linguistics: Human Language Technologies*, pages 4171–4186, Minneapolis, Minnesota. Association for Computational Linguistics.

Yanai Elazar and Yoav Goldberg. 2018. Adversarial removal of demographic attributes from text data. In *Proceedings of the 2018 Conference on Empirical Methods in Natural Language Processing*, pages 11–21, Brussels, Belgium. Association for Computational Linguistics.

Zhenxin Fu, Xiaoye Tan, Nanyun Peng, Dongyan Zhao, and Rui Yan. 2018. Style transfer in text: Exploration and evaluation. *Proceedings of the AAAI Conference on Artificial Intelligence*, 32(1).

Ruining He and Julian McAuley. 2016. Ups and downs: Modeling the visual evolution of fashion trends with one-class collaborative filtering. In *proceedings of the 25th international conference on world wide web*, pages 507–517.

Kenneth Heafield. 2011. KenLM: Faster and smaller language model queries. In *Proceedings of the Sixth Workshop on Statistical Machine Translation*, pages 187–197, Edinburgh, Scotland. Association for Computational Linguistics.

Zhiting Hu, Zichao Yang, Xiaodan Liang, Ruslan Salakhutdinov, and Eric P Xing. 2017. Toward controlled generation of text. In *International Conference on Machine Learning*, pages 1587–1596. PMLR.

P. Diederik Kingma and Lei Jimmy Ba. 2015. Adam: A method for stochastic optimization. *international conference on learning representations*.

Kalpesh Krishna, John Wieting, and Mohit Iyyer. 2020. Reformulating unsupervised style transfer as paraphrase generation. In *Empirical Methods in Natural Language Processing*.

Guillaume Lample, Sandeep Subramanian, Eric Smith, Ludovic Denoyer, Marc'Aurelio Ranzato, and Y-Lan Boureau. 2019. Multiple-attribute text rewriting. In *International Conference on Learning Representations*.

Juncen Li, Robin Jia, He He, and Percy Liang. 2018. Delete, retrieve, generate: a simple approach to sentiment and style transfer. In *Proceedings of the 2018 Conference of the North American Chapter of the Association for Computational Linguistics: Human Language Technologies*, pages 1865–1874, New Orleans, Louisiana. Association for Computational Linguistics.

Xiao Li, Guanyi Chen, Chenghua Lin, and Ruizhe Li. 2020. DGST: a dual-generator network for text style transfer. In *Proceedings of the 2020 Conference on Empirical Methods in Natural Language Processing (EMNLP)*, Online. Association for Computational Linguistics.

Yixin Liu, Graham Neubig, and John Wieting. 2021. On learning text style transfer with direct rewards. In *Proceedings of the 2021 Conference of the North American Chapter of the Association for Computational Linguistics: Human Language Technologies*, pages 4262–4273, Online. Association for Computational Linguistics.

Fuli Luo, Peng Li, Jie Zhou, Pengcheng Yang, Baobao Chang, Xu Sun, and Zhifang Sui. 2019. A dual reinforcement learning framework for unsupervised text style transfer. In *Proceedings of the Twenty-Eighth International Joint Conference on Artificial Intelligence, IJCAI-19*, pages 5116–5122. International Joint Conferences on Artificial Intelligence Organization.

Andrew L. Maas, Raymond E. Daly, Peter T. Pham, Dan Huang, Andrew Y. Ng, and Christopher Potts. 2011. Learning word vectors for sentiment analysis. In *Proceedings of the 49th Annual Meeting of the Association for Computational Linguistics: Human Language Technologies*, pages 142–150, Portland, Oregon, USA. Association for Computational Linguistics.

Aman Madaan, Amrith Setlur, Tanmay Parekh, Barnabas Poczos, Graham Neubig, Yiming Yang, Ruslan Salakhutdinov, Alan W Black, and Shrimai Prabhumoye. 2020. Politeness transfer: A tag and generate approach. In *Proceedings of the 58th Annual Meeting of the Association for Computational Linguistics*, pages 1869–1881, Online. Association for Computational Linguistics.

Kishore Papineni, Salim Roukos, Todd Ward, and Wei-Jing Zhu. 2002. Bleu: a method for automatic evaluation of machine translation. In *Proceedings of the 40th annual meeting of the Association for Computational Linguistics*, pages 311–318.

Shrimai Prabhumoye, Yulia Tsvetkov, Ruslan Salakhutdinov, and Alan W Black. 2018. Style transfer through back-translation. In *Proceedings of the 56th Annual Meeting of the Association for Computational Linguistics*, pages 866–876, Melbourne, Australia. Association for Computational Linguistics.

Juan Ramos et al. 2003. Using tf-idf to determine word relevance in document queries. In *Proceedings of the first instructional conference on machine learning*, volume 242, pages 29–48. Citeseer.

Sudha Rao and Joel Tetreault. 2018. Dear sir or madam, may I introduce the GYAFC dataset: Corpus, benchmarks and metrics for formality style transfer. In *Proceedings of the 2018 Conference of the North American Chapter of the Association for Computational Linguistics: Human Language Technologies*, pages 129–140, New Orleans, Louisiana. Association for Computational Linguistics.

Machel Reid and Victor Zhong. 2021. Lewis: Levenshtein editing for unsupervised text style transfer. In *In Findings of the 59th Annual Meeting of the Association for Computational Linguistics*.

Tianxiao Shen, Tao Lei, Regina Barzilay, and Tommi Jaakkola. 2017. Style transfer from non-parallel text by cross-alignment. In *Advances in neural information processing systems*, pages 6830–6841.

Akhilesh Sudhakar, Bhargav Upadhyay, and Arjun Maheswaran. 2019. "transforming" delete, retrieve, generate approach for controlled text style transfer. In *Proceedings of the 2019 Conference on Empirical Methods in Natural Language Processing and the 9th International Joint Conference on Natural Language Processing (EMNLP-IJCNLP)*, pages 3269–3279, Hong Kong, China. Association for Computational Linguistics.

Ashish Vaswani, Noam Shazeer, Niki Parmar, Jakob Uszkoreit, Llion Jones, Aidan N. Gomez, L. Kaiser, and Illia Polosukhin. 2017. Attention is all you need. In *NIPS*.

Chen Wu, Xuancheng Ren, Fuli Luo, and Xu Sun. 2019a. A hierarchical reinforced sequence operation method for unsupervised text style transfer. In *Proceedings of the 57th Annual Meeting of the Association for Computational Linguistics*, pages 4873–4883, Florence, Italy. Association for Computational Linguistics.

Chen Wu, Xuancheng Ren, Fuli Luo, and Xu Sun. 2019b. A hierarchical reinforced sequence operation method for unsupervised text style transfer. In *Proceedings of the 57th Conference of the Association for Computational Linguistics, ACL 2019, Florence, Italy, July 28- August 2, 2019*, pages 4873–4883.

Zhirui Zhang, Shuo Ren, Shujie Liu, Jianyong Wang, Peng Chen, Mu Li, Ming Zhou, and Enhong Chen. 2018. Style transfer as unsupervised machine translation. *CoRR*, abs/1808.07894.

Chulun Zhou, Liangyu Chen, Jiachen Liu, Xinyan Xiao, Jinsong Su, Sheng Guo, and Hua Wu. 2020. Exploring contextual word-level style relevance for unsupervised style transfer. In *Proceedings of the 58th Annual Meeting of the Association for Computational Linguistics*, pages 7135–7144, Online. Association for Computational Linguistics.

Exploiting Social Media Content for Self-Supervised Style Transfer

Dana Ruiter[1], **Thomas Kleinbauer**[1], **Cristina España-Bonet**[2,3],
Josef van Genabith[2,3], **Dietrich Klakow**[1]
[1]Spoken Language Systems Group, Saarland University, Germany
[2]Saarland Informatics Campus, Saarland University, Germany
[3]DFKI GmbH, Germany
druiter@lsv.uni-saarland.de

Abstract

Recent research on style transfer takes inspiration from unsupervised neural machine translation (UNMT), learning from large amounts of non-parallel data by exploiting cycle consistency loss, back-translation, and denoising autoencoders. By contrast, the use of self-supervised NMT (SSNMT), which leverages (near) parallel instances hidden in non-parallel data more efficiently than UNMT, has not yet been explored for style transfer. In this paper we present a novel Self-Supervised Style Transfer (3ST) model, which augments SSNMT with UNMT methods in order to identify and efficiently exploit supervisory signals in non-parallel social media posts. We compare 3ST with state-of-the-art (SOTA) style transfer models across civil rephrasing, formality and polarity tasks. We show that 3ST is able to balance the three major objectives (fluency, content preservation, attribute transfer accuracy) the best, outperforming SOTA models on averaged performance across their tested tasks in automatic and human evaluation.

1 Introduction

Style transfer is a highly versatile task in natural language processing, where the goal is to modify the stylistic attributes of a text while maintaining its original meaning. A broad variety of stylistic attributes has been considered, including formality (Rao and Tetreault, 2018), gender (Prabhumoye et al., 2018), polarity (Shen et al., 2017) and civility (Laugier et al., 2021). Potential industrial applications are manifold and range from simplifying professional language to be intelligible to laypersons (Cao et al., 2020), the generation of more compelling news headlines (Jin et al., 2020), to related tasks such as text simplification for children and people with disabilities (Martin et al., 2020).

Data-driven style transfer methods can be classified according to the kind of data they use: parallel or non-parallel corpora in the two styles (Jin et al., 2021). To learn style transfer on non-parallel monostylistic corpora, current approaches take inspiration from unsupervised neural machine translation (UNMT) (Lample et al., 2018), by exploiting cycle consistency loss (Lample et al., 2019), iterative back-translation (Jin et al., 2019) and denoising autoencoders (DAE) (Laugier et al., 2021). As these approaches are similar to UNMT they suffer from the same limitations, i.e. poor performance relative to supervised neural machine translation (NMT) systems when the amount of UNMT training data is small and/or exhibits domain mismatch (Kim et al., 2020). Unfortunately, this is precisely the case for most existing style transfer corpora.

In this paper, we follow an alternative approach inspired by self-supervised NMT (Ruiter et al., 2021) that jointly learns online (near) parallel sentence pair extraction (SPE), back-translation (BT) and style transfer in a loop. The goal is to identify and exploit supervisory signals present in limited amounts of (possibly domain-mismatched) non-parallel data ignored by UNMT. The architecture of our system–called **S**elf-**S**upervised **S**tyle **T**ransfer (3ST)–implements an online self-supervisory cycle, where learning SPE enables us to learn style transfer on extracted parallel data, which iteratively improves SPE and BT quality, and thereby style transfer learning, in a virtuous circle.

We evaluate and compare 3ST to current state-of-the-art (SOTA) style transfer models on two established tasks: formality and polarity style transfer, where 3ST is the most balanced model and reaches top overall performance.

To gain insights into the performance of 3ST on an under-explored task, we also focus on the civil rephrasing task, which is interesting as i) it has been explored only twice before (Nogueira dos Santos et al., 2018; Laugier et al., 2021) and ii) it makes an important societal contribution in order to tackle hateful content online. We focus on performance and qualitative analysis of 3ST predictions

Proceedings of the Tenth International Workshop on Natural Language Processing for Social Media (SocialNLP 2022), pages 11 - 23
July 14-15, 2022

on this task's test set and identify shortcomings of the currently available data setup for civil rephrasing. On civil rephrasing, 3ST generates more neutral sentences than the current SOTA model while being on par in overall performance.

Our contribution is threefold:

- Efficient detection and exploitation of the supervisory signals in non-parallel social media content via jointly-learning *online* SPE and BT, outperforming SOTA models on averaged performance across civility, formality and polarity tasks in automatic and human evaluation (Δ in Tables 2 and 3).

- Simple end-to-end training of a single online model without the need for additional external style-classifiers or external SPE, enabling the initialization of the 3ST network on a DAE task, which leads to SOTA-matching fluency scores during human evaluation.

- A qualitative analysis that identifies flaws in the current data, emphasizing the need for a high quality civil rephrasing corpus.

2 Related Work

Style transfer can be treated as a supervised translation task between two styles (Jhamtani et al., 2017). However, for most style transfer tasks, parallel data is scarcely available. To learn style transfer without parallel data, prior research has focused on exploiting larger amounts of monostylistic data in combination with a smaller amount of style-labeled data. One such approach is using variational autoencoders and disentangled latent spaces (Fu et al., 2018), which can be further incentivized towards generating fluent or style-relevant content by fusing them with adversarial (Shen et al., 2017) or style-enforcing (Hu et al., 2017) discriminators. Chawla and Yang (2020) use a language model as the discriminator, leading to a more informative signal to the generator during training and thus more fluent and stable results. Li et al. (2018) argue that adversarially learned outputs tend to be low-quality, and that most sentiment modification is based on simple deletion and replacement of relevant words.

The above approaches focus on separating content and style, either in latent space or surface form, however this separation is difficult to achieve (Gonen and Goldberg, 2019). Dai et al. (2019) instead train a transformer together with a discriminator,

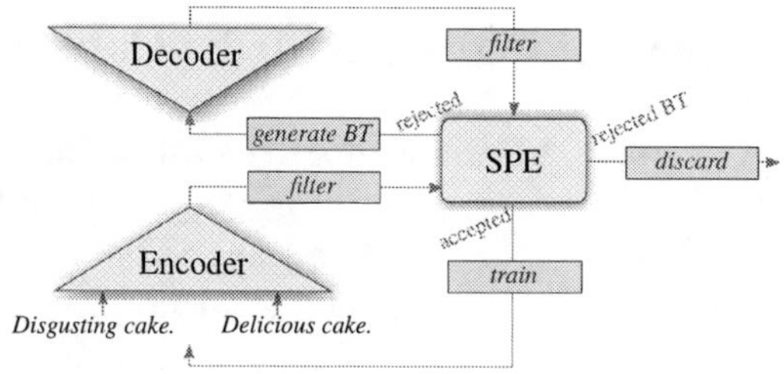

Figure 1: 3ST: joint learning of style transfer, SPE, and BT.

without disentangling the style features before decoding. Current approaches treat style transfer similar to an unsupervised neural machine translation (Artetxe et al., 2019) task. Jin et al. (2019) create pseudo-parallel corpora by extracting similar sentences offline from two monostylistic corpora to train an initial NMT model which is then iteratively improved using back-translation. Luo et al. (2019) use a reinforcement approach to further improve sentence fluency. Laugier et al. (2021) improve fluency without the need of any style-specific classifiers, giving their model a head start by initializing it on a pre-trained transformer model. Wang et al. (2020) argue that standard NMT training cannot account for the small differences between informal and formal style transfer, and apply style-specific decoder heads to enforce style differences.

Our approach differs from the two step approach of Jin et al. (2019), who first extract similar sentences from style corpora *offline* and then initialize their system by training on them. Ruiter et al. (2020) show that *joint online learning* to extract and translate in self-supervised NMT (SSNMT) leads to higher recall and precision of the extracted data. Following this observation, our 3ST approach performs similar sentence extraction and style transfer learning online with a single model in a loop. We further extend the SSNMT-based approach by combining it with UNMT methods, namely by generating additional training data via online back-translation, and by initialising our models with DAE trained in an unsupervised manner.

3 Self-Supervised Style Transfer (3ST)

Figure 1 shows the 3ST architecture, which uses the encoder outputs at training time as sentence representations to perform online (near) parallel sentence pair extraction (SPE) together with online back-translation (BT) and style transfer.

Self-Supervised NMT (SSNMT): SSNMT (Ruiter et al., 2019) is an encoder-decoder architecture that jointly learns to identify parallel data in non-parallel data and bidirectional NMT. Instead of using SSNMT on different language corpora to learn machine translation, we show how ideas from SSNMT can be used to learn a self-supervised style transfer system from non-parallel social media content. A single bidirectional encoder simultaneously encodes both styles and maps the internal representations of the two styles into the same space. This way, they can be used to compute similarities between sentence pairs in order to identify similar and discard non-similar ones for training. Formally, given two monostylistic corpora $S1$ and $S2$ of opposing styles, e.g. *toxic* and *neutral*, sentence pairs ($s_{S1} \in S1, s_{S2} \in S2$) are input to an encoder-decoder system, a transformer in our experiments. From the internal representations for the input sentences s_{S1} and s_{S2}, SSNMT uses the sum of the word embeddings $w(s)$ and the sum of the encoder outputs $e(s)$ for filtering. The embedded pairs $\{w(s_{S1}), w(s_{S2})\}$ are scored using the margin-based measure (Artetxe and Schwenk, 2019). The same is done with pairs $\{e(s_{S1}), e(s_{S2})\}$. If a sentence pair is the most similar pair for both style directions *and* for both sentence representations, it is accepted for training, otherwise it is discarded. This sequence of scoring and filtering is denoted as **sentence pair extraction (SPE)** in 3ST. SPE improves style transfer and style transfer improves SPE online in a virtuous loop, resulting in a single system that jointly learns to identify its supervision signals in the data and to perform style transfer.

To address the characteristics of the monostylistic corpora we extend basic SSNMT in two ways:

Large-Scale Extraction: SSNMT extracts parallel data from *comparable corpora*, which contain smaller topic-aligned documents $\{d_{S1}, d_{S2}\}$ of similar content, thus reducing the search space during SPE from $|S1| \times |S2|$ to $|d_{S1}| \times |d_{S2}|$. However, style transfer corpora usually consist of large collections of (unaligned) sequences of a specific style, which forces the exploration of the full space. Improving over the one-by-one comparison of vector representations, we index[1] our data using FAISS (Johnson et al., 2019).

[1]As our internal representations change during the course of training, we re-index at each iteration over the data.

Corpus	Train	Dev	Test	∅
CivCo-Neutral	136,618	500	–	–
CivCo-Toxic	399,691	500	4,878	14.9
Yahoo-Formal	1,737,043	4,603	2,100	12.7
Yahoo-Informal	3,148,351	5,665	2,741	12.4
Yelp-Pos	266,041	2,000	500	9.9
Yelp-Neg	177,218	2,000	500	10.7

Table 1: Number of sentences of the different tasks train, dev and test splits, as well as average number of tokens per sequence (∅) of the tokenized test sets. Splits with target references available are underlined.

UNMT-Style Data Augmentation: We follow Ruiter et al. (2021) and use the current models' state to generate **back-translations** *online* from sentences rejected during SPE in order to increase the amount of supervisory signals to train on. Further, we initialize our style transfer models using **denoising autoencoding** using BART-style[2] noise (Lewis et al., 2020). After pre-training a DAE on the stylistic corpora, our models will generate fluent English sentences from the beginning and only need to learn to separate the two styles $S1$ and $S2$ during style transfer learning.

4 Experimental Setup

4.1 Data

Formality For the formality task, we use the test and development (dev) splits of the GYAFC corpus (Rao and Tetreault, 2018), which is based on the Yahoo Answers L6[3] corpus. However, as GYAFC is a parallel corpus and we want to evaluate our models in a setup where only monostylistic data is available, we follow Rao and Tetreault (2018) and re-create the training split without downsampling and without creating parallel reference sentences. For this, we extract all answers from the *Entertainment & Music* and *Family & Relationships* domains in the Yahoo Answers L6 corpus. We use a BERT classifier fine-tuned on the GYAFC training split to classify sentences as either *informal* or *formal*. This leaves us with a much (46×) larger training split than the parallel GYAFC corpus, although consisting of non-parallel data where a single instance is less informative than a parallel one. We remove

[2]This is algorithmically equivalent to using a common pre-trained BART model for initialization, with the benefit that we have full control on the vocabulary size and data it is pre-trained on. We use this benefit by focusing the pre-training on in-domain data instead of generic out-of-domain data.

[3]`www.webscope.sandbox.yahoo.com/catalog.php?datatype=l`

sentences from our training data that are matched with a sentence in the official test-dev splits. We deduplicate the test-dev splits to match those used by Jin et al. (2019). For DAE pre-training, we sample sentences from Yahoo Answers L6.

Polarity We use the standard train-dev-test splits[4] of the Yelp sentiment transfer task (Shen et al., 2017). This dataset is already tokenized and lower-cased. Therefore, as opposed to the civility and formality tasks, we do not perform any additional pre-processing on this corpus. For DAE pre-training, we sample sentences from a generic Yelp corpus[5] and process them to fit the preprocessing of the Yelp sentiment transfer task, i.e. we lower-case and perform sentence and word tokenization using NLTK (Bird and Loper, 2004).

Civility The civil rephrasing task is rooted in the broader domain of hate speech research, which commonly focuses on the detection of hateful, offensive, or profane contents (Yang et al., 2019). Besides deletion, moderation, and generating counter-speech (Tekiroğlu et al., 2020), which are *reactive* measures after the abuse has already happened, there is a need for *proactive* ways of dealing with hateful contents to prevent harm (Jurgens et al., 2019). Civil rephrasing is a novel approach to fight abusive or profane contents by suggesting civil rephrasings to authors before their comments are published. So far, civil rephrasing has been explored twice before (Nogueira dos Santos et al., 2018; Laugier et al., 2021). However, their datasets are not publicly available. In order to compare the works, we reproduce the data sets used in Laugier et al. (2021). We follow their approach and create our own train and dev splits on the Civil Comments[6] (CivCo) dataset. Style transfer learning requires distinct distributions in the two opposing style corpora. To increase the distinction in our toxic and neutral datasets, we filter them using a list of slurs[7] such that the toxic portion contains only sentences with at least one slur, and the neutral portion does not contain any slurs in the list. Laugier et al. (2021) kindly provided us with the original test set used in their study. We removed sentences contained in the test set from our corpus and split the remaining sentences into train and dev. To initialize 3ST on DAE with data related to the civility task domain, i.e. user comments, we sample sentences from generic Reddit comments crawled with PRAW[8].

Preprocessing On all datasets, excluding the polarity task data which is already preprocessed, we performed sentence tokenization using NLTK as well as punctuation normalization, tokenization and truecasing using standard Moses scripts (Koehn et al., 2007). Following Rao and Tetreault (2018), we remove sentences containing URLs as well as those containing less than 5 or more than 25 words. For the civility task only, we allow longer sequences of up to 30 words due to the higher average sequence length in this task (Laugier et al., 2021). We perform deduplication and language identification using `polyglot`[9]. We apply a byte-pair encoding (Sennrich et al., 2016) of $8k$ merge-operations. We add target style labels (e.g. *<pos>*) to the beginning of each sequence. Table 1 summarizes all train, dev and test splits.

4.2 Model Specifications

We base our 3ST code on OpenNMT (Klein et al., 2017), using a transformer-base with standard parameters, a batch size of 50 sentences and a maximum sequence length of 100 sub-word units. All models are trained until the attribute transfer accuracy on the development set has converged. Each model is trained on a single Titan X GPU, which takes around 2–5 days for a 3ST model.

For DAE pre-training, we use the task-specific DAE data split into $20M$ train sentences and $5k$ dev and test sentences each. To create the noisy source-side data, we apply BART-style noise with $\lambda = 3.5$ and $p = 0.35$ for word sequence masking. We also add one random mask insertion per sequence and perform a sequence permutation.

For BERT classifiers, which we use to automatically evaluate the attribute transfer accuracy, we fine-tune a `bert-base-cased` model on the relevant classification task using early stopping with $\delta = 0.01$ and patience 5.

4.3 Automatic Evaluation

While 3ST can perform style transfer bidirectionally, we only evaluate on the *toxic→neutral* direc-

[4] www.github.com/shentianxiao/language-style-transfer

[5] www.yelp.com/dataset

[6] www.tensorflow.org/datasets/catalog/civil_comments

[7] www.cs.cmu.edu/~biglou/resources/bad-words.txt

[8] www.praw.readthedocs.io/en/latest/

[9] www.github.com/aboSamoor/polyglot

tion of the civility task, as the other direction, i.e. generation of toxic content, would pose a harmful application of our system. Similarly, the formality task is only evaluated for the *informal→formal* direction as this is the most common use-case (Rao and Tetreault, 2018). The polarity task is evaluated in both directions. We compare our model against current SOTA models: multi-class (MUL) and conditional (CON) style transformers by Dai et al. (2019), unsupervised machine translation (UMT) (Lample et al., 2019)[10] as well as models by Li et al. (2018) (DAR), Jin et al. (2019) (IMT), Laugier et al. (2021) (CAE), He et al. (2020) (DLA) and Shen et al. (2017) (SCA). Our automatic evaluation focuses on four main aspects:

Content Preservation (CP) In style transfer, the aim is to change the style of a source sentence into a target style without changing the underlying meaning of the sentence. To evaluate CP, BLEU is a common choice, despite its inability to account for paraphrases (Wieting et al., 2019), which are at the core of style transfer. Instead, we use Siamese Sentence Transformers [11] [12] to embed the source and prediction and then calculate the cosine similarity.

Attribute Transfer Accuracy (ATA) We want to transfer the style of the source sentence to the target style or attributes. Whether this transfer was successful is calculated using a BERT classification model. We train and evaluate our classifiers on the same data splits as the style-transfer models. This yields classifiers with Macro-F1 scores of 93.2 (formality), 87.4 (civility) and 97.1 (polarity) on the task-specific development sets. ATA is the percentage of generated target sentences that were labeled as belonging to the target style by the task-specific classifier.

Fluency (FLU) As generated sentences should be intelligible and natural-sounding to a reader, we take their fluency into consideration during evaluation. The perplexity of a language model is often used to evaluate this (Krishna et al., 2020). However, perplexity is unbounded and therefore difficult to interpret, and has the limitation of favoring potentially unnatural sentences containing frequent words (Mir et al., 2019). We therefore use a RoBERTa (Liu et al., 2019) model[13] trained on CoLA (Warstadt et al., 2019) to label model predictions as either *grammatical* or *ungrammatical*.

Aggregation (AGG) CP, ATA and FLU are important dimensions of style-transfer evaluation. A good style transfer model should be able to perform well across all three metrics. To compare overall style-transfer performance, it is possible to aggregate these metrics into a single value (Li et al., 2018). Krishna et al. (2020) show that corpus-level aggregation are less indicative for the overall performance of a system and we thus apply their sentence-level aggregation score, which ensures that each predicted sentence performs well across all measures, while penalizing predictions which are poor in at least one of the metrics. We also report the average AGG difference of a model m to 3ST across all tasks that m was tested on (Δ).

The automatic evaluation relies on external models, which are sensitive to hyperparameter choices during training. However, we use the same evaluation models across all style transfer model predictions and supplement the automatic evaluation with a human evaluation. As we observe consistency between the automatic and human evaluation, the underlying models used for the automatic evaluation can be considered to be sufficiently reliable.

4.4 Human Evaluation

We compare the performance of 3ST with each of the two strongest baseline systems per task, chosen based on their aggregated scores achieved in the automatic evaluation. These are: CAE and IMT for comparison in the polarity task, DAR and IMT for the formality task and CAE for the civility task. Due to the large number of models in the polarity task, we also include CON and MUL in the human evaluation, as they are strongest on ATA and CP respectively.

For each task, we sample 100 data points from the original test set and the corresponding predictions of the different models. We randomly duplicate 5 of the data points to calculate intra-rater agreement, resulting in a total of 105 evaluation sentences per system. Three fluent English speakers were asked to rate the content preservation, fluency and attribute transfer accuracy of the predictions on a 5-point Likert scale. In order to aggregate the different values, analogous to the automatic evaluation, we consider the transfer to be *successful* when a prediction was rated with a 4 or 5 across all three metrics (Li et al., 2018). The success rate

[10] Model outputs provided by He et al. (2020).

[11] Model `paraphrase-mpnet-base-v2`

[12] `https://www.sbert.net/index.html`

[13] `www.huggingface.co/textattack/roberta-base-CoLA`

Task	Model	CP	FLU	ATA	AGG	Δ
Civ.	CAE	***64.2**	***80.6**	*81.9	**39.8**	-2.9
	3ST	60.5	75.3	**89.7**	**39.0**	**0.0**
For.	DAR	*64.5	*27.9	*66.0	*14.2	-30.0
	IMT	*71.5	*73.1	*79.2	*45.2	-7.6
	SCA	*54.4	*14.7	*27.4	*4.0	-40.3
	3ST	**75.6**	**83.1**	**84.9**	**54.7**	**0.0**
Pol.	CAE	*48.3	*76.4	*84.3	*28.7	-2.9
	CON	*57.5	*32.5	***91.3**	*17.3	-18.0
	DAR	*50.4	*32.7	*87.8	*15.8	-30.0
	DLS	*50.9	*50.4	85.3	*20.1	-15.2
	IMT	*42.5	***84.4**	*84.6	*29.6	-7.6
	MUL	***62.6**	*42.3	*82.5	*20.4	-14.9
	SCA	*36.7	*19.5	*73.2	*5.5	-40.3
	UMT	*54.8	*55.7	85.4	*24.2	-11.1
	3ST	55.7	81.0	85.4	**35.3**	**0.0**

Table 2: Automatic scores for CP, FLU, ATA and their aggregated score (AGG) of SOTA models and our approach (3ST) across the Civ(ility), For(mality) and Pol(arity) tasks. Cross-task average AGG difference to 3ST under Δ. Best values per task in **bold** and models selected for human evaluation underlined. Values statistically significantly different ($p < 0.05$) from 3ST are marked with *.

(SR) is then defined as the ratio of successfully transferred instances over all instances. We also report the cross-task average SR difference of a model to 3ST (Δ).

All inter-rater agreements, calculated using Krippendorff-α, lie above 0.7, except for cases where most samples were annotated repeatedly with the same justified rating (e.g. a continuous FLU rating of 4) due to the underlying data distribution, which is sanctioned by the Krippendorff measure. Intra-rater agreement is at an average of 0.928 across all raters. A more detailed description of the evaluation task and a listing of the task- and rater-specific α-values is given in the appendix. For the ratings themselves, we calculate pair-wise statistical significance between SOTA models and 3ST using the Wilcoxon T test ($p < 0.05$).

5 Results and Analysis

5.1 Automatic Evaluation

Table 2 provides an overview of the CP, FLU, ATA and AGG results of all compared models across the three tasks.

Civility On attribute transfer accuracy, 3ST improves by +7.8 points over CAE, while CAE is stronger in content preservation (+3.7) and fluency (+5.3). There is, however, no statistically significant difference in the overall aggregated performance of the models, indicating that they are equivalent in performance.

Formality 3ST substantially outperforms SOTA models in all four categories, with an overall performance (AGG) that surpasses the top-scoring SOTA model (IMT) by +9.5 points. This is indicative, as IMT was trained on a shuffled version of the parallel GYAFC corpus, which contains highly informative human written paraphrases, while 3ST was trained on a truly non-parallel corpus.

Polarity The polarity task has more recent SOTAs to compare to, and the results show that no single model is best in all three categories. While MUL is strongest in content preservation (62.6), its fluency is low and outperformed by 3ST by +38.7 points, leading to a much lower overall performance (AGG) in comparison to 3ST (+14.9). Similarly, CON is strongest in attribute transfer accuracy (91.3) but has a low fluency (32.5), leading to a lower aggregated score than 3ST (+18). IMT is the strongest SOTA model with an overall performance (AGG) of 29.6 and the highest fluency score (84.4). Nevertheless, it is outperformed by 3ST by +5.7 points on overall performance (AGG), which is due to the comparatively better performance in content preservation (+13.2) of 3ST. Interestingly, unsupervised NMT (UMT) performs equally well on attribute transfer accuracy, while being slightly outperformed by 3ST in content preservation (+0.9). This may be due to the information-rich parallel instances automatically found in training by the SPE module. Further, 3ST has a much higher fluency than UMT (+25.3), which is due to its DAE pre-training. While 3ST is not top-performing in any of the three metrics CP, FLU and ATA, its top-scoring overall performance (AGG) shows that it is the most balanced model.

Overall Trends Table 2 shows that 3ST outperforms each of the SOTA models fielded in a single task (CON, DLS, MUL, UMT) by the respective AGG Δ, and all other models (CAE, DAR, IMT, SCA) on average AGG Δ[14]. 3ST achieves high levels of FLU, with ATA in the medium to high 80's, clear testimony to successful style transfer.

5.2 Human Evaluation

Human evaluation shows that 3ST has a high level of **fluency**, as it either outperforms or is on par with

[14]e.g. $\Delta(\text{DAR}, \text{3ST}) = \frac{14.2+15.8}{2} - \frac{54.7+35.3}{2} = -30$ across Formality and Polarity.

Task	Model	CP	FLU	ATA	SR	Δ
Civ.	CAE	**2.97**	4.01	*2.50	17.0	-8.5
	3ST	2.80	**4.05**	**3.03**	**21.0**	**0.0**
For.	DAR	*2.75	*2.87	2.72	3.0	-8.0
	IMT	3.49	4.10	**2.83**	5.0	-13.0
	3ST	**3.75**	**4.29**	2.82	**11.0**	**0.0**
Pol.	CAE	*3.64	4.46	3.90	54.0	-8.5
	CON	4.20	*3.47	3.97	44.0	-23.0
	IMT	*3.54	**4.68**	3.84	47.0	-13.0
	MUL	***4.34**	*3.66	3.68	41.0	-26.0
	3ST	3.99	4.58	**4.03**	**67.0**	**0.0**

Table 3: Average human ratings of CP, FLU, ATA and success rate (SR) on the three transfer tasks Civ(ility), For(mality) and Pol(arity). Cross-task average SR difference to 3ST (Δ). Best values per task in **bold**. Values statistically significantly different ($p < 0.05$) from 3ST are marked with *.

current SOTA models across all three tasks (Table 3), with ratings between 4.05 (civility) and 4.58 (polarity), and gains of up +1.42 (DAR, formality) points. According to the annotation protocol, a rating of 4 and 5 is to describe content written by native speakers, thus annotators deemed most generated sentences to have been written by a native speaker of English.

For **content preservation** and **attribute transfer**, there seems to be a trade-off. In the formality task, 3ST outperforms or is on par with current SOTAs on CP with gains between +0.26 (IMT) and +1.0 (DAR) points, and ATA is on par with the SOTA (−0.01, IMT). Note that for all models tested on the formality task, the success rate is low. This is due to the nature of the training data, where many sentences in the formal portion of the dataset tend to be rather neutral, i.e. neither formal nor informal, rather than truly formal sentences. For the civility task, on the other hand, 3ST outperforms the current SOTA on ATA with gains of +0.53 (CAE) while being on par on CP (−0.17). For the polarity task, the CP is slightly below the best model (−0.35, MUL).

While some models are strong on single values, 3ST has the highest success rate (SR) across all tasks. 3ST outperforms each of the single task models (DAR, CON, MUL) on SR by Δ and each of the multitask models (CAE, IMT) by average cross-task SR Δ, again highlighting that it balances best between the three capabilities CP, FLU and ATA, which leads to best-performing style transfer predictions.

	SRC	*What our ignorant PM, Mad McCallum and stupid Liberal politicians going to say?*
(1)	CAE	*what our pm, ~~trudeau~~ and his liberals are going to do about this?............*
	3ST	*Mad McCallum, what are our politicians going to say?*
	SRC	*Dear Hipster Jackass- Go to Bend.*
(2)	CAE	*dear hippie ~~- go to hawaiian to get around.......~~*
	3ST	*Dear Hipster Jackass- Go to Bend.*
	SRC	*Trump's a liar.*
(3)	CAE	*trump's a liar.*
	3ST	*Trump's a good man.*
	SRC	*Says the idiot on perpetual welfare.*
(4)	CAE	*says the ~~author on the daily basis, on the basis~~ of perpetual welfare.*
	3ST	***Says the guy on perpetual welfare.***
	SRC	*A muslim racist.*
(5)	CAE	*a muslim minority.*
	3ST	~~Not a democrat.~~
	SRC	*Quit trying to justify what this jackass did.*
(6)	CAE	*quit trying to justify what this jackass did.*
	3ST	***Quit trying to justify what he did.***
	SRC	*There was no consensus, 1 idiot and everyone else in the situation let him know he was in the wrong.*
(7)	CAE	*there was no consensus, no one in the room and everyone in the room knew he was in the wrong place.*
	3ST	***No, there was no consensus in the past, and everyone else knew he was in the wrong place.***

Table 4: 3ST and SOTA model (CAE) predictions on the CivCo test set, with **adequate** predictions, error in structure, target attribute, stance reversal, and ~~hallucinations~~ marked.

5.3 Qualitative Analysis

For our qualitative analysis, we focus on the civility task as this is a challenging, novel task and we want to understand its limitations. We analyze the same subset of the test set used for human evaluation and annotate common mistakes. Common errors in the neutral counterparts generated by 3ST can be classified into four classes. We observe fluency or *structural errors* (11% of sentences), e.g. a subject becoming a direct form of address (Table 4, Ex-1). *Attribute errors* (14%) (Ex-2), where toxic content was not successfully removed, are another common source of error. Similarly to Laugier et al. (2021), we observe *stance reversal* (14%), i.e. where a usually negative opinion in the original source sentence is reversed to a positive polarity (Ex-3). This is due to a negativity bias on the toxic side of the CivCo corpus, while the neutral side contains more positive sentences, thus introducing an incentive to

Task	Model	CP	FLU	ATA	AGG
Civ.	3ST	60.5	**75.3**	89.7	**39.0**
	-SPE	***89.5**	*39.4	*12.1	*3.7
	-BT	*44.4	*59.4	90.3	*22.8
	-DAE	*36.8	*43.3	***97.5**	*15.7
	-BT-DAE	*37.8	*43.8	*95.3	*16.4
For.	3ST	75.6	83.1	84.9	**54.7**
	-SPE	***99.3**	*73.4	*17.7	*14.8
	-BT	*66.4	***85.1**	*92.6	*52.8
	-DAE	*55.7	*64.2	*93.1	*35.1
	-BT-DAE	*57.8	*79.5	***94.0**	*44.5
Pol.	3ST	55.7	**81.0**	85.4	**35.3**
	-SPE	***100.0**	*80.5	*2.9	*1.9
	-BT	*44.0	*79.0	*88.3	*29.2
	-DAE	*29.8	*43.6	*89.7	*11.6
	-BT-DAE	*38.0	*63.3	***91.1**	*21.5

Table 5: 3ST Ablation. CP, FLU and ATA with SPE, BT, DAE removed. Best values per task in **bold**.

translate negative sentiment to positive sentiment. Unlike Laugier et al. (2021), we do not observe that hallucinations are most frequent at the end of a sequence (*supererogation*). Rather, *related hallucinations*, where unnecessary content is mixed with words from the original source sentence, are found at arbitrary positions (23%, Ex-4, CAE). We observe few hallucinations where a prediction has no relation with the source (4%, Ex-5).

Phenomena such as hallucinations can become amplified through back-translation (Raunak et al., 2021). However, as they are most prevalent in the civility task, hallucinations in this case are likely originally triggered by long source sentences that i) overwhelm the current models' capacity, and ii) add additional noise to the training. It is less likely that a complex sentence has a perfect rephrasing to match with and therefore instead it will match with a similar rephrasing that introduces additional content, i.e. noise. For reference, the average length of source sentences that triggered hallucinations was 21.9 words, while for adequate re-writings (39%), it was 8 words. Note that we capped sentence lengths to 30 words in the training data while the test data contained sentences with up to 85 words.

Successful rephrasings are usually due to one of two factors. 3ST either *replaces* profane words by their neutral counterparts (Ex-{4,6}) or *removes* them (Ex-7).

5.4 Ablation Study

To analyze the contribution of the three main components (SPE, BT and DAE) of 3ST, we remove them individually from the original architecture and observe the performance of the resulting models on the three different tasks (Table 5). Without SPE, the model merely copies source sentences without performing style transfer, resulting in a large drop in overall performance (AGG). This shows in the low ATA scores (1.9–14.8), which are in direct correlation with the extremely high scores in CP (89.5–100.0) achieved by this model. This underlines that SPE is vital to the style-transfer capabilities of 3ST, as it retrieves similar paraphrases from the style corpora and lets 3ST train on these. This pushes the system to generate back-translations which themselves are paraphrases that fulfill the style-transfer task. BT and DAE are integral parts of 3ST, too, that improve over the underlying self-supervised neural machine translation (-BT-DAE) approach. This can be seen in the drastic drops of CP and FLU scores when BT and DAE techniques are removed. Especially DAE is important for the fluency of the model. The gains in CP and FLU through BT and DAE come at a minor drop in ATA.

6 Conclusion

3ST is a style transfer architecture that efficiently uses the supervisory signals present in non-parallel social media content, by i) jointly learning style transfer and similar sentence extraction during training, ii) using online back-translation and iii) DAE-based initialization. 3ST gains strong results on all three metrics FLU, ATA and CP, outperforming SOTA models on averaged performance (Δ) across their tested tasks in automatic (AGG) and human (SR) evaluation. We present one of the first studies on automatic civil rephrasing and, importantly, identify current weaknesses in the data, which lead to limitations in 3ST and other SOTA models on the civil rephrasing task. Our code and model predictions are publicly available at `https://github.com/uds-lsv/3ST`.

Acknowledgements

We want to thank the annotators for their keen work. Partially funded by the DFG (WI 4204/3-1), German Federal Ministry of Education and Research (01IW20010) and the EU Horizon 2020 project COMPRISE (3081705). The author is responsible for the content of this publication.

References

Mikel Artetxe, Gorka Labaka, and Eneko Agirre. 2019. An effective approach to unsupervised machine translation. In *Proceedings of the 57th Annual Meeting of the Association for Computational Linguistics*, pages 194–203, Florence, Italy. ACL.

Mikel Artetxe and Holger Schwenk. 2019. Margin-based parallel corpus mining with multilingual sentence embeddings. In *Proceedings of the 57th Annual Meeting of the Association for Computational Linguistics*, pages 3197–3203, Florence, Italy. ACL.

Steven Bird and Edward Loper. 2004. NLTK: The natural language toolkit. In *Proceedings of the ACL Interactive Poster and Demonstration Sessions*, pages 214–217, Barcelona, Spain. Association for Computational Linguistics.

Yixin Cao, Ruihao Shui, Liangming Pan, Min-Yen Kan, Zhiyuan Liu, and Tat-Seng Chua. 2020. Expertise style transfer: A new task towards better communication between experts and laymen. In *Proceedings of the 58th Annual Meeting of the Association for Computational Linguistics*, pages 1061–1071, Online. ACL.

Kunal Chawla and Diyi Yang. 2020. Semi-supervised formality style transfer using language model discriminator and mutual information maximization. In *Findings of the Association for Computational Linguistics: EMNLP 2020*, pages 2340–2354, Online. ACL.

Ning Dai, Jianze Liang, Xipeng Qiu, and Xuanjing Huang. 2019. Style transformer: Unpaired text style transfer without disentangled latent representation. In *Proceedings of the 57th Annual Meeting of the Association for Computational Linguistics*, pages 5997–6007, Florence, Italy. ACL.

Zhenxin Fu, Xiaoye Tan, Nanyun Peng, Dongyan Zhao, and Rui Yan. 2018. Style transfer in text: Exploration and evaluation. In *Proceedings of the Thirty-Second AAAI Conference on Artificial Intelligence (AAAI-18)*, volume 32, pages 663–670, New Orleans, LA.

Hila Gonen and Yoav Goldberg. 2019. Lipstick on a pig: Debiasing methods cover up systematic gender biases in word embeddings but do not remove them. In *Proceedings of the 2019 Conference of the North American Chapter of the Association for Computational Linguistics: Human Language Technologies, Volume 1 (Long and Short Papers)*, pages 609–614, Minneapolis, MN. ACL.

Junxian He, Xinyi Wang, Graham Neubig, and Taylor Berg-Kirkpatrick. 2020. A probabilistic formulation of unsupervised text style transfer. In *Proceedings of ICLR*.

Zhiting Hu, Zichao Yang, Xiaodan Liang, Ruslan Salakhutdinov, and Eric P. Xing. 2017. Toward controlled generation of text. In *Proceedings of the 34th International Conference on Machine Learning*, volume 70 of *Proceedings of Machine Learning Research*, pages 1587–1596, International Convention Centre, Sydney, Australia. PMLR.

Harsh Jhamtani, Varun Gangal, Eduard Hovy, and Eric Nyberg. 2017. Shakespearizing modern language using copy-enriched sequence to sequence models. In *Proceedings of the Workshop on Stylistic Variation*, pages 10–19, Copenhagen, DK. ACL.

Di Jin, Zhijing Jin, Zhiting Hu, Olga Vechtomova, and Rada Mihalcea. 2021. Deep learning for text style transfer: A survey. *CoRR*, abs/2011.00416.

Di Jin, Zhijing Jin, Joey Tianyi Zhou, Lisa Orii, and Peter Szolovits. 2020. Hooks in the headline: Learning to generate headlines with controlled styles. In *Proceedings of the 58th Annual Meeting of the Association for Computational Linguistics*, pages 5082–5093, Online. ACL.

Zhijing Jin, Di Jin, Jonas Mueller, Nicholas Matthews, and Enrico Santus. 2019. IMaT: Unsupervised text attribute transfer via iterative matching and translation. In *Proceedings of the 2019 Conference on Empirical Methods in Natural Language Processing and the 9th International Joint Conference on Natural Language Processing (EMNLP-IJCNLP)*, pages 3097–3109, Hong Kong, China. ACL.

Jeff Johnson, Matthijs Douze, and Hervé Jégou. 2019. Billion-scale similarity search with gpus. *IEEE Transactions on Big Data*, 7(3).

David Jurgens, Libby Hemphill, and Eshwar Chandrasekharan. 2019. A just and comprehensive strategy for using NLP to address online abuse. In *Proceedings of the 57th Annual Meeting of the Association for Computational Linguistics*, pages 3658–3666, Florence, Italy. ACL.

Yunsu Kim, Miguel Graça, and Hermann Ney. 2020. When and why is unsupervised neural machine translation useless? In *Proceedings of the 22nd Annual Conference of the European Association for Machine Translation*, pages 35–44, Lisboa, Portugal. European Association for Machine Translation.

Guillaume Klein, Yoon Kim, Yuntian Deng, Jean Senellart, and Alexander Rush. 2017. OpenNMT: Open-source toolkit for neural machine translation. In *Proceedings of ACL 2017, System Demonstrations*, pages 67–72, Vancouver, Canada. ACL.

Philipp Koehn, Hieu Hoang, Alexandra Birch, Chris Callison-Burch, Marcello Federico, Nicola Bertoldi, Brooke Cowan, Wade Shen, Christine Moran, Richard Zens, Chris Dyer, Ondřej Bojar, Alexandra Constantin, and Evan Herbst. 2007. Moses: Open source toolkit for statistical machine translation. In *Proceedings of the 45th Annual Meeting of the Association for Computational Linguistics Companion Volume Proceedings of the Demo and Poster Sessions*, pages 177–180, Prague, Czech Republic. ACL.

Klaus Krippendorff. 2004. *Content Analysis, an Introduction to Its Methodology*. Sage Publications, Thousand Oaks, Calif.

Kalpesh Krishna, John Wieting, and Mohit Iyyer. 2020. Reformulating unsupervised style transfer as paraphrase generation. In *Proceedings of the 2020 Conference on Empirical Methods in Natural Language Processing (EMNLP)*, pages 737–762, Online. ACL.

Guillaume Lample, Alexis Conneau, Ludovic Denoyer, and Marc'Aurelio Ranzato. 2018. Unsupervised machine translation using monolingual corpora only. In *6th International Conference on Learning Representations, ICLR*, Vancouver, BC, Canada.

Guillaume Lample, Sandeep Subramanian, Eric Michael Smith, Ludovic Denoyer, Marc'Aurelio Ranzato, and Y-Lan Boureau. 2019. Multiple-attribute text rewriting. In *7th International Conference on Learning Representations, ICLR*, New Orleans, LA.

Léo Laugier, John Pavlopoulos, Jeffrey Sorensen, and Lucas Dixon. 2021. Civil rephrases of toxic texts with self-supervised transformers. In *Proceedings of the 16th Conference of the European Chapter of the Association for Computational Linguistics: Main Volume*, pages 1442–1461, Online. ACL.

Mike Lewis, Yinhan Liu, Naman Goyal, Marjan Ghazvininejad, Abdelrahman Mohamed, Omer Levy, Veselin Stoyanov, and Luke Zettlemoyer. 2020. BART: Denoising sequence-to-sequence pre-training for natural language generation, translation, and comprehension. In *Proceedings of the 58th Annual Meeting of the Association for Computational Linguistics*, pages 7871–7880, Online. ACL.

Juncen Li, Robin Jia, He He, and Percy Liang. 2018. Delete, retrieve, generate: a simple approach to sentiment and style transfer. In *Proceedings of the 2018 Conference of the North American Chapter of the Association for Computational Linguistics: Human Language Technologies, Volume 1 (Long Papers)*, pages 1865–1874, New Orleans, Louisiana. ACL.

Yinhan Liu, Myle Ott, Naman Goyal, Jingfei Du, Mandar Joshi, Danqi Chen, Omer Levy, Mike Lewis, Luke Zettlemoyer, and Veselin Stoyanov. 2019. Roberta: A robustly optimized bert pretraining approach.

Fuli Luo, Peng Li, Jie Zhou, Pengcheng Yang, Baobao Chang, Xu Sun, and Zhifang Sui. 2019. A dual reinforcement learning framework for unsupervised text style transfer. In *Proceedings of the Twenty-Eighth International Joint Conference on Artificial Intelligence, IJCAI-19*, pages 5116–5122. International Joint Conferences on Artificial Intelligence Organization.

Louis Martin, Angela Fan, Éric de la Clergerie, Antoine Bordes, and Benoît Sagot. 2020. Multilingual unsupervised sentence simplification. *CoRR*, abs/2005.00352.

Remi Mir, Bjarke Felbo, Nick Obradovich, and Iyad Rahwan. 2019. Evaluating style transfer for text. In *Proceedings of the 2019 Conference of the North American Chapter of the Association for Computational Linguistics: Human Language Technologies, Volume 1 (Long and Short Papers)*, pages 495–504, Minneapolis, MN. ACL.

Cicero Nogueira dos Santos, Igor Melnyk, and Inkit Padhi. 2018. Fighting offensive language on social media with unsupervised text style transfer. In *Proceedings of the 56th Annual Meeting of the Association for Computational Linguistics (Volume 2: Short Papers)*, pages 189–194, Melbourne, Australia. ACL.

Shrimai Prabhumoye, Yulia Tsvetkov, Ruslan Salakhutdinov, and Alan W Black. 2018. Style transfer through back-translation. In *Proceedings of the 56th Annual Meeting of the Association for Computational Linguistics (Volume 1: Long Papers)*, pages 866–876, Melbourne, Australia. ACL.

Sudha Rao and Joel Tetreault. 2018. Dear sir or madam, may I introduce the GYAFC dataset: Corpus, benchmarks and metrics for formality style transfer. In *Proceedings of the 2018 Conference of the North American Chapter of the Association for Computational Linguistics: Human Language Technologies, Volume 1 (Long Papers)*, pages 129–140, New Orleans, LA. ACL.

Vikas Raunak, Arul Menezes, and Marcin Junczys-Dowmunt. 2021. The curious case of hallucinations in neural machine translation. In *Proceedings of the 2021 Conference of the North American Chapter of the Association for Computational Linguistics: Human Language Technologies*, pages 1172–1183, Online. ACL.

Dana Ruiter, Cristina España-Bonet, and Josef van Genabith. 2019. Self-supervised neural machine translation. In *Proceedings of the 57th Annual Meeting of the Association for Computational Linguistics*, pages 1828–1834, Florence, Italy. ACL.

Dana Ruiter, Dietrich Klakow, Josef van Genabith, and Cristina España-Bonet. 2021. Integrating unsupervised data generation into self-supervised neural machine translation for low-resource languages. In *Proceedings of Machine Translation Summit XVIII: Research Track*, pages 76–91, Virtual. Association for Machine Translation in the Americas.

Dana Ruiter, Josef van Genabith, and Cristina España-Bonet. 2020. Self-induced curriculum learning in self-supervised neural machine translation. In *Proceedings of the 2020 Conference on Empirical Methods in Natural Language Processing (EMNLP)*, pages 2560–2571, Online. ACL.

Rico Sennrich, Barry Haddow, and Alexandra Birch. 2016. Neural machine translation of rare words with subword units. In *Proceedings of the 54th Annual Meeting of the Association for Computational Linguistics (Volume 1: Long Papers)*, pages 1715–1725, Berlin, Germany. ACL.

Tianxiao Shen, Tao Lei, Regina Barzilay, and Tommi Jaakkola. 2017. Style transfer from non-parallel text by cross-alignment. In *Advances in Neural Information Processing Systems*, volume 30, pages 6830–6841. Curran Associates, Inc.

Serra Sinem Tekiroğlu, Yi-Ling Chung, and Marco Guerini. 2020. Generating counter narratives against online hate speech: Data and strategies. In *Proceedings of the 58th Annual Meeting of the Association for Computational Linguistics*, pages 1177–1190, Online. ACL.

Yunli Wang, Yu Wu, Lili Mou, Zhoujun Li, and Wen-Han Chao. 2020. Formality style transfer with shared latent space. In *Proceedings of the 28th International Conference on Computational Linguistics*, pages 2236–2249, Barcelona, Spain (Online). International Committee on Computational Linguistics.

Alex Warstadt, Amanpreet Singh, and Samuel R. Bowman. 2019. Neural network acceptability judgments. *Transactions of the Association for Computational Linguistics*, 7:625–641.

John Wieting, Taylor Berg-Kirkpatrick, Kevin Gimpel, and Graham Neubig. 2019. Beyond BLEU:training neural machine translation with semantic similarity. In *Proceedings of the 57th Annual Meeting of the Association for Computational Linguistics*, pages 4344–4355, Florence, Italy. ACL.

Zhilin Yang, Zihang Dai, Yiming Yang, Jaime Carbonell, Russ R Salakhutdinov, and Quoc V Le. 2019. Xlnet: Generalized autoregressive pretraining for language understanding. In *Advances in neural information processing systems*, pages 5753–5763.

A Human Evaluation Task

We perform a human evaluation to assess the quality of the top performing models according to automatic metrics.

We select 3 systems for Formality, 5 systems for Polarity and the only 2 systems available for the Civility task. For each of these tasks, we sample 100 data points from the original test set and the corresponding predictions of the different models. We randomly duplicate 5 of the points for quality controls, resulting in evaluation tests with 105 sentences per system. Three fluent English speakers (*raters*) were shown with pairs source–system prediction and were asked to rate the content preservation, fluency and attribute transfer accuracy of the predictions on a 5-point Likert scale. Raters were payed around 10 Euros per hour of work.

We calculate the reliability of the ratings using Krippendorff-α (Krippendorff, 2004). Table 6 shows the inter-rater agreement measured by α for content preservation (CP), fluency (FLU) and attribute transfer accuracy (ATA). Notice that α significantly differs between tasks. The lower α on polarity CP and formality task ATA is due to the repetitive ratings of the same kind. i.e. $4, 5$ on polarity CP and 3 for formality ATA, which is sanctioned by the Krippendorff measure. For the intra-rater agreement estimated from 40 duplicated sentences per rater, we obtain values of 0.988 (Rater-1), 0.869 (Rater-2) and 0.927 (Rater-3).

Task	**Krippendorff-α**		
	CP	FLU	ATA
Civility	0.744	0.579	0.688
Formality	0.751	0.718	0.352
Polarity	0.426	0.705	0.837

Table 6: Inter-rater agreement calculated using Krippendorff-α across the different tasks and metrics.

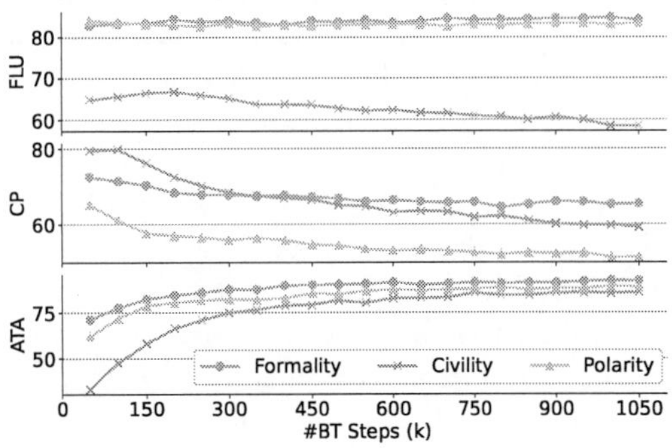

Figure 2: FLU, CP and ATA of generated back-translations (BTs) during training of 3ST on the three transfer tasks.

B Performance Evolution

The back-translations that 3ST generates during training give us a direct insight into the changing state of the model throughout the training process. We thus automatically evaluate ATA, FLU and CP on the back-translations over time.

BT **fluency** (Figure 2, top) on all three tasks is strong already at the beginning of training, due to the DAE pre-training. For the formality and polarity task, the high level of FLU remains stable ($\sim$ 80) throughout training, while for Civility it slightly drops. This underlines the observation that the Civility task is prone to hallucinations due to the sparse amount of parallel supervisory signals in the dataset, which then leads to lower FLU scores.

For all tasks, **content preservation** between the generated BTs and the source sentences is already high at the beginning of training. This is due to the DAE pre-training which taught the models to copy and denoise inputs. All of the models decay in CP over time, showing that they are slowly diverging from merely copying inputs. CP scores of the formality and the polarity tasks are close to convergence at around $1M$ train steps, while the scores of the civility task keep on decaying. This may again be due to the complexity of the data of the toxicity task, which contains longer sequences than the other two. This can lead to hallucinations when supervisory signals are lacking.

As back-translation CP decays, **attribute transfer** accuracy increases dramatically. Especially on the civility task, where the initial accuracy is low (8.2%) but grows to ATA $\sim 82\%$. For the other two tasks, the curves are less steep, and most of the transfer is learned at the beginning, within the first $300k$ generated BTs, after which they converge with ATA $\sim 95\%$ (formality) and $\sim 88\%$ (polarity). This shows the trade-off between attribute accuracy and content preservation: the higher the ATA, the lower the CP score. Nevertheless, as ATA converges earlier than CP (for formality and polarity tasks), an earlier training stop can easily benefit content preservation while having little impact on the already converged ATA.

C Sample Predictions

For each of the three tasks, Civility, Formality and Polarity, we randomly sample 5 source sentences from the respective test sets. In Table 7 we present these source sentences together with the corresponding prediction of 3ST and the two best-scoring SOTA models with respect to the AGG score per task, namely CAE for Civility, DAR and IMT for Formality and CAE and IMT for Polarity.

Civility	
SRC	*It is time to impeach this idiot judge.*
CAE	*it is time to impeach this judge.*
3ST	*It is time to impeach this judge.*
SRC	*This is classic example of collective corporate stupidity and individual managerial malice.*
CAE	*this is classic case of corporate welfare and collective bargaining.*
3ST	*This is classic example of collective corporate greed and individual managerial malice.*
SRC	*You silly goose!*
CAE	*you mean the goose, right?*
3ST	*You forgot the goose!*
SRC	*Afraid of how idiotic social engineering makes people look?*
CAE	*imagine how socially acceptable some of the people make?*
3ST	*Afraid of how social engineering works.*
SRC	*Stupid idea.*
CAE	*no idea.............*
3ST	*Not a good idea.*
Formality	
SRC	*haha julesac is funny, but mean.*
DAR	*is funny , but I understand what you mean .*
IMT	*That is funny . Those silly people annoy me !*
3ST	*Julesac is very funny.*
SRC	*DON'T LET HER RULE YOUR LIFE, SHE WILL JUST HAVE TO LEARN TO DEAL WITH IT.*
DAR	*LET HER BE , SHE WILL LEARN TO DEAL WITH IT .*
IMT	*TELL HER YOUR TRUE FEELINGS , IT MAY SHOCK HER BUT WILL WORK .*
3ST	*Do NOT LET HER RUN WITH YOU, SHE WILL NEVER HAVE TO WORK.*
SRC	*cause it's buy one take one.*
DAR	*I can not wait to buy one take one .*
IMT	*Because it is buy one take one .*
3ST	*You can buy one.*
SRC	*All my votes are going to Taylor Hicks though...*
DAR	*All my votes are , and I am going to Hicks*
IMT	*All my votes are going to Taylor .*
3ST	*All my votes are going to be Taylor Hicks.*
SRC	*but paris hilton isn't far behind.*
DAR	*I do not know but is n't far behind .*
IMT	*I ca n't read the stars , just find another way to say it .*
3ST	*Paris hilton is far behind.*
Polarity	
SRC	*even if i was insanely drunk , i could n't force this pizza down .*
CAE	*even if i was n't in the mood , i loved this place .*
IMT	*honestly , i could n't stop eating it because it was so good !*
3ST	*even if i was drunk , i could still force myself .*
SRC	*i will definitely return often !*
CAE	*i will not return often ! ! ! !*
IMT	*i will definitely not return !*
3ST	*i will not return often !*
SRC	*no massage with my manicure or pedicure .*
CAE	*great massage with great pedicure and manicure .*
IMT	*awesome relaxation and massage with my pedicure .*
3ST	*great massage with my manicure and pedicure .*
SRC	*excellent knowledgeable dentist and staff !*
CAE	*excellent dentist and dental hygienist ! ! ! !*
IMT	*not very knowledgeable staff !*
3ST	*horrible dentist and staff !*
SRC	*do not go here if you are interested in eating good food .*
CAE	*definitely recommend this place if you are looking for good food at a good price .*
IMT	*if you are looking for consistent delicious food go here .*
3ST	*if you are looking for good food , this is the place to go .*

Table 7: Examples of 3ST and SOTA model predictions.

Detecting Rumor Veracity with Only Textual Information by Double-Channel Structure

Alex Gunwoo Kim*
Seoul National University
kimgunwoo95@snu.ac.kr

Sangwon Yoon*
Artificial Society Inc.
sangwon38383@snu.ac.kr

Abstract

Kyle (1985) proposes two types of rumors: informed rumors that are based on some private information and uninformed rumors that are not based on any information (i.e. bluffing). Also, prior studies find that when people have credible source of information, they are likely to use a more confident textual tone in their spreading of rumors. Motivated by these theoretical findings, we propose a double-channel structure to determine the ex-ante veracity of rumors on social media. Our ultimate goal is to classify each rumor into true, false, or unverifiable category. We first assign each text into either certain (informed rumor) or uncertain (uninformed rumor) category. Then, we apply lie detection algorithm to informed rumors and thread-reply agreement detection algorithm to uninformed rumors. Using the dataset of SemEval 2019 Task 7, which requires ex-ante threefold classification (true, false, or unverifiable) of social media rumors, our model yields a macro-F1 score of 0.4027, outperforming all the baseline models and the second-place winner (Gorrell et al., 2019). Furthermore, we empirically validate that the double-channel structure outperforms single-channel structures which use either lie detection or agreement detection algorithm to all posts.[1]

1 Introduction

Detecting the veracity of rumors spreading out on various social media platforms has been of great importance. Indeed, several studies find that online rumors can affect human behaviors (Pound and Zeckhauser, 1990; Jia et al., 2020). However, detecting the veracity of rumors is not a simple task. Unlike news articles which are considered *ex-post*, rumors are *ex-ante* (Vosoughi et al., 2018; Shu et al., 2017). At the time when a rumor originates, the information user is not able to determine its veracity by checking whether the event has happened or not. Instead, the user can make his best guess based on the information set that he has been exposed to. In contrast, we can check the veracity of a news article immediately by comparing it with the event that the article is referring to (Cao et al., 2018). There can be diverse definitions of rumors, but in our study we define the rumors as "*information that cannot be verified at the time of origination* (Gorrell et al., 2019)".[2] Therefore, whether a rumor is false or not can only be determined afterward when the user can objectively observe the event (Zubiaga et al., 2016).

In our research, we use only the textual features of the posts and their corresponding replies, mitigating the concern that our results are driven by external information that was not readily available to the general public at the early stage of rumor origination. Also, our model shows that textual features embedded in social media posts can reasonably predict the ex-ante veracity of rumors.

Kyle (1985) provides a theoretical model that explains the motivation of spreading rumors. The model includes two types of rumor spreading: (i) rumors based on private information and (ii) rumors not based on any information (i.e. bluffing). Spreaders with private information can either deliver the correct information that they have or intentionally distort the information. On the other hand, there can be spreaders without private information. They take advantage of their social influence and spread some made-up rumors in favor of their benefits (Van Bommel, 2003). Refer to Figure 1 for the visual representation of rumor classification.

Studies on linguistics find that the perceived credibility of information source affects the tone of

*Equal contribution.

[1]The code to replicate the results of this article can be found here: https://github.com/swarso95/rumour_analysis-.

[2]This definition excludes tasks such as PHEME from our scope of analysis since they require "fact-checking" instead of "ex-ante prediction of veracity."

Proceedings of the Tenth International Workshop on Natural Language Processing for Social Media (SocialNLP 2022), pages 24 - 33
July 14-15, 2022 ©2022 Association for Computational Linguistics

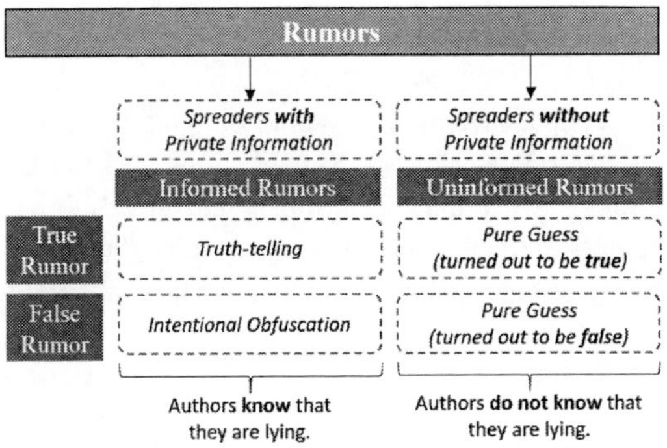

Figure 1: This figure illustrates the conceptual classification of rumors based on prior linguistics literature. Our model motivates from these two different subgroups.

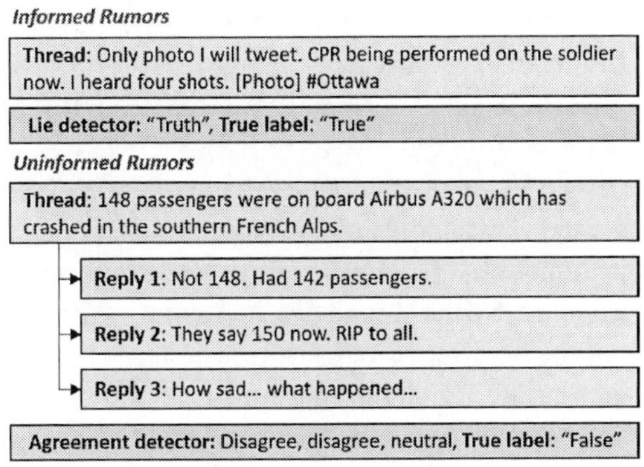

Figure 2: This figure illustrates an example of the classification results of our model.

rumors on social media (Kim et al., 2019; Kamins et al., 1997; DiFonzo, 2010). The more credible the information source is, the more confident the textual tone is. For instance, rumors based on concrete source of information are likely to include a reference link or refer to specific identities. In contrast, bluffing is less likely to encompass the source of information.

Combining these two lines of literature, rumors based on private information and rumors *not* based on private information are systematically and linguistically different. However, prior studies that intent to identify the "ex-ante" veracity of social media rumors (e.g. Enayet and El-Beltagy, 2017; Wu et al., 2015; Rao et al., 2021) treat every rumor equally. In other words, they apply the same logic or algorithm to both types of rumors. To tackle this issue, we conjecture that dividing the sample into "informed rumors" (rumors that are based on private information) and "uninformed rumors" (rumors that do not have any information background) and applying different algorithms to the two subgroups can improve the performance of veracity detection.

Motivated by the linguistic differences between the two rumor types, we first divide the sample based on the textual confidence of rumor texts. This algorithm classifies each rumor into certain (informed rumors) or uncertain (uninformed rumors) category. As in Kyle (1985), informed spreaders can strategically choose whether or not to truthfully report the private information that they have. If they choose to distort the information, the spreaders are intentionally lying. In contrast, they might opt for truth-telling. Therefore, we apply the lie detection algorithm to informed rumors to determine their ex-ante veracity.

On the other hand, for uninformed rumors, the spreaders are not intentionally lying nor are they truthfully reporting. Therefore, we do not expect lie detection algorithm to function properly. Instead, we rely on the agreement detector algorithm (Kumar and Carley, 2019; Yu et al., 2020). Prior literature finds that when primary replies are generally in accordance with the original thread, the thread is likely to be true ex-post, and vice-versa (Akhtar et al., 2018). In our model, we use primary replies and calculate their agreement scores with the main thread. The logic beyond this algorithm is that the wisdom of the crowd plays a role in social media platforms to provide accurate information (Brown and Reade, 2019; Yu et al., 2020). We leave the mathematical details for Sections 3.1 and 3.2.

In our study, we further validate this theory-motivated double-channel approach by showing that our model outperforms the single channel structures (applying lie detection algorithm or agreement detection algorithm to both channels). Section 4.1 outlines the relative performance of double-channel model compared with other structures and with other competing models of SemEval 2019. Specifically, our model achieves a macro-F1 score of 0.4027, which is approximately 12% points higher than that of the second-place winner.

Figure 2 provides an example of the classification results of our model. The uninformed thread does not refer to any source information while the informed one does so. Lie detection algorithm correctly classifies the veracity of the informed rumor. On the other hand, agreement detector captures whether each primary reply is in accordance with the main thread. The algorithm correctly classifies the thread to be false.

Our research contributes to the existing line of literature for at least two reasons. First, we are the first to employ a double-channel model to detect the veracity of rumors. This approach reflects the rumor classification (informed and uninformed) proposed by the linguistics literature. We show that the lie detection algorithm is relatively more appropriate for classifying informed rumors and that the agreement detection is more accurate when classifying uninformed rumors. After employing a BERT-based certainty classifier to divide the samples into two subgroups, we find a significant increase in our classification accuracy.

Second, we also use minimal information to obtain our results. Our F1 score falls behind the winner of SemEval 2019 Task 7, primarily due to the scope of the information that we use. The winner exploits a variety of peripheral information such as the account credibility or the number of followers (Li et al., 2019a), which explains a great portion of their results. However, such a model cannot be applied to anonymous rumors or rumors posted by relatively "new" users. In contrast, our model operates even without considering the peripheral or user-specific information, allowing it be applied to even anonymous rumors in social media. Also, since the second-place winner primarily focuses on the textual dimension of Twitter posts, we find the second-place winner more comparable to our assumptions and experiments.

2 Related Works

2.1 Information Sets

Prior literature mainly relies on two information sets to calculate the ex-ante veracity of rumors. First, several studies use user information such as the number of followers, the number of replies, the existence of hashtags and photos, and the number of previous tweets to determine the veracity of each rumor (Castillo et al., 2011; Vosoughi, 2015; Liu and Wu, 2018; Li et al., 2019a). This line of research assumes that the users who care about their accounts' reputation are likely to post true rumors. However, it is difficult to measure the account's credibility when the rumor originates since the account information is time-variant. Even though a specific account currently has many followers, we cannot guarantee that the account used to have the same number of followers when the rumor originated. Furthermore, such information is not available for anonymous rumors.

Second, several studies apply linguistic features to detect false rumors. Some studies measure the subjectivity of the posts using some attribute-based textual elements such as subjective verbs and imperative tenses (Li et al., 2019a; Ma et al., 2017; Liu et al., 2015). Vosoughi (2015) analyzes the sentiment of tweets under various circumstances and classify the tweets using the contextual information. Barsever et al. (2020) develop a better-performing lie detector with BERT, indicating that unsupervised learning can outperform traditional rule-based lie detection algorithms. However, the linguistic feature-based approach has limitations in that most of the rumors are arbitrary in nature, and lie detection, which is based on the author's intention, may not function well in the domain that contains many random posts.

Other research focuses on the network model to capture information propagation (Gupta et al., 2012; Rosenfeld et al., 2020). Also, Liu and Wu (2018) develop a model that examines the early detection of rumors with RNN classification. Also, several works aim to determine whether a given online post is a rumor or not (Kochkina et al., 2018) by implementing a multi-task learning algorithm.

2.2 Classification Algorithm

While several studies deal with improving the input dataset, others focus on improving the classification algorithm. Some early studies are based on Support Vector Machine (SVM) (Enayet and El-Beltagy, 2017; Wu et al., 2015) or neural networks (NN) to conduct the classification (Ma et al., 2017; Wang et al., 2018).

Recent works turn to unsupervised learning of rumors. Instead of inputting a number of user-specific variables, Rao et al. (2021) develop STANKER, a fine-tuned BERT model which incorporates both the textual features of posts and their comments. This model inputs comments as one of the crucial auxiliary factors, measuring the co-attention between the posts and comments. Our model differs from STANKER for at least two reasons. First, unlike STANKER which uses single-channel approach, we design a double-channel approach. This approach allows us to apply a more appropriate classifier to each thread. Second, STANKER is trained with more than 5,000 labeled observations. These observations do not include the "unverified" category as well. However, since our train set contains only 365 observations with three different labels, we utilize external open-source datasets from similar (yet slightly different) domains to further train each phase of our model. Therefore, we aim to improve the performance of the model with the minimal information and fine-tune the model to mitigate the domain-shift problem.

On the other hand, Yu et al. (2020) develops a Hierarchical Transformer which disaggregates a thread into subthreads. Then, they process the stance labels obtained from the subthreads to determine the veracity of a rumor. Their method focuses on the mutual interaction among the users but may not function properly at the early stage of rumor origination when there are not enough reply posts. Furthermore, Dougrez-Lewis et al. (2021) employ a Variational Autoencoder to filter out the topics that are useful in stance determination and achieve a macro-F1 score of 0.434 on PHEME dataset.

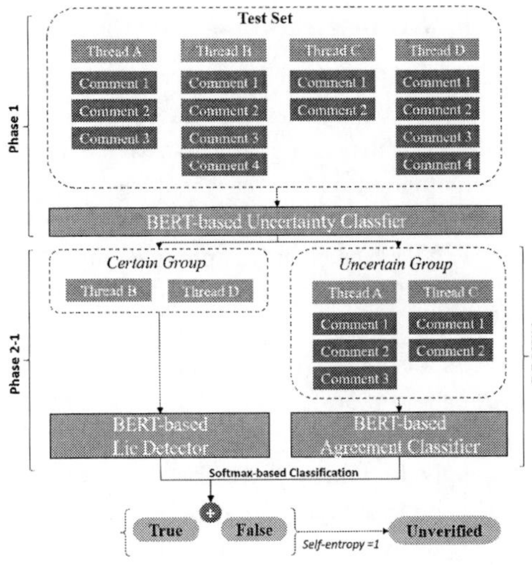

Figure 3: This figure illustrates the model pipeline. Uncertainty classifier (Phase 1) divides the sample into two subgroups, and lie detector (Phase 2-1) and agreement classifier (Phase 2-2) further classifies each thread into true or false category. We assign the observations with self-entropy of 1 to unverified category.

3 Model Design

3.1 Overall Structure

Our model is the first to introduce a double-channel approach in rumor veracity detection. We first divide the sample into two subsamples depending on the textual confidence of each thread. Here, a confidence score examines whether the author is writing the post with a strong belief or not (Farkas et al., 2010). Authors who spread informed rumors are more likely to be confident in their postings (DiFonzo, 2010). Therefore, our BERT-based uncertainty-classifier assigns each thread into one of the two categories: certain (informed rumor) and uncertain (uninformed rumor) (Devlin et al., 2018). We assume that informed rumors are based on educated belief, insider information, or other reliable sources. We name this step Phase 1.

Then, we turn to lie detection algorithms for informed rumors. Note that when the author has baseline information, it is the author's choice to decide whether or not to disclose the true information to the public. Textual lie detection focuses on lexical cues that are prevalent in intentional lies (Masip et al., 2012) and examines the author's intention – it identifies whether the writer is intentionally distorting actual information. If the authors decide to distort the information, the lie detector is expected to identify such intention (Mansbach et al., 2021; Barsever et al., 2020). We use a BERT-based lie classifier to assign the threads into a true or false category. We call this step Phase 2-1.

On the other hand, for uninformed rumors, we cannot rely on the linguistic lie detection. Uninformed rumors are written by people who do not have any specific reference when spreading the rumors. In other words, they make an uninformed guess or even write some random facts in their accounts. Since the writers do not intend to deceive other people (they do not even know what is true or false), the lie detection algorithm may not function properly. Therefore, we should take a different approach to determine the veracity of such rumors. Here, we focus on the agreement score of each reply. Users actively respond to the rumors in social media, and the wisdom of the crowd is known to generate remarkably accurate information (Brown and Reade, 2019; Navajas et al., 2018). In our study, we calculate the degree of agreement of each primary reply to the thread. Then, using the agreement score of the replies, we estimate the veracity of the thread. We call this step Phase 2-2.

For the visual representation of our pipeline, refer to Figure 3. We use Tesla V100 SXM2 32GB GPU to train our model. We use BERT in all phases of our model since BERT and its variants achieve the state-of-the-art performance in text classification tasks (Liu et al., 2019; Lan et al., 2019).

3.2 Phase 1: Detecting Linguistic Certainty

We develop a BERT-based certainty classifier. Our classifier is a binary classifier based on a BERT sentence classifier. Our goal is to assign each sentence (Twitter or Reddit thread) into one of the two categories: certain or uncertain. We first train our model with the labeled dataset provided in CoNLL-2010 Shared Task (Farkas et al., 2010). The dataset contains binary labels (certain or uncertain) and 7,363 observations. We use a batch size of 32 and a learning rate of 5e-5. We train the model for five epochs and use Adam optimizer.

We apply the trained BERT classifier to our train set. This process yields 365 distinct thread-label pairs. However, the domain of the dataset that we use to train the model slightly differs from the domain of the dataset that we have. To tackle this domain-shift issue, we sample 21 observations from each category (certain and uncertain) and re-train the model for five epochs. We select the same number of observations from the two categories to mitigate the concern arising from severely imbalanced classifications. We use a batch size of 32 and a learning rate of 5e-5. This procedure assuages the potential bias due to domain-shifting.

We set a label smoothing rate of 0.2 for both training steps. Label smoothing resolves the classification imbalance due to the differences in the two domains and the potential overfitting due to the limited number of our training samples (Szegedy et al., 2016). We apply Phase 1 to all test samples and obtain 81 distinct thread-label pairs. 17 of them are classified as informed rumors, and the remaining 64 observations are classified as uninformed rumors.

3.3 Phase 2-1: Fake Rumor Identification with Lie Detection Algorithm

We apply Phase 2-1 to informed rumors from Phase 1. We develop a BERT-based binary sentence classifier to detect lies from lexical cues. Similarly, we take a two-step approach to train the model. First, we use the open-source dataset to train a model that detects scams and lies in social media (Ott et al., 2011; Ott et al., 2013). This dataset contains 1,600 pre-labeled texts. We train the model for five epochs with a batch size of 32, a learning rate of 5e-5, and a label smoothing rate of 0.3. We also use Adam optimizer.

Then, we fine-tune the model with the train dataset of SemEval 2019 Task 7. According to the definition, unverified samples are those with zero confidence scores. Therefore, when fine-tuning our model, unverified observations are of no use. We exclude the unverified samples and use only observations with true or false labels. We fine-tune the model for one epoch using the samples that are classified as certain in Phase 1. Our batch size is 32 and learning rate is 5e-5. Unlike certainty classification of Phase 1, the domains and objectives of the external dataset that we use are similar to our primary goal – determining the veracity of a given statement. However, in Phase 1, the surrogate dataset aims at discerning non-factual and factual information. That is, the objectives of the two tasks are similar but not the same. Therefore, we train the model for five epochs in Phase 1. In Phase 2-1, since the two tasks deal with the same agenda, it suffices to fine-tune the model for one epoch.

When applied to the test set, our lie detector yields 81 distinct thread-label pairs. The label includes true and false indicators based on the softmax values. That is, when the softmax value of true is larger than the softmax of false the program returns true and vice versa. Following the definition of the unverified rumors, we classify the samples with self-entropy score of 1 into unverified category. Otherwise, we use the labels obtained from our lie detector.

The self-entropy of each observation is

$$H(x) = -\frac{1}{\log 2}\sum_{n=0}^{1} l_n(x)\log l_n(x)$$

, where x denotes each observation and $l_n(x)$ denotes the probability that x belongs to each category ($n = 0, 1$).

3.4 Phase 2-2: Fake Rumor Identification with Reply Agreement Score

We apply Phase 2-2 to uninformed rumors from Phase 1. Here, we develop a BERT-based triple sentence classifier that assigns each sentence pair into one of the three categories: agreement, disagreement, and none. Here, the input is a sentence pair composed of one thread and its corresponding primary reply. For instance, in Figure 4, since thread A has four primary replies, we construct four sentence pairs. We exclude non-primary replies (replies to the previous replies) since it is unclear whether such non-primary replies are agreeing (or disagreeing) to the thread itself or to the primary reply. Therefore, the classifier measures whether

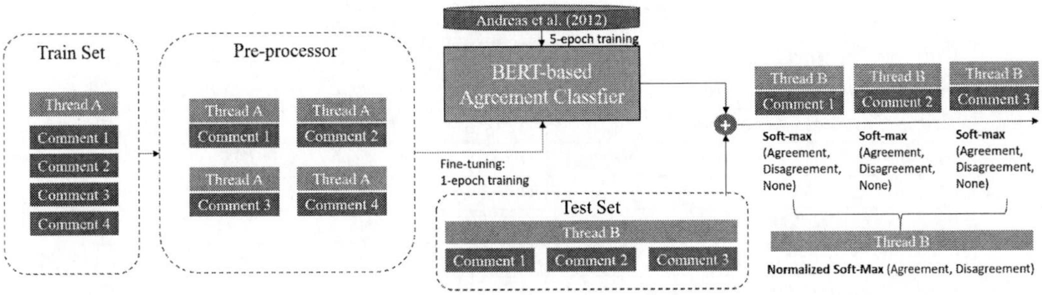

Figure 4: This figure illustrates the pipeline of Phase 2-2. We pre-train the BERT model with the dataset provided by Andreas et al. (2012) and fine-tune the model with pre-processed train set of SemEval 2019 Task 7. Then we apply the BERT-based agreement detector to thread-reply pair of the test set and obtain soft-max value vectors. We discard the soft-max values of *none* since *none* does not provide additional information about the veracity of the rumors.

the primary reply is in accordance with the thread or not. We also take a two-step approach to train the model.

First, we train the BERT-based triple classifier with an open-source dataset (Andreas et al., 2012). The dataset contains 1,163 sentence pairs with agreement labels. Specifically, it includes 609 agreement pairs and 554 disagreement pairs. We train the model for five epochs with a batch size of 32, a learning rate of 5e-5, and a label smoothing rate of 0.3. We also use Adam optimizer.

Then, we fine-tune the model with the train set of SemEval 2019 Task 7. We filter out primary responses from the dataset and create thread-reply pairs. We label the pairs with the labels pre-assigned to each thread. This process yields 2,372 distinct thread-reply pairs. Then we train the model for one epoch with batch size 32 and learning rate 5e-5. The task of Andreas et al. (2012) aims at determining whether each reply is in accordance with the thread, which is identical to our objective. Hence, we fine-tune the model for one epoch.

Applying the classifier to uninformed rumors yields the softmax values for (agreement, disagreement, none). We discard the softmax value of none and sum the softmax values of agreement and disagreement for each thread. Then, we normalize the values so that they sum up to be one. As in Phase 2-1, the program returns true when the softmax value of the agreement is larger than that of disagreement and vice versa.

For a formal representation, let X_i denote the thread and y^i_m denote the mth primary reply to X_i. Suppose that we have k threads and n_i (i is an integer between 1 and k) is the number of primary comments corresponding to X_i. We form up the pairs $(X_1, y^1_1), \cdots, (X_1, y^1_{n_1}), \cdots, (X_k, y^k_1), \cdots, (X_k, y^k_{n_k})$. BERT model returns a softmax vector of each pair (a_l, b_l, c_l), where (a, b, c) denotes the softmax vector of (agreement, disagreement, none). We obtain $\sum_{i=1}^{k} n_i$ softmax vectors. Then, for X_i, we sum up the softmax values to obtain the normalized softmax vector.

$$\left(\frac{\sum_{k=1}^{n_i} a_k}{\sum_{k=1}^{n_i} a_k + \sum_{k=1}^{n_i} b_k}, \frac{\sum_{k=1}^{n_i} b_k}{\sum_{k=1}^{n_i} a_k + \sum_{k=1}^{n_i} b_k} \right)$$

If the first softmax is larger than the second, we classify X_i to be true. If the second softmax is larger than the first, we classify X_i to be false.

Also, we assign the observations with the self-entropy value of 1 to the unverified category. We calculate the self-entropy using the same formula with Phase 2-1.

We discard the softmax values of none because replies that do not fall under either agreement or disagreement category do not have informational value. By allowing the none category and discarding the none category samples, we aim to deliberately examine the replies' intent (Li et al., 2019a). Refer to Figure 4 for the graphical illustration of Phase 2-2.

3.5 Data and Pre-processing

Our primary input data is the open-source data released in SemEval 2019 Task 7. Specifically, we aim to improve the model performance of Task 7B, in which the participants are asked to classify each rumor into one of the three categories (true, false or unverifiable). The dataset contains 365 train set observations. Each observation consists of one thread (Twitter or Reddit) post and its corresponding replies. Replies include the primary

	Macro-F1	Accuracy	Precision	Recall
Double-Channel	**0.4027**	**0.4938**	**0.5064**	**0.4043**
Single-Channel (Lie Detector)	0.3447	0.4444	0.3362	0.3706
Single-Channel (Agreement Detector)	0.3668	0.4444	0.4813	0.3700
Double-Channel with Inverse Detectors	0.3145	0.3567	0.2981	0.3374
Baseline (LSTM)	0.3364	-	-	-
Baseline (NileTMRG)	0.3089	-	-	-
Baseline (Majority class)	0.2241	-	-	-
WeST (CLEARumor)	0.2856	-	-	-
eventAI	0.5770	-	0.5960	0.6030

Table 1: This table demonstrates the relative performances of the models that we develop, the baseline models of SemEval 2019 Task 7, and the second-place winner of the task (WeST). Single-channel models include the model that applies lie detector to all observations and the model that applies agreement detector to all observations. Double-channel model with inverse detectors apply lie detection algorithm to uncertain group (uninformed rumors) and agreement detection algorithm to certain group (informed rumors).

replies (replies that respond directly to the main post) and secondary replies (replies that respond to other replies). In our task, we do not use replies other than primary replies. We first retrieve all main posts (threads) from the dataset. The threads often include hashtags or web addresses starting with http. Several studies including Li et al. (2019a) use this as auxiliary information in their analysis - they include an indicator variable that equals one when the thread has a hashtag or web address inside. However, in our research, we focus only on textual features and do not need such information. Further, given that the threads are relatively short, uninterpretable hashtags or web addresses might distort the results. Hence, we delete all hashtags and web addresses that start with "http".

Then, we turn to the comments. The dataset contains a structure file in json format for each thread. The structure file explains the format of each thread such as how many comments are there, the time when each comment is posted, the ID of the author and the ID of the comment. From the json file, we identify the primary comments and pair them with their corresponding thread. We also cleanse the texts by removing all the hashtags and web addresses.

4 Results

We present our results in Table 1. We report two main evaluation metrics, macro-F1 and accuracy, and two supplementary metrics, precision and recall. Macro-F1 is the harmonic average of the precision and recall ratios, while accuracy is the ratio of correct classifications to the total number of observations.

4.1 Justification of Double-Channel Structure

In support of our conjecture, we re-train the Phase 2-1 and Phase 2-2 classifiers with all observations, and report the results when the classifiers are applied to all posts without the certainty classification. The results yield the macro-F1 scores of 0.3447 and 0.3668, respectively. Additionally, we also report the prediction accuracy when lie detection algorithm is applied to uninformed rumors and agreement detection algorithm is applied to informed rumors. The macro-F1 score and accuracy (0.3145 and 0.3567) become even lower. As clearly indicated, dividing the total sample into two subgroups significantly improves the classification performance. This improvement is primarily because each classifier is applied to the observations that the classifier is intended to function well. These empirical results further validate our novel double-channel structure along with its theoretical background.

4.2 Overall Performance

Our double-channel model achieves a macro-F1 score of 0.4027 and an accuracy of 0.4938. In terms of precision and recall, it achieves 0.5064 and 0.4043, respectively. [3] This model outperforms all the baseline models proposed in SemEval 2019 Task 7 and the model developed by the second-place winner. Note that our program only refers to textual information of the main threads and their primary replies. We intentionally do not include

[3]The model correctly classifies 19 true rumors out of 31, 20 false rumors out of 40, and 1 unverified rumor out of 10.

user-specific peripheral information to demonstrate that the double-channel approach can significantly improve the classification outcomes.

Our model outperforms the second-best program (WeST) by approximately 12% points in terms of macro-F1. With the double-channel classification system that we develop, we manage to accurately classify false rumors at their early stage, without considering the peripheral information sets. Our model falls behind the winner of SemEval 2019 Task 7, primarily because we use limited scope of information. We intentionally discard all other information but textual information of the threads and their primary replies. In contrast, the winner exploits a wide variety of information such as account credibility and the existence of hashtags. Unlike the winner, our program can be applied to anonymous rumors without any clue about the author information.

4.3 Some Restrictions on Replies (Phase 2-2)

In our main model, we use all primary replies to the main threads, regardless of their dates created. However, we acknowledge that if it takes too much time to collect the reply data, our model cannot calculate the veracity in a timely manner. Since early veracity detection is one of our main contributions, we restrict the replies to be posted within 1-, 3-, and 5-day period from the original thread. Table 2 reports the results.

As we restrict the replies to be posted within 1 day from the original thread, we lose 3 threads. Furthermore, we experience a slight decrease in our predictive accuracy and macro-F1 score. However, as we loosen our restriction from 1-day window to 5-day window, we observe a gradual restoration in both accuracy and macro-F1. In summary, our model reasonably predicts the veracity of rumors even in a 1-day window from the origination of rumors and it gradually becomes more accurate in a 5-day window. Note that the average number of replies is 11.96 even when we restrict our window to 1-day period, allowing us to have enough replies to expect the effect of the wisdom of the crowd.[4]

[4]To further validate this argument, we repeat the same exercise after excluding the threads with only one reply in 1-day restriction sample and achieve a macro-F1 of 0.3570 and accuracy of 0.4800. When we exclude threads with less than 3 replies, we achieve a macro-F1 of 0.3637 and accuracy of 0.4857.

	F1	Accuracy	Avg #	# thr
Original	0.4027	0.4938	14.96	81
1-Day	0.3418	0.4743	11.96	78
3-Day	0.3542	0.4815	14.37	81
5-Day	0.3827	0.4938	14.58	81

Table 2: Avg # denotes the average number of replies and # thr denotes the number of distinct threads. n-Day denotes the sample when we restrict the replies to be posted within n days from the original thread (n=1,3,5).

5 Conclusion

Perfectly determining the veracity of rumors at the time of their origination is impossible. Nonetheless, an increasing number of rumors are spreading out via social media, and people are affected by those rumors. Therefore, sorting out the "likely-fraudulent" rumors at their early stage is of great importance to information users.

Our model takes minimal textual information and achieves a reasonable prediction accuracy in the SemEval 2019 Task 7 dataset. This dataset contains only 365 train samples and 81 test samples, but requires three-way classification. We achieve the macro-F1 score of 0.4027 in this task, which is approximately 12% points higher than that of the second-place winner which also focuses on the textual features of posts.

Instead of integrating a wide variety of user-specific information, our model shows that textual features have sufficient predictive power in determining the veracity of rumors. More importantly, we demonstrate that applying a uniform classifier to all Twitter and Reddit posts can harm the model's performance. Instead, we apply a double-channel approach in rumor veracity detection. We divide the sample into two subgroups depending on the textual certainty and apply two different classifiers to each subgroup. Also, by using only textual features of a post and its primary replies, this study responds to Li et al. (2019b)'s call for research that enables the early detection of rumor veracity.

Our research can be successfully implemented in the real world setting. Our model, which does not rely on user-specific information (e.g. the number of followers, the number of previous posts, etc.), can even be implemented to determine the veracity of **anonymous** rumors. The model produces a rapid veracity prediction. That is, we can produce the results almost immediately for informed rumors and within several days for uninformed rumors. Ultimately, providing users with predicted veracity information can help their potential decision making.

6 Acknowledgement

The authors deeply appreciate helpful comments from Bok Baik. Furthermore, the authors appreciate the GPU support from Artificial Society.

References

Md Shad Akhtar, Asif Ekbal, Sunny Narayan, and Vikram Singh. 2018. No, that never happened!! investigating rumors on twitter. *IEEE Intelligent Systems*, 33(5):8–15.

Jacob Andreas, Sara Rosenthal, and Kathleen R McKeown. 2012. Annotating agreement and disagreement in threaded discussion. In *LREC*, pages 818–822. Citeseer.

Dan Barsever, Sameer Singh, and Emre Neftci. 2020. Building a better lie detector with bert: The difference between truth and lies. In *2020 International Joint Conference on Neural Networks (IJCNN)*, pages 1–7. IEEE.

Alasdair Brown and J James Reade. 2019. The wisdom of amateur crowds: Evidence from an online community of sports tipsters. *European Journal of Operational Research*, 272(3):1073–1081.

Juan Cao, Junbo Guo, Xirong Li, Zhiwei Jin, Han Guo, and Jintao Li. 2018. Automatic rumor detection on microblogs: A survey. *arXiv preprint arXiv:1807.03505*.

Carlos Castillo, Marcelo Mendoza, and Barbara Poblete. 2011. Information credibility on twitter. In *Proceedings of the 20th international conference on World wide web*, pages 675–684.

Jacob Devlin, Ming-Wei Chang, Kenton Lee, and Kristina Toutanova. 2018. Bert: Pre-training of deep bidirectional transformers for language understanding. *arXiv preprint arXiv:1810.04805*.

Nicholas DiFonzo. 2010. Ferreting facts or fashioning fallacies? factors in rumor accuracy. *Social and Personality Psychology Compass*, 4(11):1124–1137.

John Dougrez-Lewis, Maria Liakata, Elena Kochkina, and Yulan He. 2021. Learning disentangled latent topics for twitter rumour veracity classification. In *Findings of the Association for Computational Linguistics: ACL-IJCNLP 2021*, pages 3902–3908.

Omar Enayet and Samhaa R El-Beltagy. 2017. Niletmrg at semeval-2017 task 8: Determining rumour and veracity support for rumours on twitter. In *Proceedings of the 11th international workshop on semantic evaluation (SemEval-2017)*, pages 470–474.

Richárd Farkas, Veronika Vincze, György Móra, János Csirik, and György Szarvas. 2010. The conll-2010 shared task: learning to detect hedges and their scope in natural language text. In *Proceedings of the fourteenth conference on computational natural language learning–Shared task*, pages 1–12.

Genevieve Gorrell, Elena Kochkina, Maria Liakata, Ahmet Aker, Arkaitz Zubiaga, Kalina Bontcheva, and Leon Derczynski. 2019. Semeval-2019 task 7: Rumoureval, determining rumour veracity and support for rumours. In *Proceedings of the 13th International Workshop on Semantic Evaluation*, pages 845–854.

Manish Gupta, Peixiang Zhao, and Jiawei Han. 2012. Evaluating event credibility on twitter. In *Proceedings of the 2012 SIAM International Conference on Data Mining*, pages 153–164. SIAM.

Weishi Jia, Giulia Redigolo, Susan Shu, and Jingran Zhao. 2020. Can social media distort price discovery? evidence from merger rumors. *Journal of Accounting and Economics*, 70(1):101334.

Michael A Kamins, Valerie S Folkes, and Lars Perner. 1997. Consumer responses to rumors: Good news, bad news. *Journal of consumer psychology*, 6(2):165–187.

Jong-Hyun Kim, Gee-Woo Bock, Rajiv Sabherwal, and Han-Min Kim. 2019. Why do people spread online rumors? an empirical study. *Asia Pacific Journal of Information Systems*, 29(4):591–614.

Elena Kochkina, Maria Liakata, and Arkaitz Zubiaga. 2018. All-in-one: Multi-task learning for rumour verification. *arXiv preprint arXiv:1806.03713*.

Sumeet Kumar and Kathleen M Carley. 2019. Tree lstms with convolution units to predict stance and rumor veracity in social media conversations. In *Proceedings of the 57th Annual Meeting of the Association for Computational Linguistics*, pages 5047–5058.

Albert S Kyle. 1985. Continuous auctions and insider trading. *Econometrica: Journal of the Econometric Society*, pages 1315–1335.

Zhenzhong Lan, Mingda Chen, Sebastian Goodman, Kevin Gimpel, Piyush Sharma, and Radu Soricut. 2019. Albert: A lite bert for self-supervised learning of language representations. *arXiv preprint arXiv:1909.11942*.

Quanzhi Li, Qiong Zhang, Luo Si, and Yingchi Liu. 2019a. Rumor detection on social media: datasets, methods and opportunities. *arXiv preprint arXiv:1911.07199*.

Quanzhi Li, Qiong Zhang, Luo Si, and Yingchi Liu. 2019b. Rumor detection on social media: datasets, methods and opportunities. *arXiv preprint arXiv:1911.07199*.

Xiaomo Liu, Armineh Nourbakhsh, Quanzhi Li, Rui Fang, and Sameena Shah. 2015. Real-time rumor debunking on twitter. In *Proceedings of the 24th ACM international on conference on information and knowledge management*, pages 1867–1870.

Yang Liu and Yi-Fang Brook Wu. 2018. Early detection of fake news on social media through propagation path classification with recurrent and convolutional networks. In *Thirty-second AAAI conference on artificial intelligence*.

Yinhan Liu, Myle Ott, Naman Goyal, Jingfei Du, Mandar Joshi, Danqi Chen, Omer Levy, Mike Lewis, Luke Zettlemoyer, and Veselin Stoyanov. 2019. Roberta: A robustly optimized bert pretraining approach. *arXiv preprint arXiv:1907.11692*.

Jing Ma, Wei Gao, and Kam-Fai Wong. 2017. Detect rumors in microblog posts using propagation structure via kernel learning. Association for Computational Linguistics.

Noa Mansbach, Evgeny Hershkovitch Neiterman, and Amos Azaria. 2021. An agent for competing with humans in a deceptive game based on vocal cues. *Proc. Interspeech 2021*, pages 4134–4138.

Jaume Masip, Maria Bethencourt, Guadalupe Lucas, MIRIAM SÁNCHEZ-SAN SEGUNDO, and Carmen Herrero. 2012. Deception detection from written accounts. *Scandinavian Journal of Psychology*, 53(2):103–111.

Joaquin Navajas, Tamara Niella, Gerry Garbulsky, Bahador Bahrami, and Mariano Sigman. 2018. Aggregated knowledge from a small number of debates outperforms the wisdom of large crowds. *Nature Human Behaviour*, 2(2):126–132.

Myle Ott, Claire Cardie, and Jeffrey T Hancock. 2013. Negative deceptive opinion spam. In *Proceedings of the 2013 conference of the north american chapter of the association for computational linguistics: human language technologies*, pages 497–501.

Myle Ott, Yejin Choi, Claire Cardie, and Jeffrey T Hancock. 2011. Finding deceptive opinion spam by any stretch of the imagination. *arXiv preprint arXiv:1107.4557*.

John Pound and Richard Zeckhauser. 1990. Clearly heard on the street: The effect of takeover rumors on stock prices. *Journal of Business*, pages 291–308.

Dongning Rao, Xin Miao, Zhihua Jiang, and Ran Li. 2021. Stanker: Stacking network based on level-grained attention-masked bert for rumor detection on social media. In *Proceedings of the 2021 Conference on Empirical Methods in Natural Language Processing*, pages 3347–3363.

Nir Rosenfeld, Aron Szanto, and David C Parkes. 2020. A kernel of truth: Determining rumor veracity on twitter by diffusion pattern alone. In *Proceedings of The Web Conference 2020*, pages 1018–1028.

Kai Shu, Amy Sliva, Suhang Wang, Jiliang Tang, and Huan Liu. 2017. Fake news detection on social media: A data mining perspective. *ACM SIGKDD explorations newsletter*, 19(1):22–36.

Christian Szegedy, Vincent Vanhoucke, Sergey Ioffe, Jon Shlens, and Zbigniew Wojna. 2016. Rethinking the inception architecture for computer vision. In *Proceedings of the IEEE conference on computer vision and pattern recognition*, pages 2818–2826.

Jos Van Bommel. 2003. Rumors. *The journal of Finance*, 58(4):1499–1520.

Soroush Vosoughi. 2015. *Automatic detection and verification of rumors on Twitter*. Ph.D. thesis, Massachusetts Institute of Technology.

Soroush Vosoughi, Deb Roy, and Sinan Aral. 2018. The spread of true and false news online. *Science*, 359(6380):1146–1151.

Yaqing Wang, Fenglong Ma, Zhiwei Jin, Ye Yuan, Guangxu Xun, Kishlay Jha, Lu Su, and Jing Gao. 2018. Eann: Event adversarial neural networks for multi-modal fake news detection. In *Proceedings of the 24th acm sigkdd international conference on knowledge discovery & data mining*, pages 849–857.

Ke Wu, Song Yang, and Kenny Q Zhu. 2015. False rumors detection on sina weibo by propagation structures. In *2015 IEEE 31st international conference on data engineering*, pages 651–662. IEEE.

Jianfei Yu, Jing Jiang, Ling Min Serena Khoo, Hai Leong Chieu, and Rui Xia. 2020. Predicting stance and rumor veracity via dual hierarchical transformer with pretrained encoders. In *Proceedings of the 2020 Conference on Empirical Methods in Natural Language Processing (EMNLP)*, pages 1392–1401.

Arkaitz Zubiaga, Maria Liakata, Rob Procter, Geraldine Wong Sak Hoi, and Peter Tolmie. 2016. Analysing how people orient to and spread rumours in social media by looking at conversational threads. *PloS one*, 11(3):e0150989.

Leveraging Dependency Grammar for Fine-Grained Offensive Language Detection using Graph Convolutional Networks

Divyam Goel
Indian Institute of Technology Roorkee
Roorkee, India
dgoel@bt.iitr.ac.in

Raksha Sharma
Indian Institute of Technology Roorkee
Roorkee, India
raksha.sharma@cs.iitr.ac.in

Abstract

The last few years have witnessed an exponential rise in the propagation of offensive text on social media. Identification of this text with high precision is crucial for the well-being of society. Most of the existing approaches tend to give high toxicity scores to innocuous statements (*e.g.*, "I am a gay man"). These false positives result from over-generalization on the training data where specific terms in the statement may have been used in a pejorative sense (*e.g.*, "gay"). Emphasis on such words alone can lead to discrimination against the classes these systems are designed to protect. In this paper, we address the problem of offensive language detection on Twitter, while also detecting the type and the target of the offense. We propose a novel approach called *SyLSTM*, which integrates syntactic features in the form of the dependency parse tree of a sentence and semantic features in the form of word embeddings into a deep learning architecture using a Graph Convolutional Network. Results show that the proposed approach significantly outperforms the state-of-the-art BERT model with orders of magnitude fewer number of parameters.

1 Introduction

Offensive language can be defined as instances of profanity in communication, or any instances that disparage a person or a group based on some characteristic such as race, color, ethnicity, gender, sexual orientation, nationality, religion, *etc.* (Nockleby, 2000). The ease of accessing social networking sites has resulted in an unprecedented rise of offensive content on social media. With massive amounts of data being generated each minute, it is imperative to develop scalable systems that can automatically filter offensive content.

The first works in offensive language detection were primarily based on a lexical approach, utilizing surface-level features such as n-grams, bag-of-words, *etc.*, drawn from the similarity of the task to another NLP task, *i.e.*, Sentiment Analysis (SA). These systems perform well in the context of foul language but prove ineffective in detecting hate speech. Consequently, the main challenge lies in discriminating profanity and hate speech from each other (Zampieri et al., 2019). On the other hand, recent deep neural network based approaches for offensive language detection fall prey to inherent biases in a dataset, leading to the systems being discriminative against the very classes they aim to protect. Davidson et al., (2019) presented the evidence of a systemic bias in classifiers, showing that such classifiers predicted tweets written in African-American English as abusive at substantially higher rates. Table 1 presents the scenarios where a tweet may be considered hateful.

Syntactic features are essential for a model to detect latent offenses, *i.e.*, untargeted offenses, or where the user might mask the offense using the medium of sarcasm (Schmidt and Wiegand, 2017). Syntactic features prevent over-generalization on specific word classes, *e.g.*, profanities, racial terms, *etc.*, instead examining the possible arrangements of the precise lexical internal features which factor in differences between words of the same class. Hence, syntactic features can overcome the systemic bias, which may have arisen from the pejorative use of specific word classes. A significant property of dependency parse trees is their ability to deal with morphologically rich languages with a relatively free word order (Jurafsky and Martin, 2009). Motivated by the nature of the modern Twitter vocabulary, which also follows a relatively free word order, we present an integration of syntactic features in the form of dependency grammar in a deep learning framework.

In this paper, we propose a novel architecture called *Syntax-based LSTM* (*SyLSTM*), which integrates latent features such as syntactic dependencies into a deep learning model. Hence, improving the efficiency of identifying offenses and their tar-

Proceedings of the Tenth International Workshop on Natural Language Processing for Social Media (SocialNLP 2022), pages 34 - 43
July 14-15, 2022 ©2022 Association for Computational Linguistics

S.No.	Hateful Tweet Scenarios
1	uses sexist or racial slurs.
2	attacks a minority.
3	seeks to silence a minority.
4	criticizes a minority (without a well-founded argument).
5	promotes but does not directly use hate speech or violent crime.
6	criticizes a minority and uses a straw man argument.
7	blatantly misrepresents truth or seeks to distort views on a minority with unfounded claims.
8	shows support of problematic hashtags. *E.g.* "#BanIslam," "#whoriental," "#whitegenocide"
9	negatively stereotypes a minority.
10	defends xenophobia or sexism.
11	contains an offensive screen name

Table 1: Hateful Tweet Scenarios (Waseem and Hovy, 2016)

gets while reducing the systemic bias caused by lexical features. To incorporate the dependency grammar in a deep learning framework, we utilize the Graph Convolutional Network (GCN) (Kipf and Welling, 2016). We show that by subsuming only a few changes to the dependency parse trees, they can be transformed into compatible input graphs for the GCN. The final model consists of two major components, a BiLSTM based Semantic Encoder and a GCN-based Syntactic Encoder in that order. Further, a Multilayer Perceptron handles the classification task with a Softmax head. The state-of-the-art BERT model requires the re-training of over $110M$ parameters when fine-tuning for a downstream task. In comparison, the *SyLSTM* requires only $\sim 9.5M$ parameters and significantly surpasses BERT level performance. Hence, our approach establishes a new state-of-the-art result for offensive language detection while being over ten times more parameter efficient than BERT.

We evaluate our model on two datasets; one treats the task of hate speech and offensive language detection separately (Davidson et al., 2017). The other uses a hierarchical classification system that identifies the types and targets of the offensive tweets as a separate task (Zampieri et al., 2019).

Our Contribution: The major contribution of this paper is to incorporate syntactic features in the form of dependency parse trees along with semantic features in the form of feature embeddings into a deep learning architecture. By laying particular emphasis on sentence construction and dependency grammar, we improve the performance of automated systems in detecting hate speech and offensive language instances, differentiating between the two, and identifying the targets for the same. Results (Section 5) show that our approach significantly outperforms all the baselines for the three tasks, *viz.*, identification of offensive language, the type of the offense, and the target of the offense.

The rest of the paper is organized as follows. In Section 2, we discuss related work in this field. Section 3 presents the design of *SyLSTM*. Section 4 elaborates on the datasets and the experimental protocol. Section 5 presents the results and discussion, and Section 6 concludes the paper.

2 Related Work

Hate speech detection, as a topical research problem, has been around for over two decades. One of the first systems to emerge from this research was called *Smokey* (Spertus, 1997). It is a decision-tree-based classifier that uses 47 syntactic and semantically essential features to classify inputs in one of the three classes ($flame$, $okay$ or $maybe$). *Smokey* paved the way for further research in using classical machine learning techniques to exploit the inherent features of Natural Language over a plethora of tasks such as junk filtering (Sahami et al., 1998), opinion mining (Wiebe et al., 2005) *etc.*

Owing to the unprecedented rise of social networks such as Facebook and Twitter, most of the research on hate speech detection has migrated towards the social media domain. To formalize this new task, a set of essential linguistic features was proposed (Waseem and Hovy, 2016). Initial research in this direction focused more on detecting profanity, pursuing hate speech detection implicitly (Nobata et al., 2016; Waseem et al., 2017). Using these systems, trained for detecting profanities, to detect hate speech reveals that they fall prey to inherent biases in the datasets while also proving ineffective in classifying a plethora of instances of hate speech (Davidson et al., 2019).

Research has also shown the importance of syntactic features in detecting offensive posts and identifying the targets of such instances (Chen et al., 2012). On social media, it was found that hate speech is primarily directed towards specific groups, targeting their ethnicity, race, gender, caste, *etc.* (Silva et al., 2016). ElSherief et al. (2018) make use of linguistic features in deep learning models, which can be used to focus on these directed instances. The problem with this approach is two-fold. First, these linguistic features learn inherent biases within the datasets, thus discriminating against the classes they are designed to protect. Second, the use of explicit linguistic features to detect hate speech leaves the model prone to the effects of domain shift. Altogether, there is a need to develop more robust techniques for hate speech detection to address the above mentioned issues. While the use of syntactic features for the task has proven useful, there has been little effort towards incorporating non-Euclidean syntactic linguistic structures such as dependency trees into the deep learning sphere.

Graph Neural Networks (GNNs) provide a natural extension to deep learning methods in dealing with such graph structured data. A special class of GNNs, known as Graph Convolutional Networks (GCNs), generalize Convolutional Neural Networks (CNNs) to non-Euclidean data. The GCNs were first introduced by Bruna et al. (2013), following which, Kipf et al. (2016) presented a scalable, first order approximation of the GCNs based on Chebyshev polynomials. The GCNs have been extremely successful in several domains such as social networks (Hamilton et al., 2017), natural language processing (Marcheggiani and Titov, 2017) and natural sciences (Zitnik et al., 2018).

Marcheggiani and Titov (2017) were the first to show the effectiveness of GCNs for NLP by presenting an analysis over semantic role labelling. Their experiments paved the way for researchers to utilize GCNs for feature extraction in NLP. Since then, GCNs have been used to generate embedding spaces for words (Vashishth et al., 2018), documents (Peng et al., 2018) and both words and documents together (Yao et al., 2019). Even though GCNs have been used in NLP, their inability to handle multirelational graphs has prevented researchers from incorporating the dependency parse tree in the deep feature space.

In this paper, we present a first approach towards transforming the dependency parse tree in a manner that allows the GCN to process it. The final model is a combination of a BiLSTM based Semantic Encoder, which extracts semantic features and addresses long-range dependencies, and a GCN-based Syntactic Encoder, which extracts features from the dependency parse tree of the sentence. Results show that the proposed approach improves the performance of automated systems in detecting hate speech and offensive language instances, differentiating between the two, and identifying the targets for the same.

3 Methodology

Traditionally, grammar is organized along two main dimensions: *morphology* and *syntax*. While morphology helps linguists understand the structure of a word, the syntax looks at sentences and how each word performs in a sentence. The meaning of a sentence in any language depends on the syntax and order of the words. In this regard, a sentence that records the occurrence of relevant nouns and verbs (*e.g.*, Jews and kill) can prove helpful in learning the offensive posts and their targets (Gitari et al., 2015). Further, the syntactic structure I $\langle intensity \rangle$ $\langle userintent \rangle$ $\langle hatetarget \rangle$, *e.g.*, "I f*cking hate white people," helps to learn more about offensive posts, their targets, and the intensity of the offense (Silva et al., 2016). Our approach incorporates both semantic features and the dependency grammar of a tweet into the deep feature space. The following subsections present a detailed discussion on the proposed methodology.

3.1 Preprocessing

Raw tweets usually have a high level of redundancy and noise associated with them, such as varying usernames, URLs, *etc.* In order to clean the data, we implement the preprocessing module described in Table 2.

3.2 Model

The proposed model *SyLSTM* (Figure 1) has the following six components:

1. Input Tokens: The tweet is passed through a word-based tokenizer after the preprocessing step. The tokenized tweet is then given as input to the model;

2. Embedding Layer: A mapping for each word to a low-dimensional feature vector;

Preprocessing	Description
Replacing usernames	replacing all usernames with '@user'. *Eg.* '@india' to '@user'.
Replacing URLs	replacing URLs in a tweet with the word 'url'.
Hashtag Segmentation	Eg. '#banislam' becomes '# banislam'.
Emoji Normalization	normalizing emoji instances with text. *Eg.* ':)' becomes 'smiley face'.
Compound Word Splitting	split compound words. *E.g.* 'putuporshutup' to 'put up or shut up'.
Reducing Word Lengths	reduce word lengths, exclamation marks, *E.g.* 'waaaaayyyy' to 'waayy'.

Table 2: Preprocessing Modules

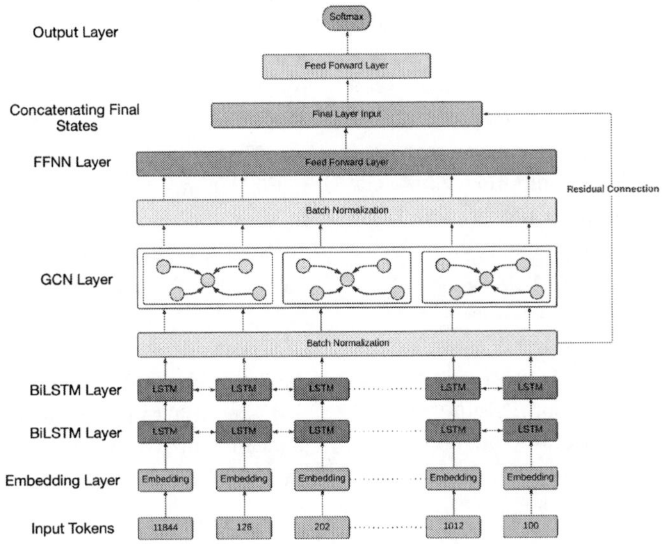

Figure 1: Model Architecture for *SyLSTM*

3. BiLSTM Layer: used to extract a high-level feature space from the word embeddings;
4. GCN Layer: produces a weight vector according to the syntactic dependencies over the high-level features from step 3. Multiply with high-level feature space to produce new features with relevant syntactic information.
5. Feed Forward Network: reduces the dimensionality of the outputs of step 4.
6. Output Layer: the last hidden states from step 3 are concatenated with the output of step 5 as a residual connection and fed as input. The feature space is finally used for hate speech detection.

The detailed description of these components is given below.

Word Embeddings: Given a sentence consisting of T words $S = \{x_1, x_2, ..., x_T\}$, every word x_i is converted to a real valued feature vector e_i. This is done by means of an embedding matrix which serves as a lookup table,

$$\mathcal{E}^{(word)} \in \mathbb{R}^{|V| \times d^{(w)}}, \tag{1}$$

where, $|V|$ is the size of the vocabulary and $d^{(w)}$ is the dimensional size of the embeddings. Each word in S is then mapped to a specific entry in this matrix,

$$e_i = \mathcal{E}^{(word)}.v_i, \tag{2}$$

where, v_i is a one hot vector of size $|V|$. The entire sentence is fed into the proceeding layers as real-valued vectors $emb = \{e_1, e_2, ..., e_T\}$. The embedding matrix can be initialized randomly and learned via backpropagation, or one can also use a set of pretrained embeddings. Twitter posts generally use the modern *internet lexicon* and hence have a unique vocabulary. For our model, we use two different instances for the embedding space - first, a randomly initialized embedding space learned at the training time. Second, a pretrained embedding space where we utilize the GloVe-Twitter Embeddings[1] ($d^{(w)} = 200$). These embeddings have been trained on 27B tokens parsed from a Twitter corpus (Pennington et al., 2014). Results indicate that models trained on the GloVe-Twitter Embeddings learn a stronger approximation of semantic

[1] `https://nlp.stanford.edu/projects/glove/`

relations in the twitter vocabulary, showcasing a more robust performance than their randomly initialized counterparts.

Semantic Encoding with BiLSTM: Most of the existing research on GCNs focuses on learning nodal representations in undirected graphs. These are suited to single relational edges and can suffer from a severe semantic gap when operating on multirelational graphs. To codify the relational edges' underlying semantics and resolve language on a temporal scale, we utilize the Bidirectional LSTM.

Using an adaptive gating mechanism, the LSTMs decide the degree of importance between features extracted at a previous time step to that at the current time step (Hochreiter and Schmidhuber, 1997). Consequently, they prove extremely useful in the context of hate speech detection, where hate speech can be distributed randomly at any part of the sentence. Standard LSTMs process sequences in a temporal order hence ignoring future context. Bidirectionality allows us access to both future and past contexts, which helps improve the cognition of hate speech in a tweet (Xu et al., 2019).

We pass the sentence embedding vectors $emb = \{e_1, e_2, ..., e_T\}$ through a two-layered BiLSTM network with 32 hidden units and a dropout of 0.4. As outputs, we extract the sequential vectors and the final hidden states for the forward and backward sequences. The final hidden states for the forward and backward sequences are concatenated and used as a residual connection at a later stage, as shown in Figure 1. The sequential vectors are passed through a batch normalization layer with a momentum of 0.6 and then fed into the GCN layer along with the dependency parse trees.

Syntactic Encoding with GCN: The dependency parse trees have specific characteristics which are rarely considered in general graphs. On the one hand, they have multirelational edges. And on the other hand, the definition of each type of edge is relatively broad, resulting in a huge difference in the semantics of edges with the same relationship. For instance, an 'amod' dependency may be presented in <Techniques, Computational> and <Techniques, Designed>, but their semantics are obviously different.

The GCN (Kipf and Welling, 2016) cannot handle such scenarios without introducing some changes to the structure of the input dependency parse tree. First, inverse edges corresponding to each of the respective dependencies are introduced between all connected nodes. Furthermore, to highlight the importance of specific words in the given context, we add self-loops over each node. The dependency parse tree of a sentence is extracted using the NLP open-source package spaCy[2].

Hence, the extracted dependency parse tree is transformed into a graph $G = (V, E)$, where V is the set of all vertices which represent the words in a tweet and E is the set of all edges which highlight the dependency and their inverse relations. The result is an undirected graph with self-loops (see Figure 2). This comes as a natural extension to the dependency structure of the sentence, highlighting the importance of word positioning and combating possible confusions in identifying the direction of the dependency. The graph is then fed into the GCN as a sparse adjacency matrix, with each dependency represented by a weight α. With the setup in place, the GCN performs a convolution operation over the graph G represented by the adjacency matrix A. Formally, the GCN performs the following computation:

$$H^{(l+1)} = \sigma(\tilde{D}^{-\frac{1}{2}}\tilde{A}\tilde{D}^{-\frac{1}{2}}H^{(l)}W^{(l)}) \qquad (3)$$

where, $\tilde{A} = A + I_N$ is the adjacency matrix of the undirected graph G with added self-connections. I_N is the identity matrix, $\tilde{D}_{ii} = \Sigma_j \tilde{A}_{ij}$ and $W^{(l)}$ is a layer-specific trainable weight matrix. $\sigma(\cdot)$ denotes an activation function, in our case the ReLU$(\cdot)$ = $\max(0, \cdot)$. $H^{(l)} \in \mathbb{R}^{N \times D}$ is the matrix of activations in the lth layer; $H^{(0)} = L$. The model learns hidden layer representations that encode both local graph structure (*the dependencies*) and nodal features (*the importance of the word in that context*). Furthermore, the Semantic Encoder complements the Syntactic Encoder by addressing the long range spatial inabilities of the GCN (Marcheggiani and Titov, 2017). The sparse adjacency matrix leads to a problem with vanishing gradients. We combat this by applying a batch normalization layer with a momentum of 0.6 and applying a dropout of 0.5. We use the Xavier distribution to initialize the weight matrix and set the output dimension of the GCN as 32.

Feed Forward Neural Network (FFNN): The output of the GCN is then passed through a single layered FFNN to learn high-level features based on dependency structure. The FFNN is activated using the non-linear ReLU activation function.

[2]`https://github.com/explosion/spaCy`

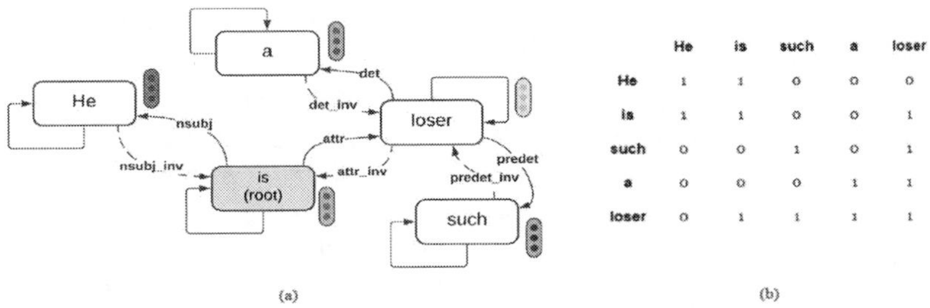

Figure 2: (a) Dependency Graph G with Nodal Embeddings (b) Adjacency Matrix A for the graph G

Output Layer: The output from the FFNN is then concatenated with the last hidden states of the BiLSTM which is added as a residual connection. The concatenated vector is then passed through a linear layer with a softmax head that produces a probability distribution over the required outputs.

4 Experimental Setup

This section describes the dataset and the experimental setup for the models reported in the paper.

4.1 Datasets

The primary motivation of this paper is the design of a methodology to integrate a neural network model with syntactic dependencies for improved performance over fine-grained offensive language detection. Keeping in line with this ideology, we test our model on two separate datasets. The following section describes these datasets at length.

Offensive Language Identification Dataset: This dataset was presented for a shared task on offensive language detection in the SemEval Challenge 2019. This was the first time that offensive language identification was presented as a hierarchical task. Data quality was ensured by selecting only experienced annotators and using test questions to eliminate individuals below a minimum reliability threshold. Tweets were retrieved using a keyword approach on the Twitter API. The dataset forms a collection of $14,000$ English tweets annotated for three subtasks proceeding in a hierarchy (Zampieri et al., 2019):

1. whether a tweet is offensive or not (A);
2. whether the offensive tweet is targeted (B);
3. whether the target of the offensive tweet is an individual, a group, or other (*i.e.*, an organization, an event, an issue, a situation) (C).

We choose this dataset because of the extended subtasks B and C. An increase in performance over these will posit that our model has been successful in tackling its objectives. We evaluate our model on all three subtasks.

Hate Speech and Offensive Language Dataset: Motivated by the central problem surrounding the separation of hate speech from other instances of offensive language, Davidson et al. (2017) curated a dataset annotating each tweet in one of three classes, hate speech (**HATE**), offensive language (**OFF**), and none (**NONE**). They use a hate speech lexicon containing words and phrases identified by internet users as hate speech, compiled by *Hatebase*. These lexicons are used to extract English tweets from the Twitter API. From this corpus, a random sample of $25k$ tweets containing terms from the lexicon was extracted. The tweets were manually coded by CrowdFlower (CF) workers, with a final inter-annotator agreement of 92%.

4.2 Baseline Models

In the following section, we describe the design of all the baseline models used for comparison.

Linear-SVM: SVMs have achieved state-of-the-art results for many text classification tasks and significantly outperform many neural networks over the OLID dataset (Zampieri et al., 2019). Hence, we use a Linear-SVM trained on word unigrams as a baseline. We employ a Grid-search technique to identify the best hyperparameters.

Two-channel BiLSTM: We design a two-channel BiLSTM as a second baseline, with the two input channels differentiated only by their embedding space. One of the input channels learns the embedding space via backpropagation after a random initialization, while the other uses the pre-trained BERT embeddings. This choice is motivated by the contextual nature of the BERT embeddings. This conforms with the ideation that certain words may be deemed offensive depending upon the context they are used in. The BiLSTM itself is two layers deep and consists of 32 hidden-units. The final hidden states for the forward and backward sequences of each channel are concatenated and passed through an MLP with a softmax head for classification.

Fine-tuned BERT: We also fine-tune a BERT model (Devlin et al., 2018) for this task. We adapt the state-of-the-art BERT model which won the SemEval Challenge 2019 (Liu et al., 2019) and tune the hyperparameters of the model to get the best performance on our preprocessing strategy. While fine-tuning this model, the choices over the loss function, optimizer, and learning rate schedule remain the same as those for the *SyLSTM*.

4.3 Training

We train our models using the standard cross-entropy loss. The AdamW optimizer (Loshchilov and Hutter, 2018) is chosen to learn the parameters. To improve the training time and chances of reaching the optima, we adopt a cosine annealing (Loshchilov and Hutter, 2017) learning rate scheduler. The vocabulary of the models is fixed to the top 30,000 words in the corpus. The initial learning rate is set to 0.001, with a regularization parameter of 0.1.

4.4 Evaluation Metric

The datasets exhibit large class imbalances over each task. In order to address this problem, we use the Weighted F1-measure as the evaluation metric. We also provide the precision and recall scores for a deeper insight into the model's performance.

5 Results

We evaluate two instances of our model, (1) with a randomly initialized embedding matrix (referred to as *SyLSTM*) and (2) utilizing the pretrained GloVe Twitter embeddings (referred to as *SyLSTM**). A paired Student's t-test using the Weighted-F1 measure of the model's performance shows that our models significantly outperform each of the baselines across all the tasks ($p < 0.001$).

5.1 Performance on Offensive Language Identification Dataset

In this section, we present performance comparisons between the baselines and the *SyLSTM* for the three subtasks. We split the training data, using 10% of the tweets to get a dev set. The hyperparameters are tuned according to the performance on the dev set. The results presented here demonstrate the performance over the predefined test set. We also present the performance metrics for the trivial case, notably where the model predicts only a single label for each tweet. By comparison, we show that the chosen baselines and our models perform significantly better than chance for each task.

Offensive Language Detection: The performance comparisons for discriminating between offensive (**OFF**) and non-offensive (**NOT**) tweets are reported in Table 3. Neural network models perform substantially better than the Linear-SVM. Our model (in gray) outperforms each of the baselines in this task.

System	Precision	Recall	F1-score
All OFF	8.4	28.2	12.1
All NOT	52.4	72.7	60.4
SVM	77.7	80.2	78.6
BiLSTM	81.7	82.8	82.0
BERT	87.3	85.8	85.7
SyLSTM	85.2	88.1	86.4
SyLSTM*	**87.6**	**88.1**	**87.4**

Table 3: Offensive Language Detection

Categorization of Offensive Language: This sub-task is designed to discriminate between targeted insults and threats (**TIN**) and untargeted (**UNT**) offenses, generally referring to profanity (Zampieri et al., 2019). Performance comparisons for the same are reported in Table 4. Our model (in gray) shows a significant 4% relative improvement in performance in comparison to the BERT model.

System	Precision	Recall	F1-score
All TIN	78.7	88.6	83.4
All UNT	1.4	11.3	12.1
SVM	81.6	84.1	82.6
BiLSTM	84.8	88.4	85.7
BERT	88.4	92.3	89.6
SyLSTM	90.6	91.6	91.4
SyLSTM*	**94.4**	**92.3**	**93.2**

Table 4: Categorization of Offensive Language

Offensive Language Target Identification: This sub-task is designed to discriminate between three possible targets: a group (**GRP**), an individual (**IND**), or others (**OTH**). The results for the same are reported in Table 5. Note that the three baselines produce almost identical results. The low F1-scores for this task may be on account of the small size of the dataset and large class imbalances, factors that make it difficult to learn the best features for classification. Our model (in gray) shows a 5.7% relative improvement over the BERT model, hence showcasing its robustness when generalizing over smaller datasets.

System	Precision	Recall	F1-score
All GRP	13.6	37.4	19.7
All IND	22.1	47.3	30.3
ALL OTH	3.4	16.2	5.4
SVM	56.1	62.4	58.3
BiLSTM	56.1	65.8	60.4
BERT	58.4	66.2	60.9
SyLSTM	60.3	**67.4**	63.4
SyLSTM*	**62.4**	66.3	**64.4**

Table 5: Offensive Language Target Identification

5.2 Performance on Hate Speech and Offensive Language Dataset

This section presents the performance comparisons between our model and the baselines for this multi-class classification problem. The task presented by the dataset complies with our main objective of integrating syntactic dependencies in a neural network model to differentiate between offensive language and hate speech more efficiently. The tweets are classified in one of three categories: hate speech (**HATE**), offensive language (**OFF**), and none (**NONE**). The Linear-SVM and the neural network baselines produce very similar results, all of which are significantly better than chance (see Table 6). The *SyLSTM* (in gray) significantly outperforms all the baselines.

System	Precision	Recall	F1-score
All HATE	0.2	6.1	0.4
All OFF	3.1	16.9	5.3
All NONE	58.8	77.2	66.7
SVM	84.9	90.1	88.2
BiLSTM	90.3	90.2	90.3
BERT	91.2	90.4	91.0
SyLSTM	90.5	91.4	91.4
SyLSTM*	**92.3**	**92.8**	**92.7**

Table 6: Hate Speech and Offensive Language Dataset

5.3 Discussion

The two-channel BiLSTM and the BERT model discussed in this paper act as strong syntax-agnostic baselines for this study. The aforementioned results indicate the superiority of the *SyLSTM* over such approaches. The inability of existing dependency parsers to generate highly accurate dependency trees for a tweet may seem like a severe problem. However, since the dependency tree has been transformed to accommodate inverse dependency edges, we find that the resulting undirected graph acts as a single-relational graph where each edge represents a "dependency". The nature of the dependency is addressed by graph convolutions operating over the dynamic LSTM features. Hence, the parser only needs to generate congruent copies of the actual dependency tree of the tweet.

We tested the utility of enriching the features generated by a BERT encoder using a GCN. Existing literature in this field integrates word embeddings learned using a GCN with the BERT model (Lu et al., 2020). In contrast, our experiments dealt with a GCN mounted over a BERT encoder. We note that this combination leads to over-parametrization and severe sparsity issues. Since BERT models have been shown to learn fairly accurate dependency structures (Clark et al., 2019), additional importance to dependency grammar over the same encoder network may be unnecessary.

6 Conclusion

In this paper, we present a novel approach called the *SyLSTM* which demonstrates how GCNs can incorporate syntactic information in the deep feature space, leading to state-of-the-art results for fine-grained offensive language detection on Twitter Data. Our analysis uncovers the Semantic and Syntactic Encoders' complementarity while revealing that the system's performance is largely unaffected for mislabeled dependencies over congruent dependency trees. Leveraging the dependency grammar of a tweet provides a practical approach to simulating how humans read such texts. Furthermore, the performance results of the *SyLSTM* indicate the robustness of the architecture in generalizing over small datasets. The added simplicity of the overall architecture promotes applicability over other NLP tasks. The *SyLSTM* can be used as an efficient and scalable solution towards accommodating graph-structured linguistic features into a neural network model.

Replication Package. The replication package for this study is available at `https://github.com/dv-fenix/SyLSTM`.

References

Joan Bruna, Wojciech Zaremba, Arthur Szlam, and Yann LeCun. 2013. Spectral networks and locally connected networks on graphs. *arXiv preprint arXiv:1312.6203.*

Ying Chen, Yilu Zhou, Sencun Zhu, and Heng Xu. 2012. Detecting offensive language in social media to protect adolescent online safety. In *2012 International Conference on Privacy, Security, Risk and Trust and 2012 International Confernece on Social Computing*, pages 71–80. IEEE.

Kevin Clark, Urvashi Khandelwal, Omer Levy, and Christopher D Manning. 2019. What does bert look at? an analysis of bert's attention. *arXiv preprint arXiv:1906.04341.*

Thomas Davidson, Debasmita Bhattacharya, and Ingmar Weber. 2019. Racial bias in hate speech and abusive language detection datasets. In *Proceedings of the Third Workshop on Abusive Language Online*, pages 25–35.

Thomas Davidson, Dana Warmsley, Michael Macy, and Ingmar Weber. 2017. Automated hate speech detection and the problem of offensive language. *arXiv preprint arXiv:1703.04009.*

Jacob Devlin, Ming-Wei Chang, Kenton Lee, and Kristina Toutanova. 2018. Bert: Pre-training of deep bidirectional transformers for language understanding. *arXiv preprint arXiv:1810.04805.*

Mai ElSherief, Vivek Kulkarni, Dana Nguyen, William Yang Wang, and Elizabeth Belding. 2018. Hate lingo: A target-based linguistic analysis of hate speech in social media. *arXiv preprint arXiv:1804.04257.*

Njagi Dennis Gitari, Zhang Zuping, Hanyurwimfura Damien, and Jun Long. 2015. A lexicon-based approach for hate speech detection. *International Journal of Multimedia and Ubiquitous Engineering*, 10(4):215–230.

William L Hamilton, Rex Ying, and Jure Leskovec. 2017. Inductive representation learning on large graphs. *arXiv preprint arXiv:1706.02216.*

Sepp Hochreiter and Jürgen Schmidhuber. 1997. Long short-term memory. *Neural computation*, 9(8):1735–1780.

Daniel Jurafsky and James H. Martin. 2009. *Speech and Language Processing (2nd Edition).* Prentice-Hall, Inc., USA.

Thomas N Kipf and Max Welling. 2016. Semi-supervised classification with graph convolutional networks. *arXiv preprint arXiv:1609.02907.*

Ping Liu, Wen Li, and Liang Zou. 2019. Nuli at semeval-2019 task 6: Transfer learning for offensive language detection using bidirectional transformers. In *Proceedings of the 13th International Workshop on Semantic Evaluation*, pages 87–91.

Ilya Loshchilov and Frank Hutter. 2017. Decoupled weight decay regularization. *arXiv preprint arXiv:1711.05101.*

Ilya Loshchilov and Frank Hutter. 2018. Fixing weight decay regularization in adam.

Zhibin Lu, Pan Du, and Jian-Yun Nie. 2020. Vgcn-bert: augmenting bert with graph embedding for text classification. In *European Conference on Information Retrieval*, pages 369–382. Springer.

Diego Marcheggiani and Ivan Titov. 2017. Encoding sentences with graph convolutional networks for semantic role labeling. *arXiv preprint arXiv:1703.04826.*

Chikashi Nobata, Joel Tetreault, Achint Thomas, Yashar Mehdad, and Yi Chang. 2016. Abusive language detection in online user content. In *Proceedings of the 25th international conference on world wide web*, pages 145–153.

John T Nockleby. 2000. Hate speech. *Encyclopedia of the American constitution*, 3(2):1277–1279.

Hao Peng, Jianxin Li, Yu He, Yaopeng Liu, Mengjiao Bao, Lihong Wang, Yangqiu Song, and Qiang Yang. 2018. Large-scale hierarchical text classification with recursively regularized deep graph-cnn. In *Proceedings of the 2018 World Wide Web Conference*, pages 1063–1072.

Jeffrey Pennington, Richard Socher, and Christopher D Manning. 2014. Glove: Global vectors for word representation. In *Proceedings of the 2014 conference on empirical methods in natural language processing (EMNLP)*, pages 1532–1543.

Mehran Sahami, Susan Dumais, David Heckerman, and Eric Horvitz. 1998. A bayesian approach to filtering junk e-mail. In *Learning for Text Categorization: Papers from the 1998 workshop*, volume 62, pages 98–105. Madison, Wisconsin.

Anna Schmidt and Michael Wiegand. 2017. A survey on hate speech detection using natural language processing. In *Proceedings of the Fifth International workshop on natural language processing for social media*, pages 1–10.

Leandro Silva, Mainack Mondal, Denzil Correa, Fabrício Benevenuto, and Ingmar Weber. 2016. Analyzing the targets of hate in online social media. *arXiv preprint arXiv:1603.07709.*

Ellen Spertus. 1997. Smokey: Automatic recognition of hostile messages. In *Aaai/iaai*, pages 1058–1065.

Shikhar Vashishth, Manik Bhandari, Prateek Yadav, Piyush Rai, Chiranjib Bhattacharyya, and Partha Talukdar. 2018. Incorporating syntactic and semantic information in word embeddings using graph convolutional networks. *arXiv preprint arXiv:1809.04283.*

Zeerak Waseem, Thomas Davidson, Dana Warmsley, and Ingmar Weber. 2017. Understanding abuse: A typology of abusive language detection subtasks. *arXiv preprint arXiv:1705.09899*.

Zeerak Waseem and Dirk Hovy. 2016. Hateful symbols or hateful people? predictive features for hate speech detection on twitter. In *Proceedings of the NAACL student research workshop*, pages 88–93.

Janyce Wiebe, Theresa Wilson, and Claire Cardie. 2005. Annotating expressions of opinions and emotions in language. *Language resources and evaluation*, 39(2-3):165–210.

G. Xu, Y. Meng, X. Qiu, Z. Yu, and X. Wu. 2019. Sentiment analysis of comment texts based on bilstm. *IEEE Access*, 7:51522–51532.

Liang Yao, Chengsheng Mao, and Yuan Luo. 2019. Graph convolutional networks for text classification. In *Proceedings of the AAAI Conference on Artificial Intelligence*, volume 33, pages 7370–7377.

Marcos Zampieri, Shervin Malmasi, Preslav Nakov, Sara Rosenthal, Noura Farra, and Ritesh Kumar. 2019. Predicting the type and target of offensive posts in social media. *arXiv preprint arXiv:1902.09666*.

Marinka Zitnik, Monica Agrawal, and Jure Leskovec. 2018. Modeling polypharmacy side effects with graph convolutional networks. *Bioinformatics*, 34(13):i457–i466.

A Comparative Study on Word Embeddings in Social NLP Tasks

Fatma Elsafoury[1], Steven R. Wilson[2] and Naeem Ramzan[1]

[1]School of Physics, Engineering, and Computing, the University of The West of Scotland, UK
[2]Department of Computer Science and Engineering, Oakland University, USA

Abstract

In recent years, grey social media platforms, those with a loose moderation policy on cyberbullying, have been attracting more users. Recently, data collected from these types of platforms have been used to pre-train word embeddings (social-media-based), yet these word embeddings have not been investigated for social NLP related tasks. In this paper, we carried out a comparative study between social-media-based and non-social-media-based word embeddings on two social NLP tasks: Detecting cyberbullying and Measuring social bias. Our results show that using social-media-based word embeddings as input features, rather than non-social-media-based embeddings, leads to better cyberbullying detection performance. We also show that some word embeddings are more useful than others for categorizing offensive words. However, we do not find strong evidence that certain word embeddings will necessarily work best when identifying certain categories of cyberbullying within our datasets. Finally, We show even though most of the state-of-the-art bias metrics ranked social-media-based word embeddings as the most socially biased, these results remain inconclusive and further research is required.

Content Warning: As part of our experiments, we show some offensive words.

1 Introduction

Distributional word representations have been successfully used for many NLP tasks. Some of these word embeddings were pre-trained on news articles like Word2vec (Mikolov et al., 2021) or Wikipedia articles like GloVe (Pennington et al., 2021b). We use the term "informational-based" to describe these word embeddings. In recent years, there have been new word embedding models pre-trained on more informal text corpora like Twitter, 4&8 Chan and Urban Dictionary. We use the term "social-media-based" to describe those word embeddings. These informal sources contain linguistic diversity, racial slurs and forms of profanity that do not exist in formal text (Türker et al., 2016). However, these social-media-based word embeddings have not been investigated for social NLP related tasks like cyberbullying detection and social bias analysis. Our intuition that social-media-based word embeddings could be better at detecting cyberbullying comes from the examples shown in Table 1, where we display the most similar five words found by each word embeddings to the word "queer". The informational-based word embeddings return non-offensive words while social-media-based word embeddings return offensive* words. Previous research has established that word embeddings, in general, contain social biases (Garg et al., 2018; Manzini et al., 2019; Sweeney and Najafian, 2019; Bolukbasi et al., 2016; Chaloner and Maldonado, 2019). Studying social bias in word embeddings includes measuring the statistical association between certain characteristics and certain groups of people. This includes racial bias (Garg et al., 2018; Manzini et al., 2019; Sweeney and Najafian, 2019) and gender bias (Garg et al., 2018; Bolukbasi et al., 2016; Chaloner and Maldonado, 2019). Prior work has focused mainly on Word2vec, Glove-WK, and glove-twitter (Badilla et al., 2020). However, this bias has not been explored in word embed-

Word Embeddings	Similar words to "queer"
Word2vec	genderqueer, LGBTQ, gay, LGBT, lesbian
Glove-WK	transgender, lesbian, lgbt, lgbtq, bisexual
Glove-Twitter	fag, faggot, feminist, gay, cunt
Urban Dictionary	fag, homo, homosexual, bumblaster, buttyman
Chan	faggot, metrosexual, fag, transvestite, homo

Table 1: Top 5 similar words retrieved by each of the word embeddings.

*Throughout this paper, we differentiate between the terms "offensive" and "profane": we use the term "offensive" to describe an expression that is offensive to a group of people but not necessarily profane e.g. "women belong to the kitchen" while we use the term "profane" to describe expressions like "b*tch".

Proceedings of the Tenth International Workshop on Natural Language Processing for Social Media (SocialNLP 2022), pages 44 - 53
July 14-15, 2022 ©2022 Association for Computational Linguistics

dings that were pre-trained on Urban Dictionary and 4&8 Chan platforms. Since those platforms are rife with offensiveness against women and racially insensitive comments (Nguyen et al., 2017; Voué et al., 2020), this motivates our investigation into the bias in social-media-based word embeddings, especially Urban Dictionary and Chan, in comparison to informational-based word embeddings.

In this paper, we compared static word embeddings based on the datasets they were pre-trained on and not models that were used to pre-train them e.g. skip-gram. While using one model to pre-train all word embeddings on different pre-training datasets would directly show the impact of the source datasets for a particular word embedding training method, we focus our work on analyzing existing, publicly released word embeddings which are often used in other downstream tasks in order to better understand the impact of using these embeddings. We examined static word embeddings instead of contextual word embeddings as they are still widely used in NLP tasks and there have not been any released contextual word embeddings pre-trained on datasets like Urban Dictionary or Chan, and pre-training these models from scratch is computationally expensive.

We set out to answer the following research questions: 1) What is the performance of the different word embeddings on offences categorisation?. 2) What is the performance of the different word embeddings on the task of cyberbullying detection? Can we use certain word embeddings to detect certain offensive categories within cyberbullying-related datasets? 3) Are social-media-based word embeddings more socially biased than informational-based word embeddings? To answer the first research question, we used the different word embeddings to categorize terms from a popular lexicon of English offensive language. Then we compared the performance of the social-media-based word embeddings and the informational-based word embeddings using statistical significance tests. Answering our first research question should help in finding out whether social-media-based word embeddings are significantly better than informational-based word embeddings at learning the semantic relationship between terms that belong to the same group of offences. We answer our second research question through a series of experiments where we used each word embedding to automatically detect cyberbullying in cyberbullying-related datasets and to detect different types of cyberbullying within each dataset. We used a statistical significance test to compare the performance of the social-media-based word embeddings and the informational-based word embeddings. Answering the second research question will help us to find out if social-media-based word embeddings improve the performance on the task of cyberbullying detection in comparison to informational-based word embeddings and to find out the ability of certain pre-trained word embeddings to detect certain types of cyberbullying. Finally, to answer our last research question and to find out which word embeddings are more socially biased, we used the state-of-the-art metrics from the literature to measure gender and racial bias in each word embedding and compared the bias scores in the social-media-based word embeddings and the informational-based word embeddings.

The contributions of this paper are: **(a)** We demonstrate that social-media-based word embeddings are better at categorizing offensive words and that social-media-based word embeddings outperform informational-based word embeddings on cyberbullying detection. **(b)** Our findings show no evidence that certain word embeddings are better than others at detecting certain offensive categories within the examined cyberbullying-related datasets. **(c)** Our results show no strong evidence that social-media-based word embeddings are more socially biased than informational-based word embeddings. We share our code with the community to reproduce our results and allow more investigation [†].

2 Related work

Recent word embeddings pre-trained on data from social media platforms have been released in the community. For example, Urban Dictionary word embeddings that was pre-trained on words and definitions from the Urban Dictionary website (Wilson et al., 2020) using the FastText framework, Chan word embeddings that was pre-trained on 4&8 Chan websites using Continuous Bag-of-Words algorithm (CBOW) (Voué et al., 2020), and a version of Glove pre-trained on Twitter data (Pennington et al., 2021a). Even though there is evidence from the literature that the data that was used in pre-training these word embeddings contain offensive-

[†] `https://github.com/efatmae/Comparative_analysis_word_embeddings_on_social_NLP_tasks`

ness and racially insensitive comments (Nguyen et al., 2017; Papasavva et al., 2020), they have not been investigated for social NLP tasks. For example, investigating the impact of social-media-based word embeddings on the task of cyberbullying detection or analysing the social bias in the social-media-based word embeddings.

Using social-media-based word embeddings could improve cyberbullying detection as they may be able to identify some offensive words or forms of profanity that are not captured by informational-based word embeddings. Comparative studies on word embeddings and deep learning models have been done for biomedical natural language processing (Wang et al., 2018) and for text classification, (Wang et al., 2020), but there have been very few similar comparative studies for the task of cyberbullying detection. Jain et al. (2021) reviewed the literature on different word embeddings: CBOW, Skip-gram, ELMo, GloVe and fastText, and then tested them with a neural networks model on hate speech detection task. They show that ELMo is the best performing followed by fastText and GloVe. However, they do not include social-media-based word embeddings like Urban Dictionary or Chan. Elsafoury et al. (2021) have shown that word embeddings pre-trained on Urban Dictionary, and Twitter outperforms embeddings like Word2vec and Glove-Wikipedia on the task of cyberbullying detection. However, they do not compare the ability of the different word embeddings to categorize offensive words or to detect different categories of offences within cyberbullying datasets.

Additionally, The research has shown that word embeddings are biased. Among the most common methods for quantifying bias in word embeddings are the word embedding association test (WEAT), the relative norm distance (RND), The relative negative sentiment bias (RNSB), and The embedding coherence test (ECT). For the WEAT metric, the authors were inspired by the Implicit Association Test (IAT) to develop a statistical test to demonstrate human-like biases in word embeddings (Caliskan et al., 2017). They used the cosine similarity and statistical significance tests to measure the unfair correlations for two different demographics, as represented by manually curated word lists. As for the RND metric, the authors used the Euclidean distance between neutral words, like professions, and a representative group vector created by averaging the word vectors for words that describe a stereotyped group (gender/ethnicity) (Garg et al., 2018). As for the RNSB metric, the authors trained a logistic regression model on the word vectors of unbiased labelled sentiment words (positive and negative) extracted from biased word embeddings. Then, that model was used to predict the sentiment of words that describe certain demographics (Sweeney and Najafian, 2019). In the ECT metric, the authors proposed a method to measure how much bias has been removed from the word embeddings after debiasing them (Dev and Phillips, 2019). These bais metrics have been used to measure the bias in Word2vec(Caliskan et al., 2017; Garg et al., 2018; Sweeney and Najafian, 2019; Dev and Phillips, 2019), Glove-WK (Dev and Phillips, 2019; Sweeney and Najafian, 2019), Glove-Twitter (Dev and Phillips, 2019). Even though research has shown that the upstream data used to pre-train the social-media-based word embeddings, especially Urban Dictionary and Chan, are full of racial slurs and profanity (Nguyen et al., 2017; Voué et al., 2020), none of these studies measured the social bias in Urban Dictionary or Chan word embeddings. In this paper, we run a series of experiments to fill the mentioned gaps in the literature and to answer our research questions.

Word embedding	Pre-training data	Type
Word2Vec	Google news articles	informational-based
Glove-Wikipedia	Wikipedia articles	informational-based
Glove-Twitter	Twitter messages	social-media-based
Chan	Text from 4&8 Chan	social-media-based
Urban Dictionary	Text from Urban Dictionary	social-media-based

Table 2: Word embedding models used in the paper.

Category	Description
PS	ethnic slurs
IS	words related to social and economic disadvantage
QAS	descriptive words with potential negative connotations
CDS	derogatory words
RE	felonies and words related to crime and immoral behavior
PR	words related to prostitution
OM	words related to homosexuality
ASF	female genitalia
ASM	male genitalia
DDP	cognitive disabilities
DDF	physical disabilities

Table 3: Hurtlex categories used in this paper.

3 Offenses categorization

In this paper, we used the word embedding models that are summarized in Table 2. To answer our research questions, we used the English offensive categories introduced in Hurtlex lexicon (Zhang et al., 2020), which is a multilingual lexicon containing

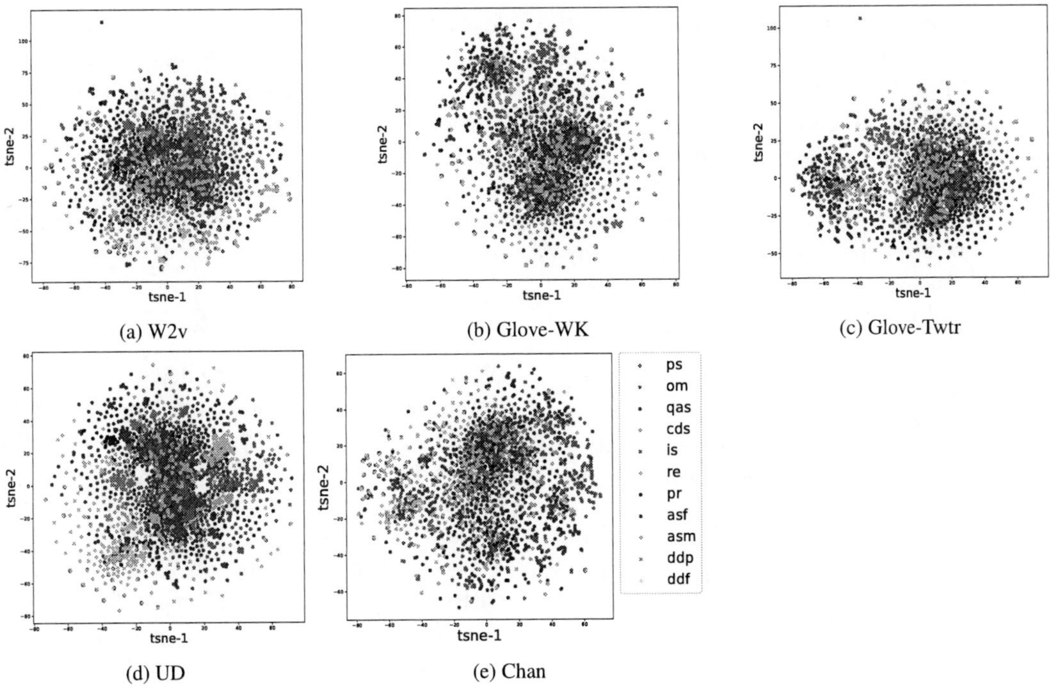

(a) W2v (b) Glove-WK (c) Glove-Twtr

(d) UD (e) Chan

Figure 1: t-SNE of the different word embeddings of the words that belong to different groups in Hurtlex lexicon.

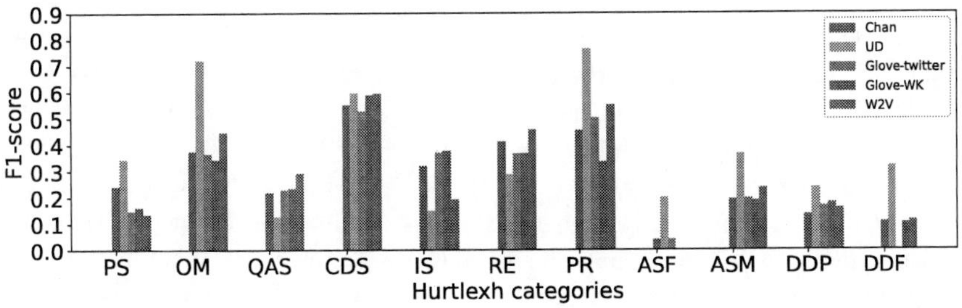

Figure 2: F1 scores of the KNN model with the different word embeddings on Hurtlext test set.

8228 offensive words and expressions, which are organized into 17 groups. We only used words that belong to 11 groups because they are related to the types of cyberbullying found in our datasets. The used categories are summarized in Table 3. We extracted the word vectors, using the different word embeddings described in Table 2, for each word in those 11 groups and projected them into a two-dimensional space using t-SNE (van der Maaten and Hinton, 2008) as shown in Figure 1. The plot shows words from some Hurtlex categories clustered better in some cases, especially, PS, PR, and ASM with Urban Dictionary. To quantitatively investigate the ability of the different word embeddings to group the words that belong to the same Hurtlex category, we used a KNN model. We first removed the words in the lexicon that belong to more than one category, which resulted in 5963 offensive words. We then split Hurtlex lexicon into training (70%) and test (30%) sets with class ratio preserved. Next, in order to understand if the neighbors of a given word typically belong to the same class as that word, we used the trained KNN model to predict the category of each word embedding in the test set based on proximity to embeddings from the training set. We measured the F1-scores and plot them in Figure 2. To answer our first question, our results show that for most of Hurtlex categories, PS, OM, PR, ASF, ASM, DDP and DDF, Urban Dictionary is the best performing, meaning that it was the best at grouping together the words that belong to these categories. For QAS and RE, Word2vec is the best performing and for IS, Glove-Wikipedia and Glove-twitter are the best performings. For CDS, all the word embeddings are performing similarly with Urban Dictionary embedding being the best performing by a small margin. We speculate that these results stem from the fact that the Urban Dictionary is pre-trained on words and definitions that are of insulting nature in general, and to women and minorities specifically, so it is better at finding more profanity related to these categories: PS, OM, PR, ASF, ASM, DDP and DDF. Word2vec, on the other hand, is better at clustering the word vectors that are related to felonies and words related to crime and immoral behaviour (RE) and words with potential negative connotations (QAS). That may be due to its pre-training on news articles, which sometimes report on crimes. Using a Friedman significance statistical test (Zimmerman and Zumbo, 1993) ($\alpha = 0.05$) between the F1 scores of each data item in the test set, we found that the F1 scores achieved by the word embeddings are significantly different. To further investigate the difference between pairs of top-scoring word embeddings, we use a Wilcoxon test (Zimmerman and Zumbo, 1993) ($\alpha = 0.05$). We found that, across all categories, Urban Dictionary scores significantly higher than Chan and Glove-Wikipedia but not significantly higher than Word2vec or Glove-Twitter. Similarly, we found that Word2vec achieves a significantly higher F1 score than Chan and Glove-Wikipedia, but not significantly higher than Glove-Twitter. The results suggest that the Urban Dictionary embeddings, along with Word2vec and Glove-twitter, place offensive words semantically close to other words from the same Hurtlex categories, indicating that these embeddings better reflect the categorization of terms outlined in Hurtlex.

4 Cyberbullying detection

In the light of our earlier results presented in Figure 2, we make two hypotheses: (1) social-media-based word embeddings will perform better than informational-based embeddings on the task of cyberbullying detection. (2) Certain word embeddings will perform better at detecting certain offensive categories within our cyberbullying-related datasets. Specifically, we expect that Urban Dictionary embeddings might perform the best on the examples in the datasets containing PS, OM, PR, ASF, ASM, DDP and DDF categories; Word2vec embeddings to perform the best on examples containing RE and QAS; and for the CDS category, we expect all the models to perform similarly. To test our hypotheses and answer our second research question, we compared the performance of the different word embeddings when used to initialize the embedding layer of a deep learning model trained on the following datasets.

4.1 Cyberbullying datasets

We used five cyberbullying-related datasets from several social media sources that contain different types of cyberbullying: (i) *Twitter-Racism*, a collection of Twitter messages containing tweets that are labelled as racist or not (Waseem and Hovy, 2016); (ii) *Twitter-Sexism*, Twitter messages containing tweets labelled as sexist or not (Waseem and Hovy, 2016); (iii) *HateEval*, a collection of tweets containing hate speech against immigrants and women in Spanish and English (Basile et al., 2019). We used only the English tweets; (iv)*Kaggle* (Kaggle, 2012), a dataset that contains social media comments that are labelled as insulting or not; and (v) *Jigsaw*, a collection of Wikipedia Talk Pages comments which have been labelled by human raters for toxicity (Jigsaw, 2018). The datasets 'statistics are described in Table 4.

To pre-process the datasets, we removed URLs, user mentions, and non-ASCII characters; All letters were lowercased; common contractions were converted to their full forms. We also removed English stop words, as proposed in (Agrawal and Awekar, 2018). However, second-person pronouns like "you", "yours" and "your", and third-person pronouns like "he/she/they", "his/her/their" and "him/her/them" were not removed because we noticed in our datasets that sometimes, profane words on their own, e.g. "f**k", are not necessarily used in an offensive way, while their combination with a pronoun, e.g. "f**k you", is used to insult someone. For Twitter datasets, we also removed the retweet abbreviation "RT". Each dataset was randomly split into training (70%) and test (30%) sets with preserved class ratios. Additionally, to find out the different categories of offences within each cyberbullying dataset, we filtered the datasets using the words in the Hurtlex lexicon. Then we sorted the data items in each dataset into the 11 Hurtlex categories based on the words present in the data items. Those that contain a mix of words from multiple Hurtlex categories were grouped in a Mixed category, and all the data items that do not contain any Hurtlex words were placed in a No-Hurtlex category. The results show that for all the datasets, the majority of data items contain words that do not belong to any Hurtlex category (No-hurtlex) with a percentage range from 40% to 66%. The second most present category in all the datasets is the Mixed category where the data items contain words from multiple Hurtlex categories with percentages ranging from 5% to 25%. For the data items that contain words from only one Hurtlex category, the datasets, are less than 10% except for the CDS category where the percentage is less than 20%. When we investigated the distribution of the different categories in the Mixed group, we found a similar distribution of the 11 categories in all the datasets with the majority belonging to the CDS category. When we investigated the data items in the No-Hurtlex category, we found some non-profane form of offensiveness.

4.2 Model settings

We used a Bi-directional LSTM (Schuster and Paliwal, 1997), with the same architecture as in (Agrawal and Awekar, 2018), who used RNN models to detect cyberbullying. To this end, we first used the Keras tokenizer (Tensorflow.org, 2020) to tokenize the input texts, using a maximum input length of 64 (maximum observed sequence length in the dataset) for the HateEval and Twitter datasets and 600 for the Kaggle and Jigsaw datasets (due to computational resource limitations). A frozen embedding layer, based on a given pre-trained word embedding model, was used as the first layer and fed to the Bi-LSTM model. To avoid over-fitting, we used L2 regularization with an experimentally determined value of 10^{-7}. The model was then trained for 100 epochs with a batch size of 32, using the Adam optimiser and a learning rate of 0.01.

4.3 Results

To answer the first part of our second research question, we analysed the overall performance of each word embeddings on each dataset, the "Average" column in Table 5, individually and across all the datasets. We used Friedman statistical significance test (Zimmerman and Zumbo, 1993) ($\alpha = 0.05$) to compare the F1-scores of each word embeddings for the 13 categories (PS, OM, QAS, CDS, IS, RE, PR, ASF, ASM, DDP, DDF, No-hurtlex and Mixed) in each dataset. Our results show that social-media-based word embeddings gave the

Dataset	Size	Pos.	Avg.	Max.
HateEval	12722	42%	21.75	93
Kaggle	7425	65%	25.28	1419
Twitter-sex	14742	23%	15.04	41
Twitter-rac	13349	15%	15.05	41
Jigsaw-tox	99738	6%	54	2321

Table 4: Cyberbullying dataset statistics. Pos. is the percentage of positive (bullying) comments. Avg. is the average number of words per comment. Max. is the maximum number of words in a comment.

best results for four out of five datasets: HateEval, Kaggle, Twitter-racism and Jigsaw-toxicity. For the HateEval dataset, performance across all the categories is at its best when Glove-Twitter, social-media-based, was used with an average F1 score of 0.620. However, the results across all the categories are not significantly better than the rest of the word embeddings with $p - value > 0.05$. Glove-Twitter also resulted in the highest average F1 score at 0.519, across all the categories on the Jigsaw-toxicity dataset which is significantly better for all the categories with $p - value < 0.05$. The best performing word embeddings on the Kaggle dataset is also the social-media-based word embeddings, Chan, with the average F1-score of 0.727 across all the categories with the results significantly better than the rest of the word embeddings for all the categories with $p - value < 0.05$. Urban Dictionary embeddings, social-media-based, gave the best results on the Twitter-racism dataset with the average F1 score of 0.663 across all the categories. These results are significantly better with $p - value < 0.05$. The informational-based word embeddings, Glove-Wikipedia, gives a significantly better average F1-score of 0.699 across all the categories on the Twitter-sexism dataset with $p - values < 0.05$. Overall, we found that although social-media-based word embeddings outperform others on four out of five datasets, the difference is only significant in three cases.

To answer the second part of the second research question, we analysed the results across the different types of cyberbullying in the datasets, we computed the mean F1-score achieved by each word embedding for each category across all datasets. When we compared the mean F1-score achieved by each word embedding for each category across all datasets using a Friedman significance statistical test ($\alpha = 0.05$), we found no significance for any of the 13 categories (PS, OM, QAS, CDS, IS, RE, PR, ASF, ASM, DDP, DDF, No-hurtlex and Mixed). This might occur because there is

HateEval														
	PS	OM	QAS	CDS	IS	RE	PR	ASF	ASM	DDP	DDF	No-Hurtlex	Mixed	Average
Chan	0.615	0.444	0.615	**0.666**	0.555	**0.647**	0.658	0.421	0.555	**0.857**	0.5	0.570	0.730	0.602
UD	**0.7**	0.444	0.571	0.603	0.533	0.562	0.678	0.4	0.603	0.571	0.375	0.508	0.734	0.560
Glove-Twitter	0.695	**0.5**	**0.736**	0.663	0.631	0.619	**0.711**	0.620	0.690	0.571	0.285	**0.605**	**0.738**	**0.620**
Glove-WK	0.583	0.222	0.571	0.616	**0.666**	0.515	0.614	**0.72**	0.691	**0.857**	0.333	0.535	0.699	0.586
W2V	0.315	**0.5**	0.666	0.648	0.631	0.514	0.614	0.714	**0.72**	0.571	**0.666**	0.593	0.705	0.604
Kaggle														
	PS	OM	QAS	CDS	IS	RE	PR	ASF	ASM	DDP	DDF	No-Hurtlex	Mixed	Average
Chan	0.380	**0.777**	**1**	**0.760**	0.571	**0.545**	0.571	**1**	**0.666**	0.916	**0.909**	0.571	0.783	**0.727**
UD	**0.72**	0.761	**1**	0.703	**0.75**	0.461	0.75	0.666	0.507	0.888	0.8	**0.611**	**0.813**	0.725
Glove-Twitter	0.454	0.727	0.444	0.627	0.727	0.285	**0.823**	0	0.520	**0.923**	0.8	0.513	0.790	0.587
Glove-WK	0.5	0.625	**1**	0.588	0.666	0.5	0.666	0.666	0.507	0.869	0.666	0.525	0.8	0.660
W2V	0.352	0.375	**1**	0.602	0.25	0.4	0.714	**1**	0.526	0.818	0.666	0.479	0.797	0.614
Twitter-sexism														
	PS	OM	QAS	CDS	IS	RE	PR	ASF	ASM	DDP	DDF	No-Hurtlex	Mixed	Average
Chan	0.666	0.829	0.421	0.523	0.695	0.4	0.45	0.6	0.510	0.666	0.56	0.561	0.586	0.574
UD	0.666	0.8	0.521	0.656	0.75	0.510	0.608	**0.923**	0.622	**0.75**	**0.687**	0.629	0.695	0.678
Glove-Twitter	0.666	**0.863**	0.380	0.640	**0.8**	0.5	0.693	**0.923**	**0.653**	0.571	0.645	0.631	0.702	0.667
Glove-WK	0.666	0.818	**0.608**	**0.686**	0.740	**0.655**	0.734	0.727	0.636	**0.75**	0.685	**0.675**	0.708	**0.699**
W2V	**0.727**	0.772	0.571	0.598	0.695	0.56	**0.769**	0.833	0.623	**0.75**	0.666	0.650	**0.730**	0.688
Twitter-racism														
	PS	OM	QAS	CDS	IS	RE	PR	ASF	ASM	DDP	DDF	No-Hurtlex	Mixed	Average
Chan	**0.76**	0.736	0.8	0.732	0.5	**0.809**	**0.4**	0	0.428	0.588	**1**	0.671	0.784	0.631
UD	0.754	**0.956**	**0.909**	0.762	**0.6**	0.8	0.333	0	0.571	0.583	0.909	0.658	0.783	**0.663**
Glove-Twitter	0.72	0.8	**0.909**	0.734	0.5	0.790	**0.4**	0	**0.666**	0.636	0.909	**0.694**	**0.813**	0.659
Glove-WK	0.703	0.8	0.833	**0.784**	0.5	0.793	0.333	0	0.615	**0.761**	0.769	0.688	0.800	0.644
W2V	0.680	0.588	0.75	0.622	0.571	0.767	0.333	0	0.545	0.631	0.8	0.654	0.748	0.591
Jigsaw-Toxicity														
	PS	OM	QAS	CDS	IS	RE	PR	ASF	ASM	DDP	DDF	No-Hurtlex	Mixed	Average
Chan	0.15	0.45	**0.461**	0.427	**0.5**	0.310	0.285	0.75	0.652	0.553	0.482	0.484	0.658	0.474
UD	0.303	**0.615**	0.387	**0.441**	0.333	0.274	0.285	0.666	0.653	0.461	0.538	0.449	0.666	0.467
Glove-Twitter	0.285	0.578	0.322	0.433	0.444	0.360	0.444	**0.888**	**0.693**	0.553	**0.571**	**0.493**	**0.687**	**0.519**
Glove-WK	0.166	0.514	0.428	0.362	0.428	**0.407**	0.25	0.75	0.615	0.558	0.363	0.454	0.661	0.458
W2V	**0.333**	0.437	0.230	0.421	0.333	0.350	**0.545**	0.571	0.543	**0.588**	0.518	0.448	0.678	0.461

Table 5: Binary F1-scores of the Bi-LSTM of each word embeddings on the different types of cyberbullying within each dataset and on the average F1 score across all the types. "Average" is the average F1 score for each datasets across all the 13 categories.

	Gender Bias				Racial Bias			
Word embeddings	WEAT	RNSB	RND	ECT	WEAT	RNSB	RND	ECT
Word2vec	4 (0.778)	2 (0.033)	2 (0.087)	4 (0.752)	2 (0.179)	1 (0.095)	1 (0.151)	4 (0.786)
Glove-WK	**5 (0.893)**	4 (0.052)	4 (0.204)	2 (0.829)	**5 (0.439)**	2 (0.118)	4 (0.253)	1 (0.903)
Glove-Twitter	2 (0.407)	3 (0.041)	3 (0.127)	1 (0.935)	4 (0.275)	3 (0.122)	2 (0.179)	2 (0.898)
UD	1 (0.346)	1 (0.031)	1 (0.051)	**5 (0.652)**	1 (0.093)	4 (0.132)	3 (0.196)	**5 (0.726)**
Chan	3 (0.699)	**5 (0.059)**	**5 (1.666)**	3 (0.783)	3 (0.271)	**5 (0.299)**	**5 (2.572)**	3 (0.835)

Table 6: The bias scores of the different word embeddings are measured using different metrics (higher scores indicate stronger bias). We report the ranking of the bias score and the actual bias score between brackets. **Bold** text represents the most biased.

no clear connection between the ability of word embeddings to cluster the Hurtlex categories and their performance on texts that contain the same offensive words in cyberbullying related datasets. Alternatively, due to the very small percentages of these categories in our datasets, it is possible that we could not get a reliable enough indication of the performance of each word embedding model on each category. More analysis and experiments with larger datasets where these categories are more prevalent are needed to fully understand the results.

5 Social bias

In this section, we answer our third research question by measuring the social bias in the different word embeddings. We studied two types of social bias: gender bias and racial bias. We hypothesise that social-media-based word embeddings, especially Urban Dictionary and Chan, are more socially biased than informational-based based word embedding. We used the WEFE framework (Badilla et al., 2020) to measure the gender bias and the racial bias in the different word embeddings using the state-of-the-art bias metrics from the literature: WEAT, RNSB, RND, and ECT. To measure the gender bias, we follow the methodology proposed in the original paper (Caliskan et al., 2017) using the WEFE framework (Badilla et al., 2020). We used two target lists: Target list 1, which contains female-related words (e.g., she, woman, and mother), and Target list 2, which contains male-related words (e.g., he, father, and son), as well as two attribute lists: Attribute list 1, which contains words related to family, arts, appearance, sensitivity, stereotypical female roles, and negative words, and Attribute list 2, which contains words related to career, science, math, intelligence, stereotypical male roles, and positive words. Then, we measured the average gender bias scores across the different attribute lists for each word embedding using the various metrics. Since the different metrics use different scales, we follow the work suggested in (Badilla et al., 2020) to rank the bias scores for each word embedding in ascending order, except for the ECT metric that was ranked in descending order, as ECT scores have an inverse relationship with the level of bias. Similarly, to measure the racial bias we follow the methodology proposed in (Garg et al., 2018) using the WEFE framework. We used two target groups: Target group 1, which contains white people's names, and Target group 2, which contains African, Hispanic, and Asian names, and two attribute lists: Attribute list 1, which contains white people's occupation names; and Attribute list 2, which contains African, Hispanic, and Asian people's occupations. Then, we measured the average racial bias scores across the different attribute lists for each word embedding using the different metrics (WEAT, RND, RNSB, ECT). Finally, we ranked the bias scores.

The results reported in Table 6 show variations between the different bias metrics. The WEAT bias metric does not support our hypothesis with Word2vec and Glove-WK being ranked as the highest two biased word embeddings regarding gender and racial biases. On the other hand, The RNSB, RND, and ECT metrics give us mixed results. As RNSB ranked Chan and Glove-WK as the highest two biased word embeddings regarding gender bias and Chan and Urban Dictionary as the highest two biased word embeddings regarding racial bias. While RND ranked Chan and Glove-WK as the highest two biased word embeddings regarding gender and racial bias. As for ECT, the metric ranked Chan and Word2vec as the highest biased embeddings regarding gender and racial bias. The results suggest that even though according to most of the metrics (RND, RNSB and ECT), the most biased word embeddings for racial and gender bias are Urban Dictionary and Chan, which supports our hypothesis, there is no consistent evidence that social-media-based word embeddings are more biased than informational-based-word embeddings. We speculate that this is the case because social bias takes different forms some include profanity and slurs which are the cases where social-media-based word embeddings are ranked the highest biased. While some times social bias takes non-offensive forms which are the cases when Glove-WK was ranked the second most biased word embeddings.

6 Conclusion

The work in this paper was motivated by the release of the new social-media-based word embeddings. We ran a series of experiments to compare social-media-based word embeddings and informational-based word embeddings regarding two social NLP tasks: cyberbullying detection and social bias analysis. We found that social-media-based word embeddings are better than informational-based embeddings at categorizing offensive words. This suggests that social-media-based word embeddings might be useful for expanding queries to collect future cyberbullying datasets. We also found that social-media-based word embeddings performed better at the task of cyberbullying detection than informational-based word embeddings. Our results also show that although some word embeddings are better at categorizing offensive words in the Hurtlex categories, these same embeddings do not necessarily perform better at detecting the corresponding offensive categories within our datasets. Hence, there is no evidence that certain word embeddings are better at detecting certain types of cyberbullying.

Our results also show that even though the different bias metrics don't agree on the ranking of the word embeddings regarding social bias, most of the bias metrics (RNSB, RND, and ECT) agree that Chan and Urban Dictionary are the highest ranked biased word embeddings regarding gender and racial bias. However, the second highest biased word embeddings is Glove-WK which is not social-media-based which means that social-media-based word embeddings are not necessarily more socially biased than informational-based word embeddings.

Our findings raise questions about some common methods currently used to detect cyberbullying and to measure social bias in word embeddings. As our findings show that state-of-the-art bias metrics did not agree on the rankings of the most biased word embeddings. Additionally, our findings show that profanity is an important feature that should be used in addition to other features to develop more reliable models to detect cyberbullying and to reveal the social bias in the different word embeddings. Future work should investigate the relationship between the bias in the word embedding and the performance of these word embeddings on cyberbullying detection.

References

Sweta Agrawal and Amit Awekar. 2018. Deep learning for detecting cyberbullying across multiple social media platforms. In *Advances in Information Retrieval - 40th European Conference on IR Research, ECIR 2018, Grenoble, France, March 26-29, 2018, Proceedings*, volume 10772 of *Lecture Notes in Computer Science*, pages 141–153. Springer.

Pablo Badilla, Felipe Bravo-Marquez, and Jorge Pérez. 2020. WEFE: the word embeddings fairness evaluation framework. In *Proceedings of the Twenty-Ninth International Joint Conference on Artificial Intelligence, IJCAI 2020*, pages 430–436. ijcai.org.

Valerio Basile, Cristina Bosco, Elisabetta Fersini, Debora Nozza, Viviana Patti, Francisco Manuel Rangel Pardo, Paolo Rosso, and Manuela Sanguinetti. 2019. SemEval-2019 task 5: Multilingual detection of hate speech against immigrants and women in Twitter. In *Proceedings of the 13th International Workshop on Semantic Evaluation*, pages 54–63, Minneapolis, Minnesota, USA. Association for Computational Linguistics.

Tolga Bolukbasi, Kai-Wei Chang, James Zou, Venkatesh Saligrama, and Adam Kalai. 2016. Man is to computer programmer as woman is to homemaker? debiasing word embeddings. In *Proceedings of the 30th International Conference on Neural Information Processing Systems*, NIPS'16, page 4356–4364, Red Hook, NY, USA. Curran Associates Inc.

Aylin Caliskan, Joanna J. Bryson, and Arvind Narayanan. 2017. Semantics derived automatically from language corpora contain human-like biases. *Science*, 356(6334):183–186.

Kaytlin Chaloner and Alfredo Maldonado. 2019. Measuring gender bias in word embeddings across domains and discovering new gender bias word categories. In *Proceedings of the First Workshop on Gender Bias in Natural Language Processing*, pages 25–32, Florence, Italy. Association for Computational Linguistics.

Sunipa Dev and Jeff M. Phillips. 2019. Attenuating bias in word vectors. In *The 22nd International Conference on Artificial Intelligence and Statistics, AISTATS 2019, 16-18 April 2019, Naha, Okinawa, Japan*, volume 89 of *Proceedings of Machine Learning Research*, pages 879–887. PMLR.

Fatma Elsafoury, Stamos Katsigiannis, Zeeshan Pervez, and Naeem Ramzan. 2021. When the timeline meets the pipeline: A survey on automated cyberbullying detection. *IEEE Access*.

Nikhil Garg, Londa Schiebinger, Dan Jurafsky, and James Zou. 2018. Word embeddings quantify 100 years of gender and ethnic stereotypes. *Proceedings of the National Academy of Sciences*, 115(16):E3635–E3644.

Minni Jain, Puneet Goel, Puneet Singla, and Rahul Tehlan. 2021. Comparison of various word embeddings for hate-speech detection. In *Data Analytics and Management*, pages 251–265, Singapore. Springer Singapore.

Jigsaw. 2018. Detecting toxic behaviour in wikipedia talk pages. `https://www.kaggle.com/c/jigsaw-toxic-comment-classification-challenge/data`. Accessed: 2021-04-07.

Kaggle. 2012. Detecting insults in social commentary. `https://www.kaggle.com/c/detecting-insults-in-social-commentary/data`. Accessed: 2020-09-28.

Thomas Manzini, Lim Yao Chong, Alan W Black, and Yulia Tsvetkov. 2019. Black is to criminal as caucasian is to police: Detecting and removing multiclass bias in word embeddings. In *Proceedings of the 2019 Conference of the North American Chapter of the Association for Computational Linguistics: Human Language Technologies, Volume 1 (Long and Short Papers)*, pages 615–621, Minneapolis, Minnesota. Association for Computational Linguistics.

Tomas Mikolov, Kai Chen, Greg Corrado, and Jeffrey Dean. 2021. word2vec embeddings. [Online] Accessed 05/11/2021.

Dong Nguyen, Barbara McGillivray, and Taha Yasseri. 2017. Emo, love, and god: Making sense of urban dictionary, a crowd-sourced online dictionary. *CoRR*, abs/1712.08647.

Antonis Papasavva, Savvas Zannettou, Emiliano De Cristofaro, Gianluca Stringhini, and Jeremy Blackburn. 2020. Raiders of the lost kek: 3.5 years of augmented 4chan posts from the politically incorrect board. *CoRR*, abs/2001.07487.

Jeffrey Pennington, Richard Socher, and Christopher D. Manning. 2021a. Glove twitter embeddings. [Online] Accessed 05/11/2021.

Jeffrey Pennington, Richard Socher, and Christopher D. Manning. 2021b. Glove wikipedia embeddings. [Online] Accessed 05/11/2021.

Mike Schuster and Kuldip K Paliwal. 1997. Bidirectional recurrent neural networks. *IEEE Transactions on Signal Processing*, 45(11):2673–2681.

Chris Sweeney and Maryam Najafian. 2019. A transparent framework for evaluating unintended demographic bias in word embeddings. In *Proceedings of the 57th Annual Meeting of the Association for Computational Linguistics*, pages 1662–1667, Florence, Italy. Association for Computational Linguistics.

Tensorflow.org. 2020. Text tokenization utility class. `https://www.tensorflow.org/api_docs/python/tf/keras/preprocessing/text/Tokenizer`. Accessed: 2020-09-28.

İlker Türker, Eftal Şehirli, and Emrullah Demiral. 2016. Uncovering the differences in linguistic network dynamics of book and social media texts. *SpringerPlus*, 5(1):1–18.

Laurens van der Maaten and Geoffrey Hinton. 2008. Visualizing data using t-sne. *Journal of Machine Learning Research*, 9(86):2579–2605.

Pierre Voué, Tom De Smedt, and Guy De Pauw. 2020. 4chan & 8chan embeddings. *CoRR*, abs/2005.06946.

Congcong Wang, Paul Nulty, and David Lillis. 2020. A comparative study on word embeddings in deep learning for text classification. In *NLPIR 2020: 4th International Conference on Natural Language Processing and Information Retrieval, Seoul, Republic of Korea, December 18-20, 2020*, pages 37–46. ACM.

Yanshan Wang, Sijia Liu, Naveed Afzal, Majid Rastegar-Mojarad, Liwei Wang, Feichen Shen, Paul R. Kingsbury, and Hongfang Liu. 2018. A comparison of word embeddings for the biomedical natural language processing. *J. Biomed. Informatics*, 87:12–20.

Zeerak Waseem and Dirk Hovy. 2016. Hateful symbols or hateful people? predictive features for hate speech detection on Twitter. In *Proceedings of the NAACL Student Research Workshop*, pages 88–93, San Diego, California. Association for Computational Linguistics.

Steven R. Wilson, Walid Magdy, Barbara McGillivray, Kiran Garimella, and Gareth Tyson. 2020. Urban dictionary embeddings for slang NLP applications. In *Proceedings of The 12th Language Resources and Evaluation Conference, LREC 2020, Marseille, France, May 11-16, 2020*, pages 4764–4773. European Language Resources Association.

Haoran Zhang, Amy X. Lu, Mohamed Abdalla, Matthew B. A. McDermott, and Marzyeh Ghassemi. 2020. Hurtful words: quantifying biases in clinical contextual word embeddings. In *ACM CHIL '20: ACM Conference on Health, Inference, and Learning, Toronto, Ontario, Canada, April 2-4, 2020 [delayed]*, pages 110–120. ACM.

Donald W Zimmerman and Bruno D Zumbo. 1993. Relative power of the wilcoxon test, the friedman test, and repeated-measures anova on ranks. *The Journal of Experimental Education*, 62(1):75–86.

Identifying Human Needs through Social Media: A study on Indian cities during COVID-19

Sunny Rai[1], Rohan Joseph[1], Prakruti Singh Thakur[2] and Mohammed Abdul Khaliq[3]

[1]Mahindra University, Hyderabad, India.
[2]Arizona State University, Tempe, USA
[3]University of Stuttgart, Stuttgart, Germany

sunny.rai@mahindrauniversity.edu.in, rohan18545@mechyd.ac.in
psthakur@asu.edu, st181091@stud.uni-stuttgart.de

Abstract

In this paper, we present a minimally-supervised approach to identify human needs expressed in tweets. Taking inspiration from Frustration-Aggression theory, we trained RoBERTa model to classify tweets expressing *frustration* which serves as an indicator of unmet needs. Although the notion of frustration is highly subjective and complex, the findings support the use of pretrained language model in identifying tweets with unmet needs. Our study reveals the major causes behind feeling *frustrated* during the lockdown and the second wave of the COVID-19 pandemic in India. Our proposed approach can be useful in timely identification and prioritization of emerging human needs in the event of a crisis.

1 Introduction

India reported its first case of COVID-19 from Kerala in the month of Jan, 2020 (Andrews et al., 2020). Several control measures including restrictions on international travel, screening of flight passengers, and institutional quarantine were undertaken shortly after to combat the transmission. The Government of India (GoI) imposed a nationwide lockdown[1] on Mar 25, 2020 as a preventive measure to curb the spread of COVID-19. *Lockdown* is an emergency protocol that restricts non-essential movement of people as well as goods. This lockdown was eventually extended till May 31, 2020, making it one of the longest lockdowns imposed during the pandemic. This resulted in a huge gap in demand and supply of goods (Mahajan and Tomar, 2021), increased stress (Rehman et al., 2021) and mass exodus of migrant workers from cities due to lack of earning opportunities in the informal economy (Das and Kumar, 2020).

Amidst the growing panic, Twitter emerged as the go to platform to express one's feelings and needs such as *travel, food, hospital beds, oxygen, cremation* and *funds*[2]. An overwhelming number of tweets seeking support, lack of timely response and inadequate after-care are a few motivating factors behind this study. We particularly study the tweets from metropolitan Indian cities posted during the COVID-19 pandemic. The main contributions are as follows:

- Using topic modeling and minimal supervision, we create a dataset of tweets labelled with needs as described in Maslow's Theory of Motivation (Maslow and Lewis, 1987). This dataset with tagged needs is available for public research[3].
- Taking inspiration from Frustration-Aggression theory (Dollard et al., 1939), we finetuned a state of the art neural language model, RoBERTa (Liu et al., 2019) to detect the unmet *needs*.

The rest of the paper is organized as follows. Section 2 describes the prior work pertinent to the research presented here. We present our approach to gather the needs from Twitter in Section 3. We introduce a RoBERTa based classifier to detect unmet needs in Section 4. We discuss the social impact of the proposed work in Section 5 and list down the limitations in Section 6. We conclude our work in Section 7.

2 Background

Understanding human needs is a widely researched domain by state agencies as well as commercial organizations (Costanza et al., 2007). Prior research has shown that fulfilled needs have a positive impact on a person's feelings of well-being

[1]'Coronavirus in India: 21-day lockdown begins; key highlights of PM Modi's speech', Business Today (Mar 25, 2020). Available at Link

[2]Reuters: https://graphics.reuters.com/HEALTH-CORONAVIRUS/INDIA-TWITTER/oakpekqlrpr/

[3]https://github.com/AxleBlaze3/Covid_19_Tweets_with_Tagged_Needs

Proceedings of the Tenth International Workshop on Natural Language Processing for Social Media (SocialNLP 2022), pages 54 - 63
July 14-15, 2022 ©2022 Association for Computational Linguistics

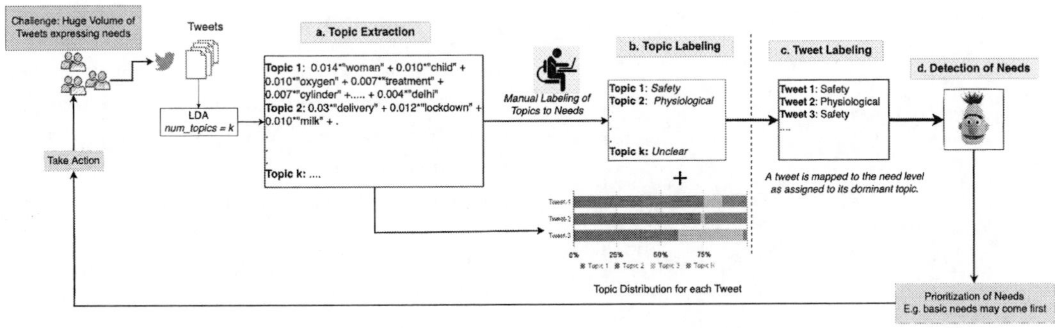

Figure 1: Block diagram for the proposed approach

(Ryff and Keyes, 1995). From stockpiling basic household items during the initial phase of the pandemic to embracing digital technologies such as *zoom*, the market witnessed quite a shift in consumer needs since the outbreak of COVID-19 (Becdach et al., 2020; Mehta et al., 2020). Identifying one's true needs, however, is a challenging task. Yang and Li (2013) took inspiration from Maslow's theory of motivation to predict consumer's needs and purchasing behavior using social media. Ko et al. (2020) used Korean twitter and blogs to discover customer's unmet needs through Hierarchical Concept Search Space algorithm. Their approach aimed to facilitate idea generation for home appliances.

More recently, Yang et al. (2021) advocated the use of Weibo[4] to identify unmet non-COVID-19 healthcare needs. Suh et al. (2021) studied the transition in needs during COVID-19 through the *search queries* on Bing. The product type in search queries were manually marked with the needs as described in Maslow's theory of motivation to automate the task of need identification. Their results affirmed a human tendency to first satisfy basic needs such as *food* and *shelter* before exploring advanced needs such as *creativity* and *love*. Jolly et al. (2020) performed a psychometric analysis of tweets posted in response to official bulletins on COVID-19 by state agencies, revealing the causality between bulletins and the feeling of medical emergency on Twitter.

Prior studies (Saha et al., 2020; Guntuku et al., 2020; Mendoza et al., 2010) have consistently demonstrated the efficacy of social media platforms such as Twitter in capturing the feelings of society at scale. However, this unfurls the challenge of annotating the posts with their expressed needs. In this paper, we propose an approach to automate labeling of tweets with their expressed needs. We also build a model to detect unmet needs from tweets. To the best of our knowledge, this is the first study on the needs expressed through tweets from Indian cities during the pandemic.

3 Identifying Human *needs* from Tweets

We illustrate the different components of the proposed model in Fig. 1. The block diagram represents the steps of the proposed approach that are, (a) *extracting key topics from Twitter discourse*, (b) *manual mapping of the topics to the expressed human needs*, (c) *mapping tweets to needs assigned to their dominant topics* and (d) detection of unmet needs from tweets. The components in green represent the use case of detecting unmet needs and categorization when given a live stream of tweets.

3.1 Tweets Collection

The GoI officially declared the nationwide lockdown on Mar 25, 2020. The second wave of COVID-19 peaked in the mid of May, 2021. Taking into account the baseline considered by Suh et al. (2021) and the number of COVID-19 cases[5] in India, we set the duration of study from Dec 1, 2019 to Jun 30, 2021, comprising a total of nineteen months. The first three months that is from Dec 1, 2019 to Feb 28, 2020 is the baseline period that serves as an indicator of pre-COVID-19 *needs pattern*. We here assume that a tweet does not need to be marked with hashtags related to COVID-19 to have a *need* affected or emerged due to ongoing COVID-19 pandemic.

Using *snscrape*[6], we extract Indian tweets posted between Dec, 2019 and June, 2021. We set the

[4]Weibo.com

[5]WHO, Coronavirus disease 2019 (COVID-19) Situation Report – 39. Feb 28, 2020. LINK

[6]`https://pypi.org/project/snscrape/`

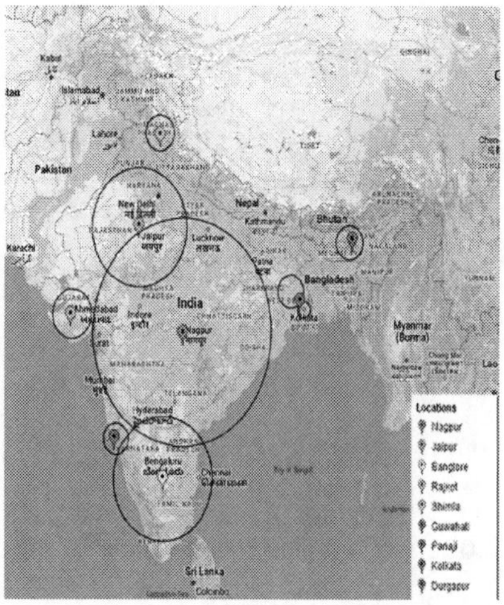

Figure 2: Areas covered during Tweet Collection

parameter "geocode" of the form [*latitude, longitude, radius*] to the (latitude, longitude) of cities namely *Nagpur, Bangalore, Jaipur, Kolkata* and *Patna* with the radii as *500km, 400km, 350km, 50km* and *100km* respectively in an attempt to encompass representative metropolitan cities situated in different parts of India. The covered region is depicted in Fig. 2.

As a pre-processing step, we removed duplicate and non-English tweets. We also filtered out tweets having less than twelve words. The word limit threshold was decided empirically after analysing the content of tweets. These tweets were either related to marketing/greetings such as *good morning*, *happy birthday* or comments on the original tweets without substantial semantic content of its own. We have a total of $1.4M$ unique tweets for further study.

3.2 Mapping Tweets to Human Needs

In this research, we study only *expressed needs* in tweets. Bradshaw (1972) defined expressed need as "*the felt need turned into action*". To identify the different types of *expressed need*, we take inspiration from Maslow's Hierarchy of Needs (MHoN) (Maslow and Lewis, 1987) which categorizes the human needs into five distinct levels namely *physiological*[L_1], *Safety* [L_2], *Love and Belonging* [L_3], *Love and Belonging* [L_3], *Esteem* [L_4] and *Self-Actualization* [L_5]. *Physiological* and *safety* needs are considered basic needs that need to be satisfied first before one begins to explore the advanced needs related to *esteem* and *self-actualization*.

3.2.1 Topic Extraction

Manual annotation of over $1.4M$ tweets with their expressed need is time consuming as well as prohibitively expensive. We therefore employ topic modeling[7] (Blei et al., 2003) to identify the major topics of discourse for monthwise set of tweets which we then manually label to a level as described in Maslow's Theory of Motivation.The number of topic words is set to 20 and the rest of the parameters were set to default values. The number of topics is decided empirically after analysing the coherence score and execution time for a randomly picked sample of three months. We set the $\#topics$ to 30 after analysing different number of topics, $\#topics = \{10, 15, 20, ...45, 50\}$. We thus obtain a set $\mathcal{T}$ having 570 topics (30 topics $*19$ months).

3.2.2 Manual Labeling of Topics

We asked a team of three human annotators to map the extracted topics $t \in \mathcal{T}$ to the levels $\{L_1, L_2, L_3, L_4, L_5\} \in$ MHoN. Each annotator is an undergraduate student, aged 19-21 years and highly proficient in the English language. Two were male and one was female. Given a topic t and few tweets elaborating its context of usage, the task is to map the topic t to either $L_i \in$ MHoN or as '*unclear*'. Annotators were encouraged to choose *unclear* if they find a topic ambiguous. A topic is assigned a *need level* from MHoN only if all annotators choose the same level.

Out of 570 topics, 59 topics were assigned to L_1, 150 topics mapped to L_2, 84 topics to L_3, 66 topics to L_4 and 95 topics to the level L_5. Rest were *unclear*.

The key categories emerged after mapping topics with needs are provided in Table 1. The *physiological* need majorly comprised *food staples and beverages*, *hygiene concerns*, *mobility*. Clearly, the meaning of safety has evolved and included topics such as *housing*, *infection*, *unemployment*, *domestic violence*, *market* and *financial liabilities*. Relationships and concern for loved one's are discussed under *love and belonging*. *Esteem* covers *online learning*, *ideologies*, postponed *examinations*, lack of internet and smart devices. Self-actualization comprises recreational tasks such as DIY, sports, entertainment and skill acquisition.

[7]Gensim LDA: `https://radimrehurek.com/gensim_3.8.3/models/wrappers/ldamallet.html`

Table 1: Mapped topics and Need Level in Maslow's Theory of Motivation

Need	#Tweets	#Topics	Key Topics
Physiological	165114	59	**staples** such as *food, beverages, apparel, household products*, **Hygiene** such as *toilet paper*, **basic daily services** such as *grocery delivery, milk, bread*, **rest**, **medicine**, **transport**
Safety	367774	150	**Housing** such as rental/mortgages, evictions, **COVID-19 Safety** such as *masks*, quarantine or *sanitizers*, **Domestic violence**, justice, **Financial liabilities** such as tax, loans, or bankruptcy, stock market, business **Job posts/application & unemployment**
Love & Belonging	192843	84	Expression of or resources for **mental health** or **emotional issues** such as *anxiety, depression, loneliness, isolation, suicide, nervousness, rejection, fear* or *sadness*; **Social media**, Search for **relationships** with significant others, dating, issues such as *divorce* or *breakup*
Esteem	151873	66	**Education** or learning materials, University/Schools; **Online classroom** learning, Examinations; Educational degrees or programs; Knowledge/Skill, zoom meetings, **Ideologies/religions**
Self-Actualization	258287	95	**Recreational tasks** such as *self-care, home decor, music* etc., parenting, wedding, **Talent/Skill acquisition**, **Life goals**, Charity/Donation, **volunteering**, **Entertainment** such as *Netflix, Prime, TV shows, movie, sports (IPL), News*

3.2.3 Mapping Tweets to MHoN

At this step, we have a list of topics mapped with the need levels as described in MHoN. We also have the probability distribution of topics for each tweet. The dominant topic of a tweet is the topic with the highest probability. A tweet t is thus marked to a need level $L_i \in$ MHoN on the basis of the mapping assigned to its dominant topic. We illustrate this process in Fig. 1 where the topic distribution along with mapped topics are used to infer the expressed need in tweets. If the tweet has multiple topics with same probability, we only assign a need level if all dominant topics are marked to the same need level else it is marked as *unclear*.

3.3 Analysis

After excluding *unclear* tweets, we have over $1.1M$ tweets marked as expressing a need. Below are few examples[8] that were mapped to their relevant level and those that were *unclear*:

"Nobody staying at hotels, So why not convert them into covid centers " –Physiological

"When I see some people attacking doctors, i get scared about the corona situation" –Safety

"Not everyone can work from home. Feeling kinda unsafe or its just fear of getting sucked up in situation and putting life of my family friends in danger." –Love and Belonging

"As a teacher I thank pm for cancelling the Std. 12th board examination." –Esteem

"xxx movie are a big hit, an average human would have to watch his movies multiple times to understand." –Self-Actualization

"Met her while traveling she was selling fruits adding on to the income of her parents, with her impressive salesman skills ." –Unclear

[8]Tweets are rephrased to protect user's privacy however, the message remains the same.

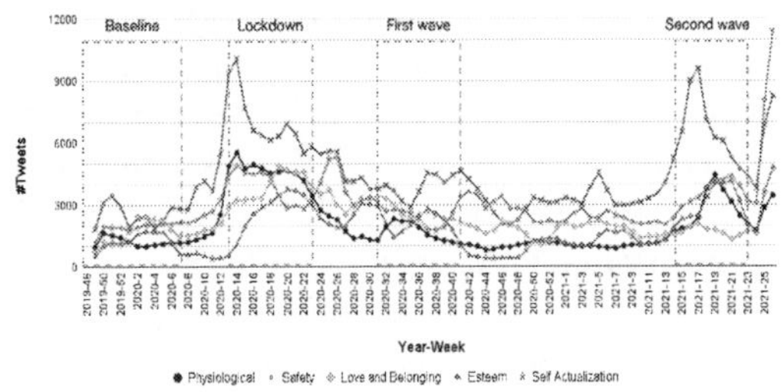

Figure 3: Volume of tweets expressing needs from Dec, 2019 to Jun, 2021.

It may be noted that we have not considered tweets on political topics such as Citizen Amendment Act (Wikipedia contributors, 2021b), National Register of Citizens (Wikipedia contributors, 2021c) and Farm laws (Wikipedia contributors, 2021a) which were part of public discourse during the time of study.

We illustrate the time-wise distribution of tweets tagged with different need levels in Fig. 3. We have considered two weeks moving average to nullify noisy fluctuations in the data. For the baseline, we consider the tweets posted in the first twelve weeks that is, between week-48'2019 to week-7'2020, to understand the pre-COVID pattern of needs. *Lockdown* phase is the period between week-13'2020 to week-23'2020. The *first wave* ranges from week-31'2020 to week-41'2021.

The *second wave* started from week-14'2021 and ended in week-23'2021. The phases namely *baseline, lockdown, first wave* and *second wave* are annotated with boxes in Fig. 3. The first peak is placed in the lockdown period and the second peak occurred during the second wave of the pandemic. The volume of needs were slightly higher than pre-COVID levels during the first wave. There is also a huge surge in self-actualization and safety needs starting *week-24'2021*.

Indian Twitter users voiced the *safety* need most often followed by *physiological* need during the lockdown. Both needs peak at the same time. A total of 45% more tweets expressing basic needs were posted during lockdown compared to the second wave of the pandemic. Over twice the number of physiological tweets was expressed during the lockdown when compared to the second wave. The relatively advanced needs namely *love and Belonging* and *esteem* display a delay during the lockdown and peak almost 3-4 weeks after the basic needs. Soon after the lockdown was lifted, the needs started to return to pre-COVID pattern of needs.

During the second phase of the pandemic, *safety* turned out to be the foremost concern and *physiological* needs peaked only after a delay of two weeks. There is no clear precedence for physiological needs over advanced needs during the second wave. Moreover, *love and belonging* needs stayed at pre-COVID levels during the second wave unlike lockdown phase where concern for loved ones was expressed in large volumes.

Safety has indeed emerged as the dominant concern in the both phases of the pandemic. Lockdown was a special scenario where essential commodities were in shortage due to lack of production as well as black marketing [9]. It is thus not conclusive from our data if physiological needs always take precedence over the advanced needs in the event of a crisis in today's world.

The most advanced need, *self-actualization* surged and ebbed through out the months of our study without any clear correlation with the different phases of pandemic. The huge surge in self-actualization and safety needs starting *week-24'2021* is due to large volume of tweets discussing Indian Premier League 2021 (Wikipedia contributors, 2022) and mass gatherings.

[9]The Hindu "Coronavirus lockdown: Invoke Essential Commodities Act to curb black marketing, Home Secretary tells States" (Apr 8, 2020). Available at Link

4 Detecting unmet Needs

Unmet needs are widely characterized by *frustration* (Dollard et al., 1939; Killgore et al., 2021). Through Frustration-Aggression theory, Dollard et al. (1939) defined *frustration* as an impediment or blockage in achieving one's needs or goals. An impediment to a goal is considered frustration if and only if the person is actively striving to reach this goal. We thus hypothesize that an unmet need can be detected by identifying whether a tweet with expressed need has *frustration* or not.

4.1 Approach

Our task is to classify whether a given tweet tagged with need is expressing *frustration* or not. We fine tuned the RoBERTa pretrained model (Wolf et al., 2020) with a learning rate of $2e^{-5}$ and dropout of 0.3 for this classification task. For training, we collected tweets containing the hashtag *#frustrated.* For negative class that is, *Not frustrated*, we extracted tweets with hashtags that symbolise satisfaction (ex: *#satisfied*, *#FeelingContent*). This dataset has a total of 13970 tweets with equal number of instances for positive and negative class. We provide a representative tweet from each class below:

> " *HOW fast does one have to be to book a slot on COWIN? I saw slots available at a hospital; I selected the time slot; entered the CAPTCHA in not more than 15 seconds... and still it didn't book the slot. And then when I refreshed, all the slots were gone*" - `Frustrated`
>
> "😀😀😀🙏*I did it! ... I officially completed my undergraduate program and received my bachelors degree. may the glory be to God for blessing me with the gifts to achieve this great milestone*" - `Not Frustrated`

As a preprocessing step, we remove hashtags and mentions from the tweet text. We consider 80% of tweets for training and the rest 20% is equally divided for validation and test set. We achieved an accuracy of 93.4% on the validation set. We obtained an accuracy of 92.2% with a precision of 91% and recall of 93% on the test set.

4.2 Performance Evaluation

Out of $1.1M$ tweets, our model predicted a total of 792533 tweets as *frustrated.* 77.36% of physiological needs and 77.5% of safety needs expressed frustration. Under advanced needs, 54.13% of love and

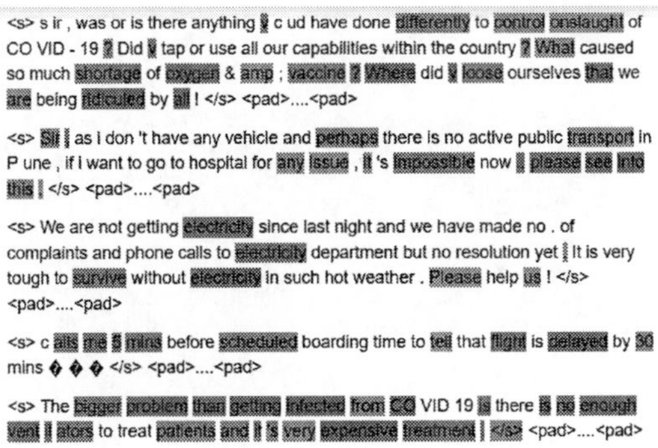

Figure 4: Tweets predicted as *Frustrated*

belonging, 70.43% of esteem needs and 62.91% of self-actualization needs were marked frustrated.

To evaluate the quality of predictions, we randomly sampled 100 tweets which were annotated as *frustrated* or *not frustrated* by three undergrad students proficient in English. The majority vote was considered as the final label. A total of 45 samples were labelled as frustrated out of 100. The inter-annotator agreement (fleiss kappa) obtained for this task was 0.638 indicating its subjective nature. The trained model achieved an accuracy of 76% with a weighted precision of 78% and weighted recall of 76% on this set of annotated tweets. Below are two example tweets which were classified as *frustrated*:

"Please complete the pending projects in Telangana State. Sir please do the needful. There is no direct train from Karimnagar to Hyderabad"

"Need of hour Free Education Free/Affordable health care No freebies , let people work".

We observe that the above tweets clearly express *frustration* as described in Dollard et al. (1939). Another point worth noting is the subjectivity when labelling frustration. Consider the below tweets predicted as *frustrated* but annotated as *not frustrated* by human annotators.

"She lost her life in line of duty. She had been performing her duty in adverse circumstances amid lockdown.She should be declared "Corona Warrior"and all benefits and compensation should be given to her family by the govt."

"Finally, I am buying an Iphone , twelfth edition but next year. As i also thought about Iphone last year."

Whether the above tweets express frustration or not, is quite debatable. Therefore, the performance metrics need to be interpreted accordingly.

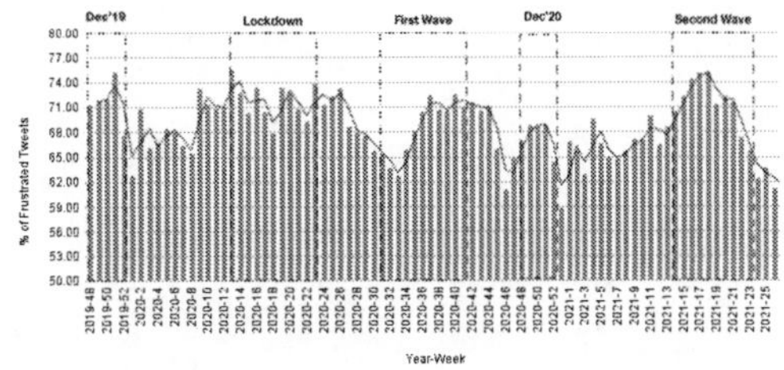

Figure 5: Percentage of Frustrated Tweets

4.2.1 Decoding *frustration* through RoBERTa

On a random sample of 30 tweets predicted as *frustrated*, we used integrated gradients method (Sundararajan et al., 2017) to identify the type of input features that attribute to the prediction to the class *frustrated.*

We provide few example tweets from this set in Fig. 4. Here, the shade of red signifies the importance of input features in prediction. The greater the significance, the deeper the hue of red. For instance, the words highlighted with deeper red such as *shortage*, *oxygen*, *where*, *loose*, *ridicule*, and *all* led to the classification into frustrated class for the first tweet in Fig. 4. Likewise for other tweets, the words namely *have*, *transport*, *electricity*, *delay*, *infected*, *ventilators*, *expensive*, *treatment* are input features that derived the prediction to the class *frustrated.* Since these terms intrinsically reflect constraints or impediments in leading a purposeful life, we may conclude that the model correctly learned to detect tweets expressing frustration.

4.3 Discussion

We illustrate the week wise percentage of tweets predicted as *frustrated* in Fig. 5. At first glance, Twitter appears to be a land of frustration with dissatisfaction rate of around 62% even before COVID-19. The jump in frustration rate in the fourth week of December'19 is due to the mulling over the passing year and eventually settled down in the next two months of Jan, 2020 and Feb, 2020.

The percentage of frustrated tweets hovered between $71-74\%$ during the *lockdown*, the *first wave* and the *second wave* of COVID-19. Clearly, there is an increment of over 4% in frustration rate when compared to non-stressful phases of the pandemic.

We illustrate the week wise transition for the volume of frustrated tweets expressing basic and advanced needs in Fig. 6. There is a huge jump

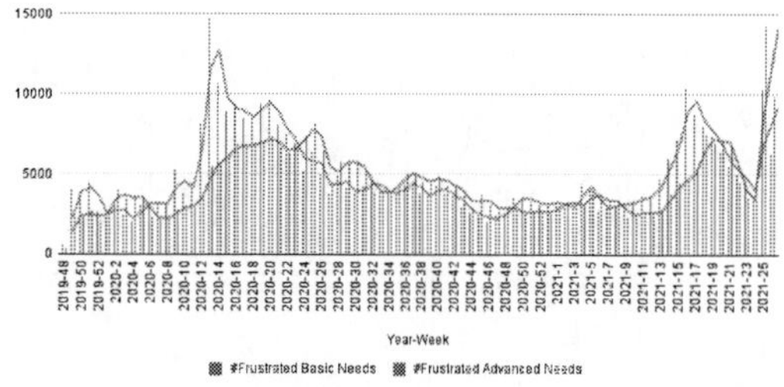

Figure 6: #Frustrated Tweets for *Basic & Advanced* Needs

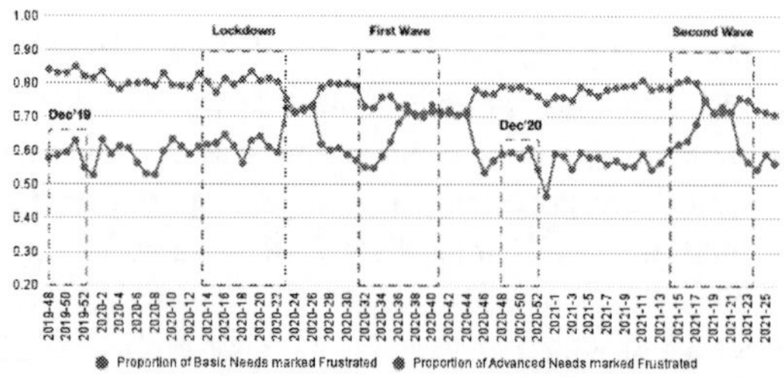

Figure 7: Proportion of Basic and Advanced Needs marked Frustrated

in the volume of both categories of tweets. More tweets expressing frustration due to basic needs were posted during the lockdown in comparison to the second wave. The volume of basic tweets during the first wave remained slightly above the pre-COVID level.

The proportion of frustrated tweets across *basic* and *advanced* level of needs is illustrated in Fig. 7. We observe that almost 80% of tweets expressing basic needs are unmet irrespective of the time of the year. Despite the fact that a large number of basic needs were posted throughout the lockdown, the dissatisfaction rate remained constant. It is thus safe to assume that users discuss basic needs only when these needs are unfulfilled. The general rate of frustration for advanced needs is 60%. We also note that as soon as the frustration due to basic needs reduces, the frustration due to advanced needs increased by over 10%. There are three such peaks in Fig. 7. This does support the belief that once the basic needs are secured, one quickly moves to the advanced needs. On analysis, education with key terms such as *board exams, national level entrance exams, graduation degree* was found to be the dominant concern across each peak. Another common concern was consumer-centric services with worries revolving around delayed *refunds*, cancelled travel plans, delayed delivery of

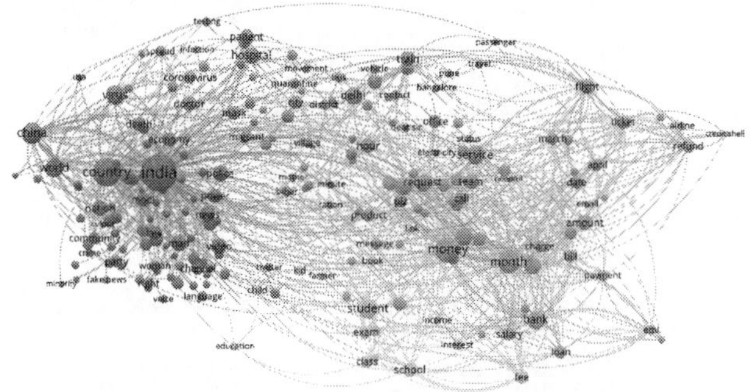

Figure 8: Themes for *frustrated* tweets: Lockdown

online orders etc.

Moreover, time specific events such as *call against products made in China*, Bollywood scandals, football, entertainment were found during the second peak (week-36'2020 - week-44'2020). In contrast, the third peak (week-18'2021 - week-22'2021 discussed the lack of availability of vaccines and further called for inclusivity and transparency in distribution.

4.3.1 Key Themes behind *frustration*

To discover the themes behind the increased volume of frustrated tweets during lockdown and the second wave of COVID-19, we used a computer program called VOSviewer (van Eck and Waltman, 2011) to create a term co-occurrence map for the tweets labelled as *frustrated*. Fig. 8 and Fig. 9 illustrate the oft-discussed terms in frustrated tweets posted during the lockdown and the second wave respectively.

Lockdown: Travel concerns due to the imposed nationwide lockdown are evident from the terms in cluster **blue** in Fig. 8. Major Indian cities namely *bengaluru, bihar, pune* coupled with transportation choices such as *bus, train, vehicle* can be seen. We also note terms such as *quarantine, doctor, patient, office* in the same cluster indicating the traveling problems faced during daily life activities. The nodes in **green** reveal the challenges faced by logistics and travel industry. Terms such as *refund, ticket, airline, flight, credit* reflect the chief complaints by customers along with *bill* and other *payments*.

The nodes in cluster **red** highlight the discussion on digital media and news channels. Growing concern due to increasing toll of infections in the *USA* and a sense of anger towards *China* were expressed through tweets. *Fake news, channel, minority* and *economy* were also a few topics of online discussion. The nodes in cluster **yellow** depict the

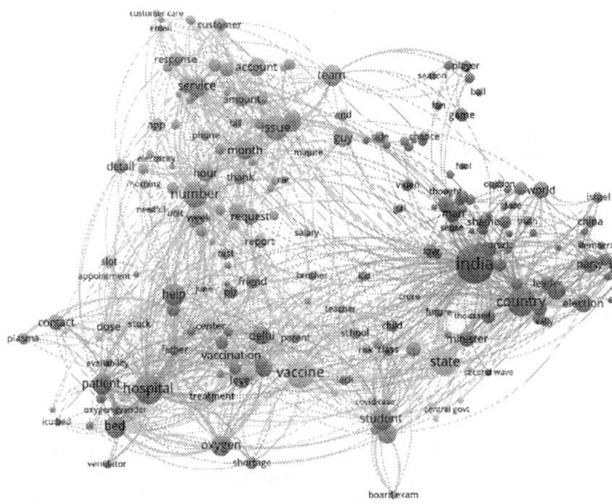

Figure 9: Themes for *frustrated* tweets: Second wave

concerns revolving around closed educational institutions, payment of *fees*, *online classes* and *exams*.

Second Wave: The usual customer care complaints are depicted in cluster **green**. The nodes in cluster **red** particularly reveal the frustration against political parties and elections. There are also terms such as *player, season, ball, game* due to upcoming IPL cricket matches. The anxiety due to shortage of *ventilator, patient, hospital, icu bed* and *oxygen cylinder* is captured through nodes in cluster **blue**. Words such as *refer, friend, help* reveal anxious attempts to locate healthcare through contacts on Twitter. Availability of *vaccine* and booking of *slots* were also a cause of frustration amongst Indians. Education remained a concern during the second wave as evident from nodes marked in **purple**.

5 Social Impact

Tsao et al. (2021) highlighted the paucity of action driven research on the COVID-19 data. Early detection of human needs will enable public agencies and independent organizations to provide prompt support including *food supplies*, *medical care*, *transport* and timely awareness about the crisis amongst masses. Our approach can facilitate timely identification and prioritization of emerging human needs in the event of a crisis. When coupled with geo-location tag, the proposed approach can be customized to retrieve closest support available. *Unmet needs scoping* can help in designing public policies to cater to emerging needs of a society. During the COVID-19 pandemic in India, people expressed distinct needs at different stages of each wave. Public needs on social media can thus serve as an immediate feedback mechanism for public agencies to improvise their relief efforts and policies. Our model to detect unmet needs leverages a pre-trained neural language model that generalises well and is capable of transfer learning from previously labelled data at the start of a crisis. It is thus easy to extend our approach for other languages using publicly available pre-trained multilingual language models.

6 Limitations

Due to our focus on understanding the pattern of needs emerged in India during the COVID-19 pandemic, we performed rigorous filtering to retain only those tweets geo-tagged with locations within India. This significantly reduced the quantity of tweets gathered for our study. Human needs are innately complex and ever evolving concept. As we transition from basic to advanced needs, the needs become more obscure and implicit. To optimize the time and effort for human annotation, we assumed that the dominant topic of a tweet would reflect its need type as discussed in Section 3. This had an impact on the quality of tweet-need mapping and resulted in incorrect labeling in some cases.

7 Conclusion

In this paper, we examined the human needs expressed in Indian cities during the COVID-19 pandemic. We described a minimally supervised approach to annotate tweets with their need level as in Maslow's Hierarchy of Needs. This greatly reduced the time and human effort without much impact on the quality of annotation. We observed a recurring pattern in the needs, indicating predictability in the emerging needs in the event of a crisis. The results support the use of pretrained language model for the task of unmet needs detection. In future, we will extend the proposed model to detect needs in regional languages. We will further work upon incorporating theories better suited to capture advanced psychological needs.

References

MA Andrews, Binu Areekal, KR Rajesh, Jijith Krishnan, R Suryakala, Biju Krishnan, CP Muraly, and PV Santhosh. 2020. First confirmed case of COVID-19 infection in India: A case report. *The Indian Journal of Medical Research* 151, 5 (2020), 490.

Camilo Becdach, Brandon Brown, Ford Halbardier, Brian Henstorf, and Ryan Murphy. 2020. Rapidly forecasting demand and adapting commercial plans in a pandemic. *URL https://www. mckinsey. com/industries/consumer-packaged-goods/our-insights/rapidly-forecasting-demand-and-adapting-commercial-plans-in-a-pandemic* (2020).

David M Blei, Andrew Y Ng, and Michael I Jordan. 2003. Latent dirichlet allocation. *the Journal of machine Learning research* 3 (2003), 993–1022.

Jonathan Bradshaw. 1972. The concept of social need. *New society* 30 (1972).

Robert Costanza, Brendan Fisher, Saleem Ali, Caroline Beer, Lynne Bond, Roelof Boumans, Nicholas L Danigelis, Jennifer Dickinson, Carolyn Elliott, Joshua Farley, et al. 2007. Quality of life: An approach integrating opportunities, human needs, and subjective well-being. *Ecological economics* 61, 2-3 (2007), 267–276.

Ritanjan Das and Nilotpal Kumar. 2020. Chronic crisis: migrant workers and India's COVID-19 lockdown. *South Asia@ LSE* (2020).

John Dollard, Neal E Miller, Leonard W Doob, Orval Hobart Mowrer, and Robert R Sears. 1939. Frustration and aggression. (1939).

Sharath Chandra Guntuku, Garrick Sherman, Daniel C Stokes, Anish K Agarwal, Emily Seltzer, Raina M Merchant, and Lyle H Ungar. 2020. Tracking mental health and symptom mentions on Twitter during COVID-19. *Journal of general internal medicine* 35, 9 (2020), 2798–2800.

Baani Leen Kaur Jolly, Palash Aggrawal, Amogh Gulati, Amarjit Singh Sethi, Ponnurangam Kumaraguru, and Tavpritesh Sethi. 2020. Psychometric Analysis and Coupling of Emotions Between State Bulletins and Twitter in India during COVID-19 Infodemic. *arXiv preprint arXiv:2005.05513* (2020).

William DS Killgore, Sara A Cloonan, Emily C Taylor, Ian Anlap, and Natalie S Dailey. 2021. Increasing aggression during the COVID-19 lockdowns. *Journal of affective disorders reports* 5 (2021), 100163.

Taehoon Ko, Ilsun Rhiu, Myung Hwan Yun, and Sungzoon Cho. 2020. A Novel Framework for Identifying Customers' Unmet Needs on Online Social Media Using Context Tree. *Applied Sciences* 10, 23 (2020), 8473.

Yinhan Liu, Myle Ott, Naman Goyal, Jingfei Du, Mandar Joshi, Danqi Chen, Omer Levy, Mike Lewis, Luke Zettlemoyer, and Veselin Stoyanov. 2019. Roberta: A robustly optimized bert pretraining approach. *arXiv preprint arXiv:1907.11692* (2019).

Kanika Mahajan and Shekhar Tomar. 2021. COVID-19 and Supply Chain Disruption: Evidence from Food Markets in India. *American journal of agricultural economics* 103, 1 (2021), 35–52.

Abraham Maslow and KJ Lewis. 1987. Maslow's hierarchy of needs. *Salenger Incorporated* 14 (1987), 987.

Seema Mehta, Tanjul Saxena, and Neetu Purohit. 2020. The New Consumer Behaviour Paradigm amid COVID-19: Permanent or Transient? *Journal of Health Management* 22, 2 (2020), 291–301.

Marcelo Mendoza, Barbara Poblete, and Carlos Castillo. 2010. Twitter under crisis: Can we trust what we RT?. In *Proceedings of the first workshop on social media analytics*. 71–79.

Usama Rehman, Mohammad G Shahnawaz, Neda H Khan, Korsi D Kharshiing, Masrat Khursheed, Kaveri Gupta, Drishti Kashyap, and Ritika Uniyal. 2021. Depression, anxiety and stress among Indians in times of Covid-19 lockdown. *Community mental health journal* 57, 1 (2021), 42–48.

Carol D Ryff and Corey Lee M Keyes. 1995. The structure of psychological well-being revisited. *Journal of personality and social psychology* 69, 4 (1995), 719.

Koustuv Saha, John Torous, Eric D Caine, Munmun De Choudhury, et al. 2020. Psychosocial effects of the COVID-19 pandemic: large-scale quasi-experimental study on social media. *Journal of medical internet research* 22, 11 (2020), e22600.

Jina Suh, Eric Horvitz, Ryen W White, and Tim Althoff. 2021. Population-scale study of human needs during the covid-19 pandemic: Analysis and implications. In *Proceedings of the 14th ACM International Conference on Web Search and Data Mining*. 4–12.

Mukund Sundararajan, Ankur Taly, and Qiqi Yan. 2017. Axiomatic attribution for deep networks. In *International Conference on Machine Learning*. PMLR, 3319–3328.

Shu-Feng Tsao, Helen Chen, Therese Tisseverasinghe, Yang Yang, Lianghua Li, and Zahid A Butt. 2021. What social media told us in the time of COVID-19: a scoping review. *The Lancet Digital Health* 3, 3 (2021), e175–e194.

Nees Jan van Eck and Ludo Waltman. 2011. Text mining and visualization using VOSviewer. arXiv:1109.2058 [cs.DL]

Wikipedia contributors. 2021a. 2020 Indian agriculture acts — Wikipedia, The Free Encyclopedia. `https://en.wikipedia.org/w/index.php?title=2020_Indian_agriculture_acts&oldid=1025817251`. [Online; accessed 9-July-2021].

Wikipedia contributors. 2021b. Citizenship (Amendment) Act, 2019 — Wikipedia, The Free Encyclopedia. `https://en.wikipedia.org/w/index.php?title=Citizenship_(Amendment)_Act,_2019&oldid=1032618250` [Online; accessed 9-July-2021].

Wikipedia contributors. 2021c. National Register of Citizens — Wikipedia, The Free Encyclopedia. https://en.wikipedia.org/w/index.php?title=National_Register_of_Citizens&oldid=1028089793. [Online; accessed 9-July-2021].

Wikipedia contributors. 2022. 2021 Indian Premier League — Wikipedia, The Free Encyclopedia. https://en.wikipedia.org/w/index.php?title=2021_Indian_Premier_League&oldid=1079776521. [Online; accessed 1-April-2022].

Thomas Wolf, Lysandre Debut, Victor Sanh, Julien Chaumond, Clement Delangue, Anthony Moi, Pierric Cistac, Tim Rault, Rémi Louf, Morgan Funtowicz, Joe Davison, Sam Shleifer, Patrick von Platen, Clara Ma, Yacine Jernite, Julien Plu, Canwen Xu, Teven Le Scao, Sylvain Gugger, Mariama Drame, Quentin Lhoest, and Alexander M. Rush. 2020. HuggingFace's Transformers: State-of-the-art Natural Language Processing. arXiv:1910.03771 [cs.CL]

Huahai Yang and Yunyao Li. 2013. Identifying user needs from social media. *IBM Research Division, San Jose* (2013), 11.

Wei-Fa Yang, Danping Zheng, Reynold CK Cheng, Jingya Jane Pu, and Yu-Xiong Su. 2021. Identifying unmet non-COVID-19 health needs during the COVID-19 outbreak based on social media data: a proof-of-concept study in Wuhan city. *Annals of Translational Medicine* 9, 18 (2021).

Towards Toxic Positivity Detection

Ishan Sanjeev Upadhyay and **KV Aditya Srivatsa** and **Radhika Mamidi**
International Institute of Information Technology, Hyderabad
{ishan.sanjeev, k.v.aditya}@research.iiit.ac.in
radhika.mamidi@iiit.ac.in

Abstract

Over the past few years, there has been a growing concern around toxic positivity on social media which is a phenomenon where positivity is used to minimize one's emotional experience. In this paper, we create a dataset for toxic positivity classification from Twitter and an inspirational quote website. We then perform benchmarking experiments using various text classification models and show the suitability of these models for the task. We achieved a macro F1 score of 0.71 and a weighted F1 score of 0.85 by using an ensemble model. To the best of our knowledge, our dataset is the first such dataset created.

1 Introduction

Toxic positivity can be defined as the overgeneralization of a positive state of mind that encourages using positivity to suppress and displace any acknowledgement of stress and negativity (Sokal et al., 2020; Bosveld, 2021). The popularity of the term "toxic positivity" peaked during the COVID 19 pandemic (refer to figure 1) where it was used to identify advice that focused on just looking at the positive at a time when people were hurting due to loss of life, loss of jobs and other traumatic events.

Toxic positivity results in one minimizing one's own negative feelings and suppressing negativity instead of acknowledging, processing and working through it. Some examples of toxic positivity include telling someone to focus on the positive aspects of a loss, telling someone that positive thinking will solve all their problems, suggesting that things could be worse and shaming someone for expressing negative emotions. This suppression of emotions is not only unhelpful but also leads to poorer recovery from the negative effects of the emotion. Accepting and working through one's emotions is the better route to take while dealing with negative emotions (Campbell-Sills et al., 2006).

Macro level events like COVID 19 and climate change disasters have distressed many people in the past few years (Marazziti et al., 2021). Social media is used by people having mental health issues or going through a tough time to find community, support, advice and encouraging messages (Gowen et al., 2012). However, it becomes important to be able to differentiate between messages that may help uplift an individual and those that may look positive but promote suppression of emotions and cause great harm in the long term recovery from negative emotions. The harms of toxic positivity are not only limited to its deleterious mental health outcomes but it can also be used to uphold oppression by making people ignore the oppression that is going on and encouraging them to "just be positive".

In this paper, we aim to create a dataset for toxic positivity and perform text classification using various transformer based models to establish the baseline results for this task.

2 Related Work

There have been studies that show the ineffectiveness and deleterious effects of emotion suppression. Gross and John (2003) showed that people who suppressed their emotions had a greater experience of negative emotions while also expressing lesser positive emotion. They also showed that using suppression is related negatively to well being. A study done by Campbell-Sills et al. (2006) involved dividing 60 participants diagnosed with anxiety and mood disorders into two groups. One group was given a rationale for suppressing their emotions while the other was given a rationale for accepting emotions. It was found that suppression was ineffective in reducing distress while watching an emotion-provoking film. It was also seen that the suppression group showed a poorer recovery from the changes in negative affect after watching the film compared to the acceptance group. A

Proceedings of the Tenth International Workshop on Natural Language Processing for Social Media (SocialNLP 2022), pages 64 - 71
July 14-15, 2022

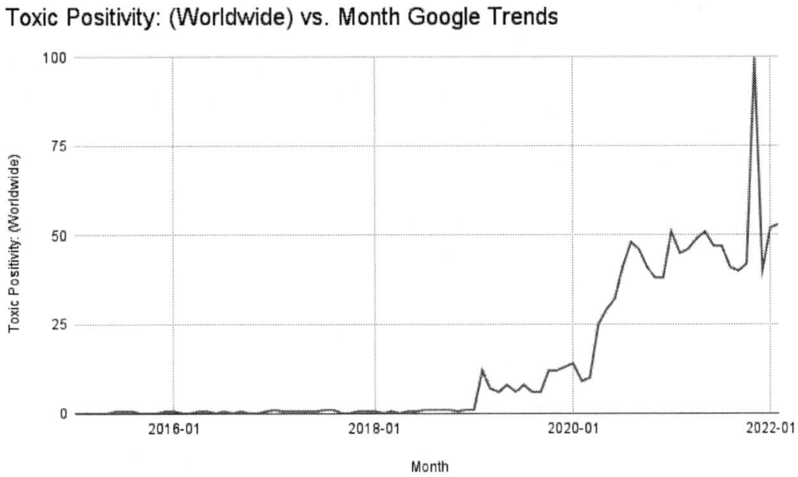

Figure 1: Worldwide Google Trends showing search interest of the term "Toxic Positivity".

similar observation is seen in the case of physical pain as well. Cioffi and Holloway (1993) divided participants into three groups during a cold-pressor pain induction (CPT) where participants would dip their hands in cold water for as long as tolerable. The first group was told to pay attention to the pain, the second was told to focus on their room at home as a distraction, and the third was told to suppress the sensations they felt. It was seen that the group that focused on the pain had a faster recovery from the pain and the suppression group had the slowest recovery from pain. Suppressing pain has shown to have negative outcomes, while accepting it is observed to be as a better strategy. Ford et al. (2018) through longitudinal and lab studies showed that habitually accepting mental experiences broadly predicted psychological health and that it reduced negative emotional response and experience. Hence toxic positivity, with its overemphasis on thinking positively and having a positive state of mind, encourages emotion suppression rather than emotional acceptance which has negative consequences for the person who engages in it.

Lecompte-Van Poucke (2022) conducted a critical discourse analysis of toxic positivity as a discursive construct on Facebook. Two corpora of posts from organizations that promoted endometriosis awareness (an invisible chronic condition) were analyzed using systematic functional linguistics, pragma-dialectics and critical theory. The study showed that users on social media platforms often engage in toxic positivity or forced positive discourse which is inspired by the neoliberal "positive thinking" ideology, leading to a less inclusive online community.

In the field of NLP, there have been many papers focusing on hate speech detection using support vector machine (SVM), long short term memory networks (LSTM),convolutional neural network (CNN), transformers and other machine learning models (Wang et al., 2019b; Zhang et al., 2018; Ousidhoum et al., 2019; Basile et al., 2019). These works use Twitter posts (tweets) to create datasets. YouTube and Reddit comments have also been used in some works (Mollas et al., 2022; Mandl et al., 2020). There have been recent efforts in hope speech detection as well (Palakodety et al., 2020). The HopeEDI dataset (Chakravarthi, 2020) is a hope speech dataset that contains Youtube comments that have been marked for hope and not-hope speech. There has been a shared task on this dataset where participants have used various machine learning models for hope speech detection like multilingual transformer-based models, recurrent neural networks (RNN) and CNN-LSTMs (Chakravarthi and Muralidaran, 2021).

However, to the best of our knowledge, there has been no prior work on creating datasets and classification models for toxic positivity.

3 Dataset Creation

3.1 Data Extraction and Pre-processing

We sourced our data from two sources. Twitter and inspirational quote website BrainyQuote[1] which is one of the largest quotation websites.

The reason for sourcing data from BrainyQuotes was that we observed that a lot of motivational quotes being shared on Twitter were ones that were said by famous personalities. Hence, including popular quotes from a quotation website is helpful. We made a web scraper using Beautiful Soup 4[2] library in python to extract a subset of quotations from the website.

For the Twitter data, we extracted tweets using Twitter API [3] we queried using hashtags like #MondayMotivation to #SundayMotivation and hashtags like #InspirationalQuotes, #Motivation, #SelfLove and #AdviceForSuccess. We also took quotes from widely followed inspirational or motivational twitter accounts.

After collecting the data, pre-processing was performed. Bylines of quotes were removed because it was not useful information for annotation and to also to ensure that there was no annotator bias. For tweets, hashtags and "@" tags were removed. The Twitter data and BrainyQuotes data was also manually filtered to remove sentences that were not inspirational, motivational or advisory in nature. Examples of the kind of data removed are given in Table 4. A total of 4,250 quotes and tweets were collected for annotation after the data elimination and pre-processing steps.[4].

3.2 Dataset Annotation

Two annotators annotated the data for toxic positivity. The annotators were linguistics students. An annotation workshop was conducted for the annotators where they were sensitized to the topic of toxic positivity through academic works as described in the related works section and examples of toxic positivity. The annotators were then asked to annotate 50 sentences separately and then their annotator agreement was measured and was found to have a Kappa score of 0.72.We used Cohen's Kappa coefficient to calculate Inter Annotator Agreement (Fleiss and Cohen, 1973) . The annotators then discussed their disagreements and came to a better understanding of the annotation guidelines. They annotated another 50 sentences and got a better Kappa score of 0.76. They again had a discussion about their disagreements. After this exercise, they were told to annotate the dataset separately without communicating with each other. The 100 sentences used for training the annotators were discarded and are not a part of this dataset of 4,250 sentences. It was observed that sentences that had the following general characteristics were marked as toxic positive:

- Encouraging hiding or suppressing negative emotions.
  - Example: "A negative mind will never give you a positive life."
- Encouraging focusing on positivity rather than processing negative emotions.
  - Example: "Every time I hear something negative, I will replace it with a positive thought."
- Minimizing someone's negative feelings.
  - Example: "You cannot be lonely if you like the person you're alone with."

A few categories of sentences or quotes we emerged when were studying the dataset. We decided to annotate for them as well. The categories of the sentences were as follows.

- **Worldview**: sentences that are philosophical, abstract and provide an insight into the worldview of the writer. Example: "Things may come to those who wait, but only the things left by those who hustle"
- **Personal Experience**: sentences that provide insights based on the writer's personal experience. Example: "I always did something I was a little not ready to do. I think that's how you grow. When there's that moment of 'Wow, I'm not really sure I can do this,' and you push through those moments, that's when you have a breakthrough."
- **Advice**: sentences that are more instructional in nature and provide straightforward recommendations and advice. Example: "Do one thing every day that scares you."

[1] http://www.brainyquote.com
[2] BeautifulSoup Documentation
[3] Twitter API Documentation
[4] Dataset Link

Class	Number of sentences
Toxic Positive	512
Non-Toxic Positive	3738

Table 1: Distribution of toxic positive and non-toxic positive sentences.

Type of sentence	Number of sentences
Worldview	3128
Advice	709
Personal Experience	253
Affirmation	160

Table 2: Distribution of the various types of sentences occurring in the dataset.

- **Affirmation**: First-person sentences that are used as affirmations. Example: "I choose to make the rest of my life, the best of my life."

The same annotators annotated the categories of sentences as well. The same process of annotating 100 sentences, 50 sentences at a time and discussing disagreements was followed to train the annotators.

3.3 Dataset Statistics

Out of the 4,250 sentences, 512 were annotated as toxic positive, which constitutes 12% of the dataset.The rest of the 3738 sentences were non-toxic positive. Examples of toxic and non-toxic positive sentences are presented in Table 3.

Worldview was the most common category of sentence occurring 73.6% of the time with advice occurring 16.7% of the time and the rest occurring less than 10% of the time in the dataset. Exact figures are presented in Table 2.

It was also seen that 44% of the sentences that belonged to the affirmation category were toxic positive. 21% of the sentences belonging to the advice category were toxic positive, while 14% and 8% of sentences belonging to the personal experience and the worldview category respectively were toxic positive. We noticed that in our dataset, most affirmation sentences were focused on emotion suppression, and hence they were marked as toxic positive. The non-toxic positive affirmations focused on gratitude, having a growth mindset and self-acceptance, although they were fewer in number.

We got a Kappa score of 0.82 for the toxic positivity (toxic or non-toxic) annotation and a Kappa score of 0.74 for category annotations (worldview, advice, personal experience or affirmation).

4 Methodology

We used the following transfomer-based models for text classification:

- **BERT**: BERT (Devlin et al., 2019) is a transformer encoder with several encoder layers, each with several self-attention heads. It is trained using two tasks, Masked Language Modelling (MLM), and Next Sentence Prediction (NSP). MLM has been shown to help incorporate both the left and the right contexts into the bidirectional embeddings generated. We have fine-tuned the "bert-base-uncased" model in our implementation.
- **RoBERTa**: RoBERTa (Liu et al., 2019) is a transformer-based encoder built by modifying the original BERT architecture. It utilizes more data with longer average sequence lengths and larger batches. It is solely trained on MLM and makes use of dynamic masking (i.e. the set of masked tokens is subject to change while training). It performs better on the GLUE benchmark (Wang et al., 2019a) in comparison to BERT and XLNet. For the classifier, we have fine-tuned the "roberta-base" model.
- **ALBERT**: ALBERT (Lan et al., 2020) is yet another transformer encoder based on BERT but aimed at being lighter than its predecessor. The core parameter reduction methods include factorizing the vocabulary embedding matrix into smaller sub-matrices and utilizing repeating layers distributed across groups for increased parameter sharing. These techniques help reduce the parameter count by almost 80% with minimal changes to the overall performance. We have fine-tuned the "albert-base-v2" model in our implementation.

We also experimented with an ensemble based classifier for which we additionaly used the following:

- **XGBoost Random Forest Classifier**: Random Forest Classifiers (Ho, 1995) are widely used for ensemble classification. They consist

Sentence	Class
When people say there is a 'reason' for the depression, they insult the person who suffers, making it seem that those in agony are somehow at fault for not 'cheering up.' The fact is that those who suffer - and those who love them - are no more at fault for depression than a cancer patient is for a tumor.	Non-Toxic Positive
Just like it's not healthy to think overly negative thoughts, exaggeratedly positive thoughts can be equally detrimental. If you overestimate how much of a positive impact a particular change will have on your life, you may end up feeling disappointed when reality doesn't live up to your fantasy.	Non-Toxic Positive
Do what you feel in your heart to be right	Non-Toxic Positive
The secret of getting ahead is getting started.	Non-Toxic Positive
Being positive is like going up a mountain. Being negative is like sliding down a hill. A lot of times, people want to take the easy way out, because it's basically what they've understood throughout their lives.	Toxic Positive
You must not under any pretense allow your mind to dwell on any thought that is not positive, constructive, optimistic, kind.	Toxic Positive
While you're going through this process of trying to find the satisfaction in your work, pretend you feel satisfied. Tell yourself you had a good day. Walk through the corridors with a smile rather than a scowl. Your positive energy will radiate. If you act like you're having fun, you'll find you are having fun.	Toxic Positive
You can't live a positive life with a negative mind and if you have a positive outcome you have a positive income and just to have more positivity and just to kind of laugh it off.	Toxic Positive

Table 3: Examples of toxic positive and non-toxic positive sentences in the dataset.

Removed Text	Source
Check out this new print for SPRING! #SpringForArt #ThisSpringBuyArt #gardeners #gardens #Inspire #InspirationalQuotes	Twitter
A future Metaverse, a social network for the people by the people, around jobs and finance in the decentralised world.Tomorrow's job fair in 3 dimensions at your fingertips. #MondayMotivation #cryptocurrency #blockchain #Crypto #jobseeker #Trader #Jobs #trading #ICO	Twitter
The failure of Lehman Brothers demonstrated that liquidity provision by the Federal Reserve would not be sufficient to stop the crisis; substantial fiscal resources were necessary.	BrainyQuote
Museums are managers of consciousness. They give us an interpretation of history, of how to view the world and locate ourselves in it. They are, if you want to put it in positive terms, great educational institutions. If you want to put it in negative terms, they are propaganda machines.	BrainyQuote

Table 4: Examples of the text removed during dataset creation.

Model	Macro Precision	Weighted Precision	Macro Recall	Weighted Recall	Macro F1	Weighted F1
BERT	0.78	0.84	0.6	0.86	0.63	0.83
RoBERTa	0.71	0.85	0.7	0.84	0.68	0.85
ALBERT	0.71	0.83	0.65	0.85	0.67	0.84
Ensemble	**0.76**	**0.85**	**0.69**	**0.86**	**0.71**	**0.85**

Table 5: Classification results of various models used on the dataset.

of a large number of decision trees, each set to only a subset of the overall feature-set of the data. This helps create numerous weak learners with relatively low correlation. The majority verdict of these weak learners tends to outperform an individual predictor tasked with the entire feature-set. In this paper, we have made use of the implementation of the Random Forest Classifier by XGBoost (Chen and Guestrin, 2016).

- **Bayesian Optimization**: Bayesian Optimization (Mockus, 1989) is a sequential global optimization strategy for various black-box functions and is used for models across Machine Learning. It attempts to determine the prior distribution of the system (i.e model hyperparameters), which yields the optimal posterior distribution (i.e objective function) by iteratively testing the prior and updating the posterior accordingly. It provides a more computationally efficient yet fine-grained search space than more exhaustive methods such as grid search. In our work, Bayesian optimization is used for tuning the hyperparameters (i.e. number of tree estimators, train subsample ratio, and column subsample ratio) of the Random Forest Classifier. We make use of the implementation by the bayesian-optimization Python library (Fernando, 2014).

5 Experiments and Results

We experimented with 3 transformer models BERT, RoBERTa, and ALBERT. Each of the classification models utilizes a pretrained Transformer encoder, i.e. BERT-Base, RoBERTa-Base, and ALBERT-Base. The pooled output layer from each encoder is passed through respective dropout layers ($p = 0.3$) for further regularization and linear layers (mapping from a vector size of 768 to the number of classification categories, i.e. 2). A softmax function is applied to each of the size-2 vectors for normalized likelihoods of the two classes. The results from these models are provided in Table 5.

We also experimented with an ensemble-based classifier. The classifier is an ensemble of three predictors with a random forest classifier on top (as shown in Figure 2). The predictors were the three text classification transformer based models as mentioned above.

The likelihoods from each of the predictors were concatenated and passed as features to an XGBoost Random Forest Classifier to generate an ensemble class prediction. After a Bayesian Search for the classifier parameters on the validation set, the number of tree estimators w set to 149, subsample ratio of the training samples to 0.50, and subsample ratio of columns for each split to 0.33.

Each of the Transformer encoder predictors were trained using AdamW optimizer ($\beta_1 = 0.9$, $\beta_2 = 0.999$, $\epsilon = 10^{-8}$), with Cross Entropy loss, using a linear training scheduler. The encoder pipelines were trained with an initial learning rate of $2e^{-5}$ and the XGBoost ensemble classifier with a learning rate of 1.0. The predictors were trained for 6 epochs . The predictions from the epoch with the best validation weighted macro F1 score were utilized for the ensemble classification. The overall batch size for the pipeline was set to 16.

The ensemble model generalized better than the individual models producing the highest macro F1 score of 0.71 and a weighted F1 score of 0.85 as seen in Table 5. As the toxic tweets comprise of only a small portion of the data (14.5%), models performing well on non-toxic tweets tend to have inflated weighted-F1 scores. Therefore we opted for macro-F1 as the main performance metric for this task.

6 Conclusion and Future Work

In this work, we created a dataset for toxic positivity detection. We scraped 4,250 sentences from Twitter and the inspirational quote website BrainyQuote. We then annotated them and

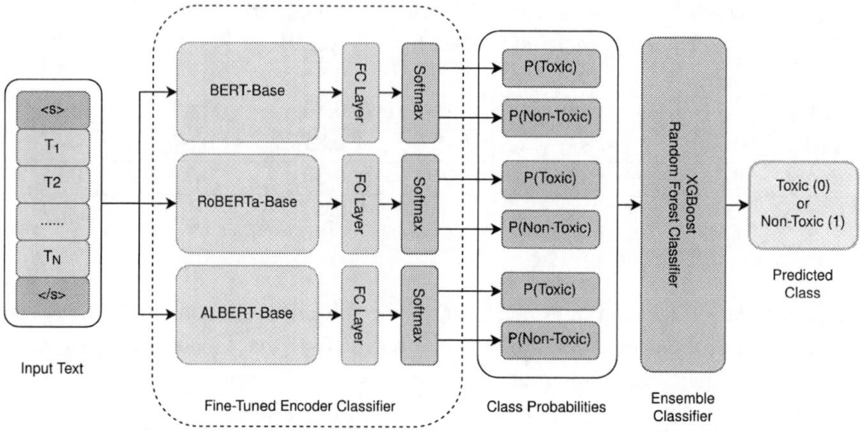

Figure 2: Schematic overview of the architecture of our model.

achieved a Kappa score of 0.82 for toxic positivity classification. We then performed experiments using transformer-based models for text classification. Our ensemble model gave us the best results achieving a macro F1 score of 0.71 and a weighted F1 score of 0.85. As more people turn to social media to get help when they are going through a tough time, it becomes important for them to be able to differentiate between positive and toxic positive messages. Furthermore, being able to recognize toxic positivity is also important for chatbots and other automated systems that aim to provide mental health assistance. We hope that our work contributes to further research in this field. In the future, we plan to extend the study by introducing a larger dataset in English as well as other languages.

References

Valerio Basile, Cristina Bosco, Elisabetta Fersini, Debora Nozza, Viviana Patti, Francisco Manuel Rangel Pardo, Paolo Rosso, and Manuela Sanguinetti. 2019. SemEval-2019 task 5: Multilingual detection of hate speech against immigrants and women in Twitter. In *Proceedings of the 13th International Workshop on Semantic Evaluation*, pages 54–63, Minneapolis, Minnesota, USA. Association for Computational Linguistics.

Eva Bosveld. 2021. *Positive Vibes Only: The Downsides of a Toxic Cure-All.*

Laura Campbell-Sills, David H. Barlow, Timothy A. Brown, and Stefan G. Hofmann. 2006. Effects of suppression and acceptance on emotional responses of individuals with anxiety and mood disorders. *Behaviour Research and Therapy*, 44(9):1251–1263.

Bharathi Raja Chakravarthi. 2020. HopeEDI: A multilingual hope speech detection dataset for equality, diversity, and inclusion. In *Proceedings of the Third Workshop on Computational Modeling of People's Opinions, Personality, and Emotion's in Social Media*, pages 41–53, Barcelona, Spain (Online). Association for Computational Linguistics.

Bharathi Raja Chakravarthi and Vigneshwaran Muralidaran. 2021. Findings of the shared task on hope speech detection for equality, diversity, and inclusion. In *Proceedings of the First Workshop on Language Technology for Equality, Diversity and Inclusion*, pages 61–72, Kyiv. Association for Computational Linguistics.

Tianqi Chen and Carlos Guestrin. 2016. XGBoost: A scalable tree boosting system. In *Proceedings of the 22nd ACM SIGKDD International Conference on Knowledge Discovery and Data Mining*, KDD '16, pages 785–794, New York, NY, USA. ACM.

Delia Cioffi and James Holloway. 1993. Delayed costs of suppressed pain. *Journal of Personality and Social Psychology*, 64(2):274–282.

Jacob Devlin, Ming-Wei Chang, Kenton Lee, and Kristina Toutanova. 2019. BERT: Pre-training of deep bidirectional transformers for language understanding. In *Proceedings of the 2019 Conference of the North American Chapter of the Association for Computational Linguistics: Human Language Technologies, Volume 1 (Long and Short Papers)*, pages 4171–4186, Minneapolis, Minnesota. Association for Computational Linguistics.

Nogueira Fernando. 2014. Bayesian Optimization: Open source constrained global optimization tool for Python.

Joseph L. Fleiss and Jacob Cohen. 1973. The equivalence of weighted kappa and the intraclass correlation coefficient as measures of reliability. *Educational and Psychological Measurement*, 33(3):613–619.

Brett Q. Ford, Phoebe Lam, Oliver P. John, and Iris B. Mauss. 2018. The psychological health benefits of accepting negative emotions and thoughts: Laboratory, diary, and longitudinal evidence. *Journal of Personality and Social Psychology*, 115(6):1075–1092.

Kris Gowen, Matthew Deschaine, Darcy Gruttadara, and Dana Markey. 2012. Young adults with mental health conditions and social networking websites: Seeking tools to build community. *Psychiatric Rehabilitation Journal*, 35(3):245–250.

James J. Gross and Oliver P. John. 2003. Individual differences in two emotion regulation processes: Implications for affect, relationships, and well-being. *Journal of Personality and Social Psychology*, 85(2):348–362.

Tin Kam Ho. 1995. Random decision forests. In *Proceedings of 3rd international conference on document analysis and recognition*, volume 1, pages 278–282. IEEE.

Zhenzhong Lan, Mingda Chen, Sebastian Goodman, Kevin Gimpel, Piyush Sharma, and Radu Soricut. 2020. Albert: A lite bert for self-supervised learning of language representations.

Margo Lecompte-Van Poucke. 2022. "you got this!": A critical discourse analysis of toxic positivity as a discursive construct on facebook. *Applied Corpus Linguistics*, 2(1):100015.

Yinhan Liu, Myle Ott, Naman Goyal, Jingfei Du, Mandar Joshi, Danqi Chen, Omer Levy, Mike Lewis, Luke Zettlemoyer, and Veselin Stoyanov. 2019. Roberta: A robustly optimized bert pretraining approach.

Thomas Mandl, Sandip Modha, Anand Kumar M, and Bharathi Raja Chakravarthi. 2020. Overview of the hasoc track at fire 2020: Hate speech and offensive language identification in tamil, malayalam, hindi, english and german. In *Forum for Information Retrieval Evaluation*, FIRE 2020, page 29–32, New York, NY, USA. Association for Computing Machinery.

Donatella Marazziti, Paolo Cianconi, Federico Mucci, Lara Foresi, Chiara Chiarantini, and Alessandra Della Vecchia. 2021. Climate change, environment pollution, covid-19 pandemic and mental health. *Science of The Total Environment*, page 145182.

Jonas Mockus. 1989. *Bayesian approach to global optimization*. Kluwer Academic.

Ioannis Mollas, Zoe Chrysopoulou, Stamatis Karlos, and Grigorios Tsoumakas. 2022. Ethos: a multi-label hate speech detection dataset. *Complex Intelligent Systems*.

Nedjma Ousidhoum, Zizheng Lin, Hongming Zhang, Yangqiu Song, and Dit-Yan Yeung. 2019. Multilingual and multi-aspect hate speech analysis. In *Proceedings of the 2019 Conference on Empirical Methods in Natural Language Processing and the 9th International Joint Conference on Natural Language Processing (EMNLP-IJCNLP)*, pages 4675–4684, Hong Kong, China. Association for Computational Linguistics.

Shriphani Palakodety, Ashiqur R. KhudaBukhsh, and Jaime G. Carbonell. 2020. Hope speech detection: A computational analysis of the voice of peace. *ECAI 2020*, page 1881–1889.

Laura Sokal, Lesley Eblie Trudel, and Jeff Babb. 2020. It's okay to be okay too. why calling out teachers' "toxic positivity" may backfire. *EdCan*, 60.

Alex Wang, Amanpreet Singh, Julian Michael, Felix Hill, Omer Levy, and Samuel R. Bowman. 2019a. GLUE: A multi-task benchmark and analysis platform for natural language understanding. In the Proceedings of ICLR.

Bin Wang, Yunxia Ding, Shengyan Liu, and Xiaobing Zhou. 2019b. Ynu_wb at HASOC 2019: Ordered neurons LSTM with attention for identifying hate speech and offensive language. In *Working Notes of FIRE 2019 - Forum for Information Retrieval Evaluation, Kolkata, India, December 12-15, 2019*, volume 2517 of *CEUR Workshop Proceedings*, pages 191–198. CEUR-WS.org.

Ziqi Zhang, David Robinson, and Jonathan Tepper. 2018. Detecting hate speech on twitter using a convolution-gru based deep neural network. In *The Semantic Web*, pages 745–760, Cham. Springer International Publishing.

OK Boomer: Probing the socio-demographic Divide in Echo Chambers

Henri-Jacques Geiss[†] **Flora Sakketou**[‡] **Lucie Flek**[‡]

[†]Department of Computer Science, Technical University of Darmstadt
henri-jacques.geiss@stud.tu-darmstadt.de

[‡]Conversational AI and Social Analytics (CAISA) Lab
Department of Mathematics and Computer Science,
University of Marburg, Germany
{flora.sakketou, lucie.flek}@uni-marburg.de

Abstract

Social media platforms such as Twitter or Reddit have become an integral part in political opinion formation and discussions, accompanied by potential echo chamber forming. In this paper, we examine the relationships between the interaction patterns, the opinion polarity, and the socio-demographic characteristics in discussion communities on Reddit. On a dataset of over 2 million posts coming from over 20k users, we combine network community detection algorithms, reliable stance polarity annotations, and NLP-based socio-demographic estimations, to identify echo chambers and understand their properties at scale. We show that the separability of the interaction communities is more strongly correlated to the relative socio-demographic divide, rather than the stance polarity gap size. We further demonstrate that the socio-demographic classifiers have a strong topical bias and should be used with caution, merely for the relative community difference comparisons within a topic, rather than for any absolute labeling.

1 Introduction

Social media platforms such as Twitter or Reddit have become an integral part in political opinion formation and discussions, as users exchange opinions on numerous polarising topics such as gun control, abortion or healthcare. This process is accompanied by the forming of echo chambers, i.e. clusters formed by users with a homogeneous content production and diffusion (Cota et al., 2019), where users mostly see posts reinforcing their preexisting belief (DiFranzo and Gloria-Garcia, 2017; Barberá, 2015). At the same time, humans tend to be *homophile* in their social connections and interactions in general, implying that socio-demographic similarities in categories such as age, gender, ethnicity, religion or political ideology significantly increase the chance of a connection between two individuals in social networks (McPherson et al., 2001; Li et al., 2015; Himelboim et al., 2013).

So while we do know that similarities foster connections and *common identities* (Ren et al., 2007; McPherson et al., 2001) as well as that online communities can become echo chambers, by combining network-based community modeling, stance annotations, and socio-demographic projections from natural language of self-identified authors, it is possible to coarsely estimate the extent to which these phenomena inter-play such that this socio-demographic clustering is intensified in online echo chambers.

Based on that, we explore the following hypotheses in this paper: (i) key societal topics on Reddit shape network interaction communities indicating the echo chamber phenomenon, (ii) stance polarity mean values are further apart in more separated network communities, (iii) a distinct socio-demographic divide exists between groups of interacting users with diverse stance polarities showing echo chamber characteristics, (iv) automated socio-demographic profiling tools suffer from a strong topical bias, which hinders their ability to characterize the communities.

This paper provides the following contributions:

- We create a Reddit dataset of over 20k users (over 2M posts) within 8 current societal topics (Sec. 3), aligned with manual stance polarity annotations of 640 users (Sec. 4).
- We quantify the presence and extent of echo chambers in these discussions, employing network-based community detection metrics, such as separability and expansion, and the stance polarity annotations (Sec. 5).

Proceedings of the Tenth International Workshop on Natural Language Processing for Social Media (SocialNLP 2022), pages 72 - 94
July 14-15, 2022 ©2022 Association for Computational Linguistics

- We develop classification models for socio-demographic variable estimates (age, gender, ideology) and find a strong topical bias, validating their use only for relative comparison of differences between communities rather than absolute labels (Sec. 6).
- By applying our socio-demographic classifiers on the detected and quantified network communities, we assess the echo-chamber phenomenon by identifying correlations between the relative difference in socio-demographic variables, the stance polarity differences, and the separability as well as expansion scores of the communities (Sec. 7).

2 Related Work

Recent works have either studied social-media data with regards to their graph-theoretical properties to detect echo-chamber-like phenomena from the user interactions (Barberá et al., 2015; Colleoni et al., 2014; Conover et al., 2011; Duseja and Jhamtani, 2019; Garimella et al., 2018) or estimated socio-demographic properties of social media users with NLP methods in isolation (Wiegmann et al., 2019; Wood-Doughty et al., 2018; Volkova and Bachrach, 2016; Burger et al., 2011). However, the combination of these two procedures in order to study a potential socio-demographic divide in such user groups at scale has, to the best of our knowledge, not been investigated so far.

In the broader context of analysing the political orientation of users in combination with their demographics, Barberá (2015) studies how Twitter users cluster with respect to different political leanings and shows that women tend to be on average slightly more liberal than men. A similar study demonstrated that there are differences in the average political leaning depending on gender, age, marital status and possession of a college degree (Bond and Messing, 2015), and observed that stronger ties between friends lead to a stronger correlation between their ideologies, which inspired us to the hypotheses explored in this paper.

On a similar note, Bamman et al. (2014) showed that mutual @-connections are more likely to appear between same-gender individuals. Comparable clustering effects were found for age as well as ideology (Li et al., 2015; Himelboim et al., 2013). Furthermore, Bastos et al. (2018) studied the relationship between echo chambers concerning the Brexit referendum on Twitter and the geographic location of its members, while Ebrahimi et al. (2016) found clear differences in the predicted stance towards Donald Trump between users from different US states, both embodying the idea of extracting social media stance-wise user groups and analysing their characteristics.

Regarding content-based models for the prediction of stance and socio-demographic properties, Durmus and Cardie (2018) studied discriminating tokens in the joined prediction of gender and stance towards abortion, finding that these correlate to the two labels differently, hinting towards our hypothesized topical bias for tokens that correlate more with stance than gender.

In the proposed work, we combine the users' political orientation, their estimated socio-demographic properties and their social media network, while previous works combine only a subset of these concepts, as shown in Table 1. Through a multifaceted analysis of the communities formed, we provide a more spherical insight into the relative differences of their members, in an attempt to analyze political opinion formation.

Authors	Demographics	Networks	Political stance
Barberá (2015)	✓		✓
Bond and Messing (2015)	✓		✓
Durmus and Cardie (2018)	✓		✓
Bamman et al. (2014)	✓	✓	
Li et al. (2015)	✓	✓	
Himelboim et al. (2013)		✓	✓
Bastos et al. (2018)		✓	✓
Ebrahimi et al. (2016)		✓	✓
Proposed method	✓	✓	✓

Table 1: Concepts covered by the related works

3 Dataset Characteristics

We used the API of Reddit to build our dataset. We chose Reddit as our source of data since it provides (i) rich content, due to the fact that there is no word limit, and (ii) a clear relationship between the text and the target topic, since users post within a subreddit. Previous work (Matthes et al., 2018) showed that the controversiality of the topic is one of the main drivers of opinion formation. Therefore, we manually compiled a set of contemporary discussion topics together with subreddits devoted to them (Table 7 in supplementary material for the 8 topics that were included). We crawled threads from these subreddits between November 2019 and June 2021 and periodically extended a database of posts and authors, preserving also the thread hier-

Topic	Reddit #Users	#Posts	#Posts/User
Abortion	3,747	631,177	168.4
Brexit	2,857	423,294	148.2
Capitalism	2,757	418,476	151.8
Climate change	1,117	269,032	240.9
Feminism	3,613	510,768	141.4
Gun control	5,192	667,477	128.6
Veganism	1,467	277,786	189.4
Nuclear-Energy	535	157,082	293.6
Total	**20,571**	**2,716,998**	**132**

Table 2: Amount of users, posts and posts per user for the studied topics. A user can be present in multiple topics, as we study in-topic interactions only.

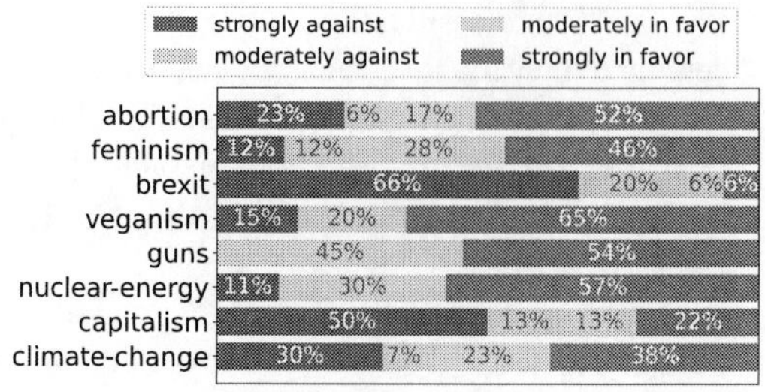

Figure 1: Average user stance distribution per topic

archy.

For the study at hand, we selected the 8 most active topics, and for each of those, we extracted all users with at least 10 posts. The final dataset statistics are provided in Table 2.

4 Stance Polarity and Intensity Labels

As the opinion of the users towards the investigated topics is a central dimension when studying the echo chamber phenomenon, we discarded our automated stance classification efforts (F1-score around 60% on three classes) and utilized the human labels of the SPINOS dataset instead (Sakketou et al., 2022)[1]. Since the SPINOS dataset resembles a proper subset of the data that will be studied in this paper, it was deemed a feasible source for human labeled user stance samples. The stance labels and their corresponding numeric values are: *strongly against* (-2), *moderately against* (-1), *stance not inferrable* (0), *moderately in favor* (1) and *strongly in favor* (2).

The dataset consists of 3526 manually annotated posts from 640 users, which fully overlap with our Reddit data. We analyzed the annotated stances of each user and verified that most users consistently persist on a particular stance polarity. There are a few users with vacillating stances, who seem to mostly persist on one pole (either in favor or against) and express strong stance intensity only for that pole. We therefore compute each user's average stance based on the individual stances of their posts.

Figure 1 shows the distribution of the averaged user stances for each topic. We note that, based on the annotation guidelines, a positive stance in the topic of feminism means being *in favor of equal rights for all genders*, a positive stance against climate change means believing that *climate change is caused by humans and constitutes a potential threat on survival* and a positive stance in the case of gun control means argumenting *in favor of the public availability of guns*.

5 Identifying Echo Chambers

Apart from the stance, a central aspect in the analysis of network structures, and especially echo chambers, in social media datasets is the definition of the interaction itself. Researchers have used retweets (Barberá et al., 2015; Conover et al., 2011) or follows (Colleoni et al., 2014; Duseja and Jhamtani, 2019; Garimella et al., 2018) to represent edges between user nodes. These however do not involve an explicit effort of content production (Cota et al., 2019), which is why we, following the work of Trabelsi and Zaiane (2018), focus on replies in the downward subtree of the post to extract the social network topologies. Figure 2 shows an example of how the post-reply tree of a social media post is transformed into the connecting edges of a user interaction network.

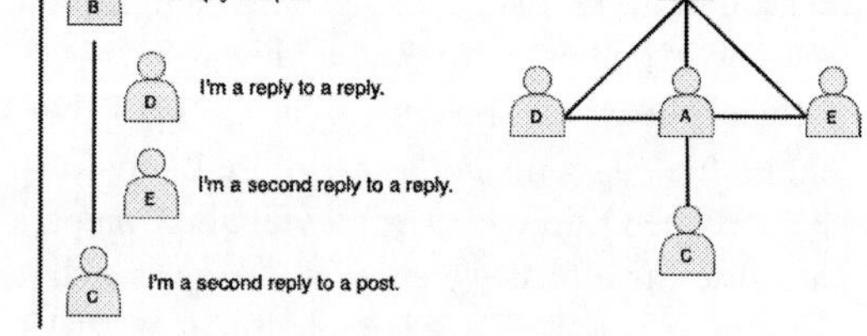

Figure 2: Examples of user interaction under a post and the resulting interaction network edges.

[1]https://github.com/caisa-lab/SPINOS-dataset

Detection Approach Similar to the studies of Conover et al. (2011) or Duseja and Jhamtani (2019), we search for interconnected user groups to detect echo-chamber-resembling structures in the extracted interaction topology. We experimented with the Louvain algorithm (Cota et al., 2019), the label propagation algorithm from Conover et al. (2011), and the Fluid algorithm (Parés et al., 2017). The latter yielded the best qualitative results.

To choose the optimal amount of communities, we encompass the fluid community detection with a meta-algorithm based on the notion of *modularity* of the detected communities. The meta algorithm runs the fluid community detection on the extracted network graphs from 2 up until 7 communities, and keeps track of the *modularity* of the created partitions, which is defined as:

$$\text{modularity} = m(p) = \sum_{c=1}^{n} \left[\frac{i_c}{m} - \gamma \left(\frac{k_c}{2m} \right)^2 \right]$$

where for a certain community c in a graph with m total edges, its number of internal edges is defined by i_c, the sum of degrees of the nodes in the community by k_c and the resolution parameter γ (Clauset et al., 2004; Hagberg et al., 2008).

In the end, the partition with the highest modularity score is returned. We chose *modularity* since it measures the division of the network into communities, i.e., whether there are only a few connections between the communities, while the nodes within them are densely connected (Clauset et al., 2004), which aligns with our goal of finding echo chambers. To ensure the consistency of our results even despite the elements of randomness in the community detection, 30 runs of the detection function are performed for each community amount, while still maximizing for *modularity*.

Based on these created partitions, we capture three graph community metrics (Yang and Leskovec, 2015), in order to measure the degree to which each distinct community represents an echo chamber in the network topology on variables that are not explicitly optimized during the community detection. We utilize *separability*, *expansion* and *density*, defined as follows for a community c:

$$\text{separability} = s(c) = \frac{i_c}{o_c}$$

$$\text{expansion} = e(c) = \frac{o_c}{n_c}$$

$$\text{density} = d(c) = \frac{i_c}{n_c(n_c - 1) \times 0.5}$$

here, the number of community-internal edges is defined by i_c, outbound edges by o_c, and community node count by n_c

The higher the values for *separability* and *density* of a detected community are, the more the interactions of its users are segregated from the rest of the network and rather take place with people from the same "bubble" and therefore represent an echo chamber. *Expansion* resembles echo chamber effects anti-proportionally as it is increased, when users of a community have more interactions with members from the other groups. To visualize the network nodes, we use the Fruchterman-Reingold force-directed placement (Fruchterman and Reingold, 1991).

We further provide the average manually annotated user stance, as described in section 4, for each of the detected interaction communities to explore if these also represent distinct stance clusters. Additionally, a weighted average stance for a community is determined by weighting the sampled stance values by the node degree of the users that contribute them.

Echo Chamber Identification Results We observe that the Reddit discussions take place in different network topology shapes, not all of them representing the echo chamber phenomenon. Rather, we distinguish three typical shapes:

1. Characteristic properties of the first structure, represented by the topic of nuclear-energy in the studied topics, are low values for *separability* (≤ 0.5), a high minimum *expansion* (around 20), a rather uniform distribution of the sampled stances, as well as no visually separated cluster of user-nodes. In discussions of this type, there are no separated communities with opposing stances, rather all discussion participants acting as one community. Such is the case for nuclear energy (Figure 3a). This can be further validated by the manual stance annotations on this topic, where the majority of the average user stances is 'in favor of the use of nuclear energy' (Figure 1).
2. The second and most frequent structure is characterized by average *separability* and *expansion* values, presence of at least one cluster with a rather neutral stance, and visually clearly distinct communities that are spatially close to each other. While for the topics of gun control and Brexit all communities show a similar average sampled stance, in the cases of capitalism and abortion a cluster with strongly parti-

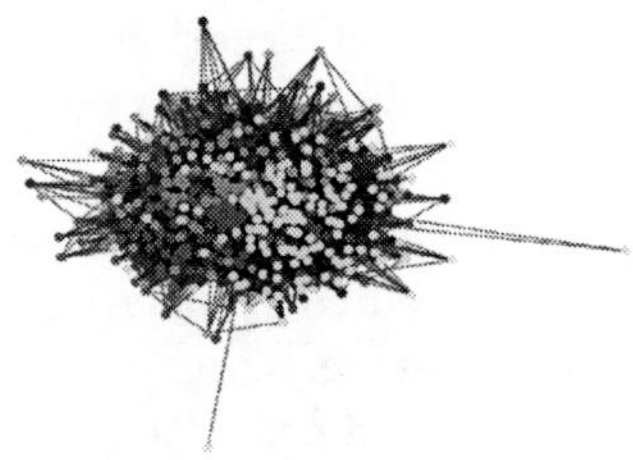

$max(s(c_i)) = 0.446$
$min(e(c_i)) = 19.373$

Community				
Stance	1.5	0.53	0.7	1.02

(a) Nuclear-Energy

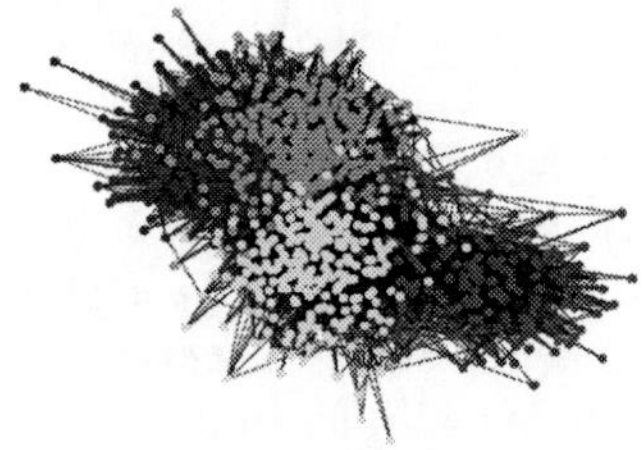

$max(s(c_i)) = 1.559$
$min(e(c_i)) = 4.213$

Community				
Stance	-0.01	0.96	-0.05	0.24

(b) Climate-Change

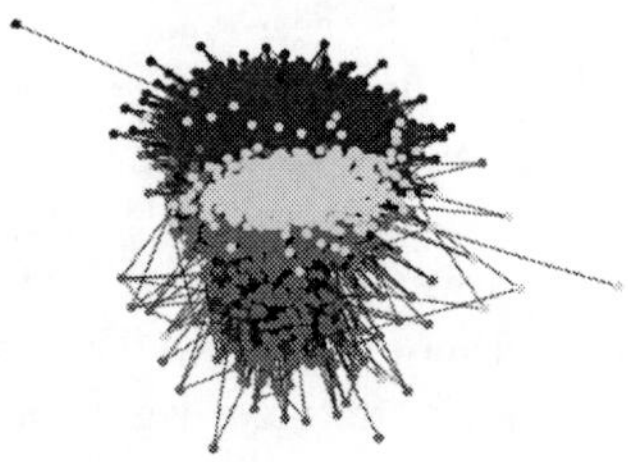

$max(s(c_i)) = 2.024$
$min(e(c_i)) = 10.443$

Community			
Stance	-0.23	1.19	0.12

(c) Abortion

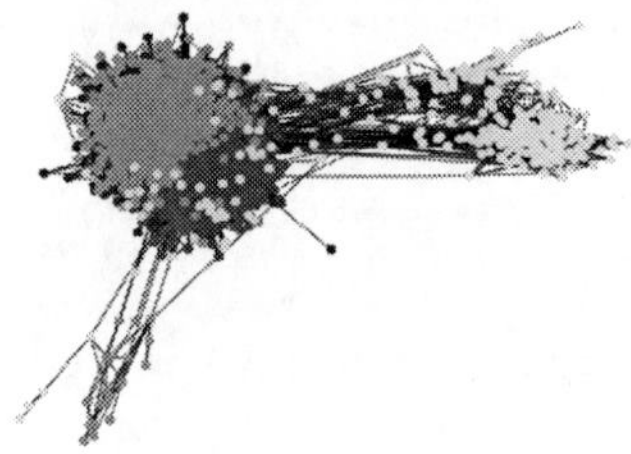

$max(s(c_i)) = 3.78$
$min(e(c_i)) = 1.511$

Community				
Stance	-1	-0.34	0.11	0.73

(d) Feminism

Figure 3: Four examples of topic interaction topologies and their detected communities on Reddit. $max(s(c_i))$ and $min(s(e_i))$ are the maximum *separability* and minimum *expansion* among the detected communities

san stances can be observed, hinting towards an echo-chamber-like "homogeneous content production and diffusion"(Cota et al., 2019).

3. The third structure type in the discussion topology, embodied by the topic of feminism in our analyzed data (Figure 3d), resembles the echo chamber phenomenon the most. In this case there is at least one detected community with a high *separability* score (≥ 4), a low minimum *expansion* (≤ 2) and at least one cluster with a clearly partisan average stance. The detected communities are also more spatially separated than in the other structure types. Here, like-minded individuals interact segregated from the rest of the network; an echo chamber is formed.

6 Socio-Demographic Prediction

To study how these community structures relate to their participants' socio-demographic traits we train interpretable supervised classifiers on datasets from previous social-media (Twitter) studies on gender, age, and political ideology (Preotiuc-Pietro et al., 2016; Preoţiuc-Pietro et al., 2017; Preoţiuc-Pietro and Ungar, 2018). For all three of these dimensions, it has been previously shown that social media users cluster along their labels (Bamman et al., 2014; Li et al., 2015; Himelboim et al., 2013). Following previous studies, and considering the available data volumes, we approach these tasks as classification.[2] We acknowledge the sub-optimality of predicting binary gender labels and using self-reported training data with users having

[2]We are aware of the limitations and ethical risks that this simplification entails, as discussed in the Ethics section.

Label / Data	Tw1	Tw2	Tw3	Reddit
Male	34.3%	38.1%	34.8%	55.2%
Female	65.7%	61.9%	65.1%	44.8%
≤ 30	38.9%	39.9%	54.3%	37.3%
≤ 45	41.2%	43.7%	32.2%	31.2%
> 45	19.9%	16.4%	13.4%	31.5%
Liberal	-	-	50.3%	28.2%
Moderate	-	-	26.8%	-
Conservative	-	-	22.9%	71.8%

Table 3: Class distribution in training datasets

only binary option (Larson, 2017). We interpret the predictions in line with (Bem, 1974), examining if the discussion communities differ in constituent features around the class modes. The self-reported labels were obtained through the survey platforms Qualtrics and Amazon Mechanical Turk. Note that the actual posts of the twitter timelines we retrieved for each user might differ from the previous studies. We predict the user's: (i) self-reported age (three classes: below 30, between 30-45, and 46+), (ii) self-reported gender (male/female), and (iii) political ideology (conservative, moderate, or liberal).

Our training data from Twitter for age and gender consists of 3960 users. In order to directly include also users from reddit in the training data, we employ an automatic annotation generation for the dimensions of gender and age group based on regex-matching of 'I am'-statements in the user posts (Welch et al., 2020). For instance we annotate gender by searching for statements such as 'I am a guy/girl' or age with phrases such as 'I am X years old' or 'My grandson/granddaughter'. Users with multiple contradicting 'I am'-statements are excluded from the dataset. This way, we enhance our training data with 966 users from reddit, annotated for gender and 289 users for age. We then enhance the ideology training data with 1223 users from subreddits *r/Liberal* and *r/Conservative*, excluding users with less than 5 posts.

Feature settings (1) `TF-IDF`: We use the Porter Stemmer together with the TF-IDF weighting scheme (Manning et al., 2008).
(2) `Unigrams`: A user vector is calculated by summing up the appearances of every token, used by at least one percent of the training user base, across all the posts of one user and normalizing these values with the number of posts (Preoţiuc-Pietro and Ungar, 2018).
(3) `word2vec`: Spectral clustering of word embeddings creating a feature vector for a given set of posts from a user by calculating the proportion of tokens that belong to each of the topic clusters (Preoţiuc-Pietro and Ungar, 2018). These however didn't outperform the unigram and TF-IDF results.

We intentionally apply only easily interpretable classification models; linear SVM, logistic regression, and random forest. The best-performing setup for each of the user traits, which is used further in paper, is highlighted in Table 4.

	LinSVM	LogReg	RForest	Base
	Gender (Class-Balanced Down)			
tf-idf	0.735	0.693	0.769	0.5
word2vec	0.696	0.659	0.728	0.5
unigrams	**0.786**	0.7652	0.756	0.5
	Age (Class-Balanced Down)			
tf-idf	0.549	0.51	0.542	0.33
word2vec	0.516	0.492	0.546	0.33
unigrams	**0.577**	0.56	0.564	0.33
	Ideology (Class-Balanced Up)			
tf-idf	**0.587**	0.574	0.506	0.33
word2vec	0.563	0.557	0.524	0.33
unigrams	0.585	0.6	0.516	0.33

Table 4: Socio-demographic predictor accuracies with 5-fold cross-validation on balanced data

Socio-Demographic Prediction Analysis In the cases of gender and age group, the best-performing predictor(LinSVM) uses unigram-based user vectors, with accuracies of 79% and 58% respectively. For the prediction of political ideology, tf-idf features perform the best with 59%, more than 20% above the random prediction baseline.

We then analyze the predictive unigrams, extracting the feature score for each class from the LinSVM coefficient vector as per (Guyon and Elisseeff, 2003; Guyon et al., 2002). The results (Appendix) align with previous work, e.g. self-identified female users referring more to emotions (Burger et al., 2011; Carpenter et al., 2017).

Furthermore, Table 5 compares the predicted gender distribution of users participating in each topic with the more accurate, but sparser information detected by the regular expressions. We see that our content-based predictor tends to generally over-estimate the percentage of male users for most political topics. The two predictors are in more agreement on the three topics with the lowest amount of male participants, namely abortion, veganism-animalrights and feminism.

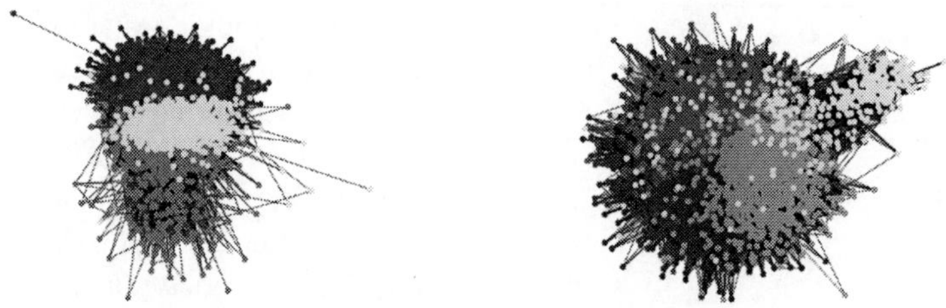

Cluster	Gender	Age	Ideology
	Socio-demographics		
Violet (-0.457)	M: 64.1% F: 35.9%	≤ 30: 58.7% ≤ 45: 19.7% > 45: 21.6%	Con: 52% Mod: 0.6% Lib: 47.5%
Green (1.05)	M: 25.5% F: 74.5%	≤ 30: 60.6% ≤ 45: 21.2% > 45: 18.2%	Con: 25.1% Mod: 6.6% Lib: 68.3%
Yellow (0.635)	M: 53.5% F: 46.5%	≤ 30: 64.4% ≤ 45: 22.6% > 45: 13%	Con: 44.3% Mod: 0.4% Lib: 55.3%

Cluster	Gender	Age	Ideology
	Socio-demographics		
Violet (0.503)	M: 94.1% F: 5.9%	≤ 30: 29.7% ≤ 45: 25.6% > 45: 44.8%	Con: 79.8% Mod: 0.3% Lib: 19.9%
Blue (0.362)	M: 95. % F: 5%	≤ 30: 22.9% ≤ 45: 27.6% > 45: 49.6%	Con: 79.9% Mod: 0.4% Lib: 19.8%
Green (0.372)	M: 96.6% F: 3.4%	≤ 30: 23.6% ≤ 45: 25.4% > 45: 51%	Con: 81.6% Mod: 0.4% Lib: 18%
Yellow (0.055)	M: 92.5% F: 7.5%	≤ 30: 21.9% ≤ 45: 22.6% > 45: 55.5%	Con: 77.1% Mod: 1% Lib: 21.9%

Figure 4: Predicted socio-demographic distributions of the detected communities in the discussion about **abortion** (left) and **gun control** (right) on Reddit. The clusters' degree-weighted average sampled stance is given in brackets.

Topic	**Predicted Gender** (M-F)	**Regex Gender** (M-F)	**Regex #Users**
abortion	53%-47%	39%-61%	222
climate-change	91%-9%	64%-36%	14
feminism	76%-24%	59%-41%	301
gun control	95%-5%	8-%2%	49
veganism	65%-35%	47%-53%	47
Brexit	94%-6%	71%-29%	24
capitalism	92%-8%	82%-18%	39
nuclear-energy	95%-5%	100%-0%	5

Table 5: Comparison of predicted gender proportions

7 Result of Combining the Studies

Labeling the posts of each user yields a percentage distribution for socio-demographic labels in the communities we extract from the interaction graphs of each topic. Figure 4 shows two examples of the determined socio-demographic distributions of a topic's communities and visually explains how we combined the systems derived in sections 5 and 6 for the following analyses (see Appendix for results on the rest of the topics).

Generally, we observe that diverse topics show diverse socio-demographic community profiles. For Abortion, the violet and green communities have opposing stances and large differences in the predicted gender and ideology distributions. In contrast, for Gun Control, all socio-demographic labels only differ by a small margin.

To formalize our hypothesis that the *relative* socio-demographic differences between the intra-topic community groups grow with the groups becoming more resembling to an echo chamber, we propose to measure, across all 8 topics, the correlation between the *separability* and *expansion* values of each community and the average RMSE (Equation 2) of each of the socio-demographic variables (Equation 1) of the detected clusters from the topic's baseline (i.e. the distribution for all users in the topic). A positive correlation in this case means that the more the communities of one topic resemble an echo chamber, the more they also differ in their socio-demographics. In Equation 1, d is the analyzed socio-demographic label, t is a certain topic with the corresponding full user base for this topic b_t and the ith detected community $c_{t,i}$, and $\text{pred}_d(x)$ is a function yielding the distribution of

	Stance	Stance σ	Gender	Age	Ideology
Separability	0.483	0.317	0.630	0.110	0.498
Expansion	-0.549	-0.090	-0.403	-0.170	-0.585

Table 6: Pearson's correlation of the *separability* and *expansion* values of the detected communities to (a) their mean stance, (b) their stance standard deviation (σ) and (c) their deviations from the full in-topic socio-demographics (Equation 1)

label d in a user group:

$$\text{sd-value}_d(b_t, c_{t,i}) = \text{rmse}(\text{pred}_d(b_t) - \text{pred}_d(c_{t,i})) \quad (1)$$

$$\text{rmse}(x) = \sqrt{\frac{1}{N}\sum_{i=1}^{N}(x_i)^2}, \quad x \in \mathbb{R}^N \quad (2)$$

Additionally, we measure the correlation of the two community metrics to the community's difference in stance from the complete topic's contributor average as well as the absolute values of standard deviation (σ). In the four stance-related correlations values, only communities with at least 5 stance-user-samples were considered.

Correlation Results The results in Table 6 indicate that values of *separability* and *expansion* that model the presence of an echo-chamber-resembling interaction network structure (high *separability* and low *expansion*) correlate with a larger separation of a sub-community in terms of gender and ideology of the topic's user average. Hence hypothesis (iii) holds - a distinct socio-demographic divide exists between groups of interacting users with diverse stance polarities showing echo chamber characteristics.

Furthermore, increased *separability* and decreased *expansion* also correlate with a stronger stance-wise segregation, confirming our hypothesis (ii) that stance polarity mean values are further apart in more separated network communities. That being said, these communities also show an increased standard deviation of stances, indicating that at least some variance in the opinion of contributing users is present, while more uniform network structures also tend to have more uniform stances.

8 Discussion and Limitations

The topic- and platform-specific environment underlines the limits of text-based user studies such as ours, indicating a lexical issue in the predictors used, confirming our hypothesis (iv) that the automated socio-demographic profiling tools suffer from a strong topical bias. While words such as *problem*, *understand*, or *politics* tend to be in general statistically more often used by self-identified men (Table 8), this does not hold when comparing discussions within a given topic. Similarly, while words like *women*, *mom* or *girl* are in general strong lexical cues for an author being female (compare Table 8), they tend to be used frequently by both genders just as a part of discussion about abortion or feminism. Similar issues occur with age models, leading to prediction biases. However, note that comparing *relative* differences (gaps) in estimated demographics between communities within one topic, as we did in Equation 1, is possible, as the bias merely shifts the distribution. In line with (Bem, 1974), we can still examine if the communities differ in constituent features around the class modes.

9 Summary and Conclusions

We explore the social media phenomenon of echo chambers with regards to its socio-demographic implications. To quantify the forming of these structures, we employed an interaction graph-based algorithm, exploring the *separability*, *density* and *expansion* of the detected communities. For the network topologies of abortion, capitalism, and feminism, we found a moderate to high resemblance of the echo-chamber phenomenon. Bridging the gap between theory and practice, these algorithm and measures could also be used by actual social-media platforms to track where its communities are structurally 'echo-chambered' and potential counter-measures are needed.

To capture the socio-demographic distributions of the detected communities, we trained interpretable socio-demographic estimation models, scrutinized by keyphrase-based approaches. By merging the network and content information, we found that more 'echo-chambered' topic communities also show an increased separation in their stance and gender and ideology profiles. These results reinforce the call for incorporating socio-demographic and network information into data sets and models for tasks like sentiment analysis, text generation and stance prediction (Hovy, 2015; Hovy and Yang, 2021), while keeping in mind that a lexical topic-related bias can be a source of misinterpretation in domain-specific user modeling.

Ethical Considerations

We acknowledge the suboptimality of predicting binary gender labels and using self-reported training data with users having only binary option (Larson, 2017). The topic- and platform-specific environment underlines the limits of such user studies. Any user-augmented classification efforts risk invoking stereotyping and essentialism, which can cause harm even if they are accurate on average differences (Rudman and Glick, 2008), and can be emphasized by the semblance of objectivity created by the use of a computer algorithm (Koolen and van Cranenburgh, 2017). It is important to be mindful of these effects when interpreting the model results in its application context. Use of any user data for socio-demographic estimates shall be transparent, and limited to the given aggregated purpose (Williams et al., 2017), no individual posts shall be republished and the study authors were advised to take account of users' privacy expectations (Williams et al., 2017; Shilton and Sayles, 2016; Townsend and Wallace, 2016) when collecting online data for user-based predictions. In our case, we utilize publicly available Reddit data in a purely observational, community-aggregated, and non-intrusive manner (Norval and Henderson, 2017) and restrain from any verbatim citations of the post contents.

Acknowledgements

This work has been supported by the German Federal Ministry of Education and Research (BMBF) as a part of the Junior AI Scientists program under the reference 01-S20060.

References

David Bamman, Jacob Eisenstein, and Tyler Schnoebelen. 2014. Gender identity and lexical variation in social media. *Journal of Sociolinguistics*, 18(2):135–160.

Pablo Barberá. 2015. Birds of the same feather tweet together: Bayesian ideal point estimation using twitter data. *Political analysis*, 23(1):76–91.

Pablo Barberá, John T Jost, Jonathan Nagler, Joshua A Tucker, and Richard Bonneau. 2015. Tweeting from left to right: Is online political communication more than an echo chamber? *Psychological science*, 26(10):1531–1542.

Marco Bastos, Dan Mercea, and Andrea Baronchelli. 2018. The geographic embedding of online echo chambers: Evidence from the brexit campaign. *PloS one*, 13(11):e0206841.

Sandra Bem. 1974. The measurement of psychological androgyny. *Journal of Consulting and Clinical Psychology*, 42(2):155–162.

Robert Bond and Solomon Messing. 2015. Quantifying social media's political space: Estimating ideology from publicly revealed preferences on facebook. *American Political Science Review*, 109(1):62–78.

John D Burger, John Henderson, George Kim, and Guido Zarrella. 2011. Discriminating gender on twitter. In *Proceedings of the 2011 Conference on Empirical Methods in Natural Language Processing*, pages 1301–1309.

Jordan Carpenter, Daniel Preotiuc-Pietro, Lucie Flekova, Salvatore Giorgi, Courtney Hagan, Margaret L Kern, Anneke EK Buffone, Lyle Ungar, and Martin EP Seligman. 2017. Real men don't say "cute" using automatic language analysis to isolate inaccurate aspects of stereotypes. *Social Psychological and Personality Science*, 8(3):310–322.

Aaron Clauset, Mark EJ Newman, and Cristopher Moore. 2004. Finding community structure in very large networks. *Physical review E*, 70(6):066111.

Elanor Colleoni, Alessandro Rozza, and Adam Arvidsson. 2014. Echo chamber or public sphere? predicting political orientation and measuring political homophily in twitter using big data. *Journal of communication*, 64(2):317–332.

Michael D Conover, Bruno Gonçalves, Jacob Ratkiewicz, Alessandro Flammini, and Filippo Menczer. 2011. Predicting the political alignment of twitter users. In *2011 IEEE third international conference on privacy, security, risk and trust*, pages 192–199. IEEE.

Wesley Cota, Silvio C Ferreira, Romualdo Pastor-Satorras, and Michele Starnini. 2019. Quantifying echo chamber effects in information spreading over political communication networks. *EPJ Data Science*, 8(1):35.

Dominic DiFranzo and Kristine Gloria-Garcia. 2017. Filter bubbles and fake news. *XRDS: Crossroads, The ACM Magazine for Students*, 23(3):32–35.

Esin Durmus and Claire Cardie. 2018. Understanding the effect of gender and stance in opinion expression in debates on "abortion". In *Proceedings of the Second Workshop on Computational Modeling of People's Opinions, Personality, and Emotions in Social Media*, pages 69–75.

Nikita Duseja and Harsh Jhamtani. 2019. A sociolinguistic study of online echo chambers on twitter. In *Proceedings of the Third Workshop on Natural Language Processing and Computational Social Science*, pages 78–83.

Javid Ebrahimi, Dejing Dou, and Daniel Lowd. 2016. Weakly supervised tweet stance classification by relational bootstrapping. In *Proceedings of the 2016 conference on empirical methods in natural language processing*, pages 1012–1017.

Thomas MJ Fruchterman and Edward M Reingold. 1991. Graph drawing by force-directed placement. *Software: Practice and experience*, 21(11):1129–1164.

Kiran Garimella, Gianmarco De Francisci Morales, Aristides Gionis, and Michael Mathioudakis. 2018. Political discourse on social media: Echo chambers, gatekeepers, and the price of bipartisanship. In *Proceedings of the 2018 World Wide Web Conference*, pages 913–922.

Isabelle Guyon and André Elisseeff. 2003. An introduction to variable and feature selection. *Journal of machine learning research*, 3(Mar):1157–1182.

Isabelle Guyon, Jason Weston, Stephen Barnhill, and Vladimir Vapnik. 2002. Gene selection for cancer classification using support vector machines. *Machine learning*, 46(1-3):389–422.

Aric Hagberg, Pieter Swart, and Daniel S Chult. 2008. Exploring network structure, dynamics, and function using networkx. Technical report, Los Alamos National Lab.(LANL), Los Alamos, NM (United States).

Itai Himelboim, Stephen McCreery, and Marc Smith. 2013. Birds of a feather tweet together: Integrating network and content analyses to examine cross-ideology exposure on twitter. *Journal of computer-mediated communication*, 18(2):154–174.

Dirk Hovy. 2015. Demographic factors improve classification performance. In *Proceedings of the 53rd annual meeting of the Association for Computational Linguistics and the 7th international joint conference on natural language processing (volume 1: Long papers)*, pages 752–762.

Dirk Hovy and Diyi Yang. 2021. The importance of modeling social factors of language: Theory and practice. In *Proceedings of the 2021 Conference of the North American Chapter of the Association for Computational Linguistics: Human Language Technologies*, pages 588–602, Online. Association for Computational Linguistics.

Corina Koolen and Andreas van Cranenburgh. 2017. These are not the stereotypes you are looking for: Bias and fairness in authorial gender attribution. In *Proceedings of the First ACL Workshop on Ethics in Natural Language Processing*, pages 12–22, Valencia, Spain. Association for Computational Linguistics.

Brian N Larson. 2017. Gender as a variable in natural-language processing: Ethical considerations. *EACL 2017*, page 1.

Peter Li, Jiejun Xu, and Tsai-Ching Lu. 2015. Leveraging homophily to infer demographic attributes: Inferring the age of twitter users using label propagation. In *Proceedings of Workshop on Information In Networks (WIN15)*.

Christopher D Manning, Prabhakar Raghavan, and Hinrich Schütze. 2008. *Introduction to information retrieval*. Cambridge university press.

Jörg Matthes, Johannes Knoll, and Christian von Sikorski. 2018. The "spiral of silence" revisited: A meta-analysis on the relationship between perceptions of opinion support and political opinion expression. *Communication Research*, 45(1):3–33.

Miller McPherson, Lynn Smith-Lovin, and James M Cook. 2001. Birds of a feather: Homophily in social networks. *Annual review of sociology*, 27(1):415–444.

Chris Norval and Tristan Henderson. 2017. Contextual consent: Ethical mining of social media for health research. *CoRR*, abs/1701.07765.

Ferran Parés, Dario Garcia Gasulla, Armand Vilalta, Jonatan Moreno, Eduard Ayguadé, Jesús Labarta, Ulises Cortés, and Toyotaro Suzumura. 2017. Fluid communities: A competitive, scalable and diverse community detection algorithm. In *International Conference on Complex Networks and their Applications*, pages 229–240. Springer.

Daniel Preotiuc-Pietro, Jordan Carpenter, Salvatore Giorgi, and Lyle Ungar. 2016. Studying the dark triad of personality through twitter behavior. In *Proceedings of the 25th ACM international on conference on information and knowledge management*, pages 761–770.

Daniel Preoţiuc-Pietro, Ye Liu, Daniel Hopkins, and Lyle Ungar. 2017. Beyond binary labels: political ideology prediction of twitter users. In *Proceedings of the 55th Annual Meeting of the Association for Computational Linguistics*, pages 729–740.

Daniel Preoţiuc-Pietro and Lyle Ungar. 2018. User-level race and ethnicity predictors from twitter text. In *Proceedings of the 27th International Conference on Computational Linguistics*, pages 1534–1545.

Yuqing Ren, Robert Kraut, and Sara Kiesler. 2007. Applying common identity and bond theory to design of online communities. *Organization studies*, 28(3):377–408.

Laurie A Rudman and Peter Glick. 2008. The social psychology of gender: How power and intimacy shape gender relations.

Flora Sakketou, Allison Lahnala, Liane Vogel, and Lucie Flek. 2022. Investigating user radicalization: A novel dataset for identifying fine-grained temporal shifts in opinion.

Katie Shilton and Sheridan Sayles. 2016. " we aren't all going to be on the same page about ethics": Ethical practices and challenges in research on digital and social media. In *2016 49th Hawaii International Conference on System Sciences (HICSS)*, pages 1909–1918. IEEE.

Leanne Townsend and Claire Wallace. 2016. Social media research: A guide to ethics. *University of Aberdeen*, 1:16.

Amine Trabelsi and Osmar Zaiane. 2018. Unsupervised model for topic viewpoint discovery in online debates leveraging author interactions. In *Proceedings of the International AAAI Conference on Web and Social Media*, volume 12.

Svitlana Volkova and Yoram Bachrach. 2016. Inferring perceived demographics from user emotional tone and user-environment emotional contrast. In *Proceedings of the 54th Annual Meeting of the Association for Computational Linguistics*, pages 1567–1578.

Charles Welch, Jonathan K. Kummerfeld, Verónica Pérez-Rosas, and Rada Mihalcea. 2020. Compositional demographic word embeddings. In *Proceedings of the 2020 Conference on Empirical Methods in Natural Language Processing*.

Matti Wiegmann, Benno Stein, and Martin Potthast. 2019. Celebrity profiling. In *Proceedings of the 57th Annual Meeting of the Association for Computational Linguistics*, pages 2611–2618.

Matthew L Williams, Pete Burnap, and Luke Sloan. 2017. Towards an ethical framework for publishing twitter data in social research: Taking into account users' views, online context and algorithmic estimation. *Sociology*, 51(6):1149–1168.

Zach Wood-Doughty, Nicholas Andrews, Rebecca Marvin, and Mark Dredze. 2018. Predicting twitter user demographics from names alone. In *Proceedings of the Second Workshop on Computational Modeling of People's Opinions, Personality, and Emotions in Social Media*, pages 105–111.

Jaewon Yang and Jure Leskovec. 2015. Defining and evaluating network communities based on ground-truth. *Knowledge and Information Systems*, 42(1):181–213.

A Supplemental Material

A.1 Annotated List of Subreddits for each of the Studied Topics

Topic	Subreddits
Abortion	'abortion', 'Abortiondebate', 'prochoice', 'prolife', 'trueprochoice', 'Insaneprochoice', 'ProLifeLibertarians', 'ThingsProChoicersSay', 'AskProchoice', 'insaneprolife', 'abortionopinions'
Brexit	'brexit', 'brealism'
Capitalism	'CapitalismVSocialism', 'DebateCommunism', 'SocialismVCapitalism', 'occupywallstreet', 'Capitalism', 'communism'
Climate Change	'climate', 'climatechange', 'climateskeptics', 'GlobalClimateChange', 'FridaysForFuture'
Feminism	'DebateFeminism', 'feminisms', 'feministtheory', 'GenderCritical', 'RadicalFeminism', 'INeedFeminismBecause', 'meToo', 'masculinism', 'Egalitarianism', 'masculism', 'MensRights', 'MRActivism', 'MenGetRapedToo', 'LeftistsForMen', 'feminismformen', 'mensrightslinks', 'antifeminists', 'Feminism', 'Radical_Feminists', 'RadicalFeminismUSA'
Gun control	'guncontrol', 'GunDebates', 'gunpolitics', 'GunResearch', 'GunsAreCool', 'progun', 'liberalgunowners', 'Firearms'
Nuclear-Energy	'nuclear', 'NuclearEnergy', 'NuclearPower'
Veganism-Animalrights	'AnimalRights', 'animalwelfare', 'VeganActivism', 'Veganism', 'Vegetarianism', 'Veganity', 'vegproblems', 'AntiVegan', 'DebateAVegan', 'debatemeateaters', 'exvegans'

Table 7: The subreddits that were crawled to creat the dataset from which the studied users, their posts and the interaction graphs were extracted

A.2 Unigram Coefficients

Female		Male	
2.805	girl	-2.597	game
2.723	love	-2.224	men
2.572	♀	-2.088	wife
1.781	book	-2.05	♂
1.653	bodi	-1.89	man
1.611	so	-1.751	good
1.611	about	-1.627	bro
1.606	woman	-1.509	some
1.583	omg	-1.506	back
1.482	women	-1.481	#x200b
1.469	no	-1.439	🔥
1.442	oh	-1.404	guy
1.41	senat	-1.349	beat
1.338	cute	-1.287	doe
1.321	🖤	-1.281	player
1.317	pleas	-1.266	look
1.29	friend	-1.264	war
1.281	😊	-1.263	problem
1.279	thing	-1.225	coronaviru
1.27	mom	-1.215	enjoy
1.267	:)	-1.195	year
1.263	hous	-1.167	en
1.239	are	-1.159	3
1.218	birthday	-1.143	mplusreward
1.208	husband	-1.13	harm
1.198	ad	-1.126	should
1.193	excit	-1.11	great
1.179	sticker	-1.097	shit
1.178	color	-1.09	check
1.175	ye	-1.07	time
1.156	stop	-1.049	much
1.137	he	-1.048	comic
1.135	didn't	-1.043	If
1.118	okay	-1.039	understand
1.089	public	-1.03	valu
1.08	cooki	-1.023	#es161
1.074	serious	-1.02	complet
1.062	danc	-1.013	down
1.061	mental	-0.996	against
1.061	heart	-0.986	youtub
1.061	night	-0.981	mpoint
1.06	text	-0.978	app
1.055	tweet	-0.971	hi

Table 8: Gender svc-model coefficients for unigrams

≤ 30	
1.712	be
1.688	actual
1.433	is
1.334	my
1.305	i’m
1.299	Me
1.295	it’
1.284	gonna
1.238	life
1.199	so
1.129	
1.097	like
1.078	an
1.076	class
1.055	day
1.013	becaus
0.996	😞
0.977	😊
0.945	y’all
0.944	wanna
0.924	:)
0.889	pop
0.881	3
0.878	
0.876	<3
0.876	i
0.86	okay
0.85	give
0.847	punchcard
0.836	you’r
0.833	can’t
0.825	–
0.825	shop
0.82	1,000
0.818	nigga
0.796	dailylook
0.796	charact
0.777	no
0.777	#cochlearimpl
0.767	berni
0.766	chang

≤ 45	
2.037	right
1.278	movi
1.269	mean
1.173	excit
1.166	tri
1.139	fun
1.124	or
1.087	🙏
1.057	aquariu
1.056	awesom
1.022	ago
1.016	teacher
0.989	white
0.969	wait
0.953	kid
0.949	babi
0.941	leo
0.935	bad
0.933	product
0.921	man
0.887	some
0.886	...
0.884	chat
0.825	year
0.817	idea
0.816	exactli
0.806	free
0.796	episod
0.791	#winterofzombi
0.788	odd
0.782	#saveforev
0.768	week
0.761	narcissist
0.759	great
0.756	mayb
0.753	total
0.748	#debatenight
0.745	then
0.743	guess
0.738	can’t
0.737	wow

> 45	
1.411	she
1.228	enter
1.216	have
1.194	pleas
1.181	those
1.096	via
1.04	thank
1.01	he
1.008	well
1.006	hi
1.004	ani
0.989	great
0.973	#ifb
0.965	by
0.964	must
0.954	read
0.953	#photographi
0.925	they
0.921	veri
0.903	place
0.893	most
0.875	die
0.873	100
0.849	❤
0.847	scorpio
0.819	video
0.816	there
0.809	oia
0.798	trump
0.795	daughter
0.789	see
0.779	use
0.778	safe
0.776	would
0.759	your
0.746	happi
0.744	were
0.741	:)
0.74	stay
0.739	now
0.734	here

Table 9: Age group svc-model coefficients for unigrams

Conservative		Moderate		Liberal	
1.405	polic	1.225	wow	1.347	❤️
1.154	leftist	1.107	back	1.206	omg
1.132	chat	1.087	by	1.177	prize
1.114	polit	1.075	😊	1.137	write
1.103	protest	1.07	money	1.112	save
1.046	kid	1.052	love	1.111	tweet
1.036	👦	0.995	stream	1.092	📷
1.027	littl	0.97	can	1.044	serious
1.009	they	0.963	🙏	1.025	We
1.005	it’	0.926	😽	0.987	still
1.004	blm	0.917	dot	0.977	episod
0.98	😘	0.909	😍	0.967	women
0.974	democrat	0.877	pack	0.938	so
0.972	call	0.857	Me	0.934	work
0.962	On	0.833	. . .	0.909	#voicesaveindia
0.941	left	0.804	summer	0.903	fox
0.923	💗	0.791	show	0.881	movi
0.904	kind	0.786	realli	0.872	chang
0.9	jesu	0.779	game	0.855	damn
0.889	state	0.773	time	0.853	pandem
0.879	that’	0.755	play	0.851	spnwithlov
0.876	know	0.749	enter	0.848	law
0.861	hillari	0.748	get	0.847	anyth
0.86	mani	0.748	#stevenunivers	0.844	he’
0.851	😺	0.744	need	0.84	again
0.85	school	0.737	when	0.828	right
0.845	also	0.733	👀	0.821	food
0.843	seem	0.731	befor	0.819	trump
0.842	legal	0.728	come	0.819	+
0.835	which	0.728	->	0.807	think
0.814	look	0.724	🔥	0.792	today
0.81	china	0.717	school	0.774	|
0.808	hospit	0.715	app	0.773	white
0.794	rather	0.712	best	0.772	youtub
0.787	viru	0.696	free	0.756	stay
0.774	these	0.685	coronaviru	0.753	&
0.771	down	0.681	reach	0.751	mean
0.762	’	0.679	awesom	0.749	protect
0.759	own	0.666	learn	0.748	gay
0.759	bill	0.663	y	0.741	kat
0.756	ye	0.657	reward	0.741	stori
0.743	clinton	0.65	join	0.736	everi
0.737	illeg	0.647	from	0.727	dog
0.737	around	0.646	$	0.725	and
0.732	sens			0.724	beauti

Table 10: Ideology svc-model coefficients for unigrams

A.3 Full results of community detection and socio-demographic prediction

The following are the complete study results for all eight topics. They include the interaction graph with its detected communities as well as a table presenting each communities' user count, weighted and unweighted annotated stance, graph community metrics and predicted socio-demographic distributions. All correlations and analyses in the paper were based on these results.

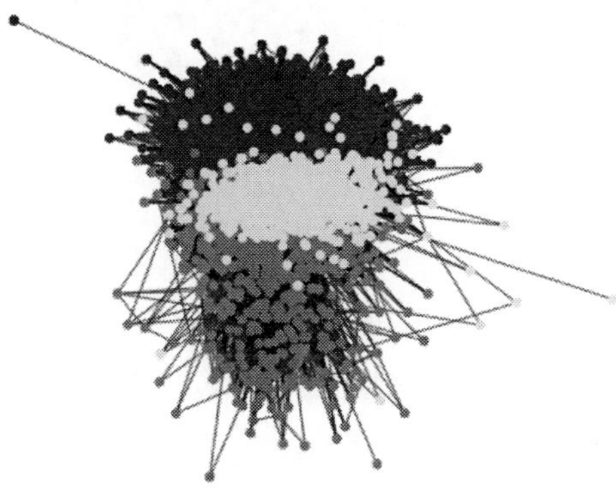

Cluster				Metrics			Sociodemographics		
	#Users	stance	weighted stance	d(c)	s(c)	e(c)	Gender	Age	Ideology
0	1776	⌀: -0.231 Std: 0.924 #Users: 36.0	⌀: -0.457 Std: 0.706	0.024	2.024	10.443	M: 0.641 F: 0.359	$\leq$ 30: 0.587 $\leq$ 45: 0.197 $>$ 45: 0.216	Con: 0.52 Mod: 0.006 Lib: 0.475
1	797	⌀: 1.185 Std: 0.584 #Users: 33.0	⌀: 1.05 Std: 0.693	0.027	0.687	15.764	M: 0.255 F: 0.745	$\leq$ 30: 0.606 $\leq$ 45: 0.212 $>$ 45: 0.182	Con: 0.251 Mod: 0.066 Lib: 0.683
2	1168	⌀: 0.199 Std: 1.051 #Users: 118.0	⌀: 0.635 Std: 0.947	0.047	1.273	21.452	M: 0.535 F: 0.465	$\leq$ 30: 0.644 $\leq$ 45: 0.226 $>$ 45: 0.13	Con: 0.443 Mod: 0.004 Lib: 0.553

Figure 5: Sampled stance (unweighted and weighted average), *separability* s(c), *density* d(c), *expansion* e(c) and predicted socio-demographics of the detected communities in the discussion around **abortion** on Reddit. The weighted stance is calculated based on the user's degree in the graph

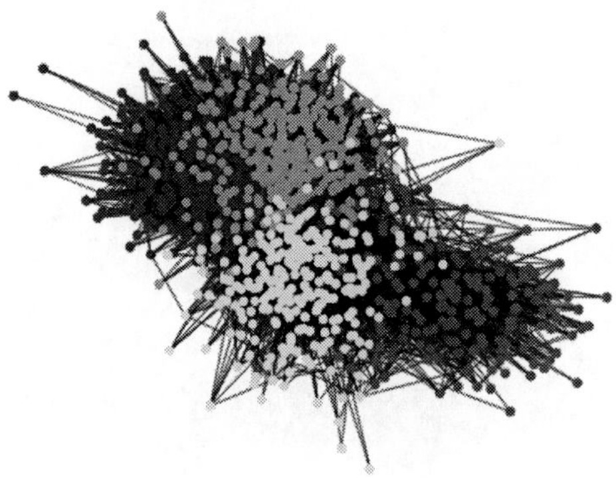

Cluster				Metrics			Sociodemographics		
	#Users	**stance**	**weighted stance**	**d(c)**	**s(c)**	**e(c)**	**Gender**	**Age**	**Ideology**
0	337	⌀: -0.007 Std: 1.042 #Users: 8.0	⌀: -0.372 Std: 0.896	0.059	0.764	12.896	M: 0.899 F: 0.101	$\leq$ 30: 0.291 $\leq$ 45: 0.237 $>$ 45: 0.472	Con: 0.656 Mod: 0.009 Lib: 0.335
1	178	⌀: 0.963 Std: 0.129 #Users: 4.0	⌀: 0.97 Std: 0.101	0.074	1.559	4.213	M: 0.933 F: 0.067	$\leq$ 30: 0.152 $\leq$ 45: 0.309 $>$ 45: 0.539	Con: 0.438 Mod: 0.011 Lib: 0.551
2	336	⌀: -0.047 Std: 0.751 #Users: 6.0	⌀: -0.281 Std: 0.455	0.068	0.829	13.688	M: 0.905 F: 0.095	$\leq$ 30: 0.321 $\leq$ 45: 0.196 $>$ 45: 0.482	Con: 0.634 Mod: 0.009 Lib: 0.357
3	262	⌀: 0.243 Std: 1.226 #Users: 15.0	⌀: 0.521 Std: 1.002	0.065	0.986	8.553	M: 0.927 F: 0.073	$\leq$ 30: 0.248 $\leq$ 45: 0.279 $>$ 45: 0.473	Con: 0.531 Mod: 0.031 Lib: 0.439

Figure 6: Sampled stance (unweighted and weighted average), *separability* s(c), *density* d(c), *expansion* e(c) and predicted socio-demographics of the detected communities in the discussion around **climate-change** on Reddit. The weighted stance is calculated based on the user's degree in the graph

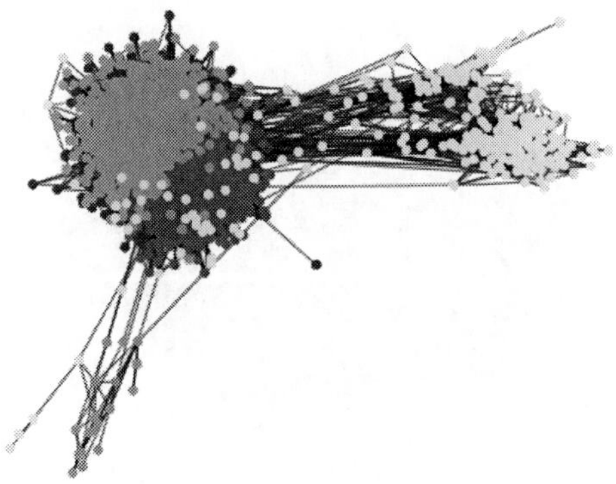

Cluster				Metrics			Sociodemographics		
	#Users	stance	weighted stance	d(c)	s(c)	e(c)	Gender	Age	Ideology
0	930	⌀: -1.0 Std: 0.4 #Users: 2.0	⌀: -0.761 Std: 0.321	0.018	0.421	20.289	M: 0.824 F: 0.176	$\leq$ 30: 0.487 $\leq$ 45: 0.298 > 45: 0.215	Con: 0.499 Mod: 0.013 Lib: 0.488
1	1176	⌀: -0.34 Std: 0.694 #Users: 16.0	⌀: -0.589 Std: 0.42	0.022	0.733	17.426	M: 0.798 F: 0.202	$\leq$ 30: 0.367 $\leq$ 45: 0.355 > 45: 0.277	Con: 0.493 Mod: 0.019 Lib: 0.488
2	1168	⌀: 0.113 Std: 1.012 #Users: 26.0	⌀: -0.604 Std: 0.796	0.023	0.757	17.997	M: 0.782 F: 0.218	$\leq$ 30: 0.447 $\leq$ 45: 0.347 > 45: 0.206	Con: 0.427 Mod: 0.011 Lib: 0.562
3	331	⌀: 0.728 Std: 0.9 #Users: 32.0	⌀: 0.538 Std: 0.944	0.035	3.78	1.511	M: 0.353 F: 0.647	$\leq$ 30: 0.344 $\leq$ 45: 0.369 > 45: 0.287	Con: 0.269 Mod: 0.012 Lib: 0.719

Figure 7: Sampled stance (unweighted and weighted average), *separability* s(c), *density* d(c), *expansion* e(c) and predicted socio-demographics of the detected communities in the discussion around **feminism** on Reddit. The weighted stance is calculated based on the user's degree in the graph

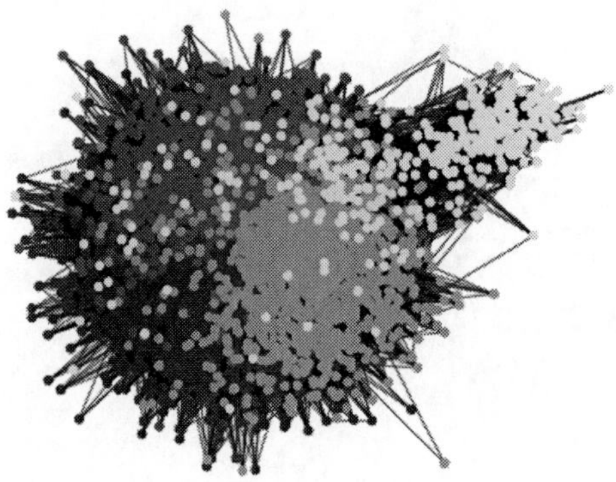

Cluster				Metrics			Sociodemographics		
	#Users	stance	weighted stance	d(c)	s(c)	e(c)	Gender	Age	Ideology
0	1705	⌀: 0.472 Std: 0.572 #Users: 9.0	⌀: 0.503 Std: 0.615	0.018	0.597	26.266	M: 0.941 F: 0.059	$\leq$ 30: 0.297 $\leq$ 45: 0.256 $>$ 45: 0.448	Con: 0.798 Mod: 0.003 Lib: 0.199
1	1574	⌀: 0.517 Std: 0.717 #Users: 12.0	⌀: 0.362 Std: 0.636	0.02	0.535	28.745	M: 0.95 F: 0.05	$\leq$ 30: 0.229 $\leq$ 45: 0.276 $>$ 45: 0.496	Con: 0.799 Mod: 0.004 Lib: 0.198
2	1509	⌀: 0.435 Std: 0.548 #Users: 8.0	⌀: 0.372 Std: 0.571	0.023	0.549	31.557	M: 0.966 F: 0.034	$\leq$ 30: 0.236 $\leq$ 45: 0.254 $>$ 45: 0.51	Con: 0.816 Mod: 0.004 Lib: 0.18
3	398	⌀: 0.333 Std: 0.333 #Users: 2.0	⌀: 0.055 Std: 0.183	0.043	0.867	9.872	M: 0.925 F: 0.075	$\leq$ 30: 0.219 $\leq$ 45: 0.226 $>$ 45: 0.555	Con: 0.771 Mod: 0.01 Lib: 0.219

Figure 8: Sampled stance (unweighted and weighted average), *separability* s(c), *density* d(c), *expansion* e(c) and predicted socio-demographics of the detected communities in the discussion around **guncontrol** on Reddit. The weighted stance is calculated based on the user's degree in the graph

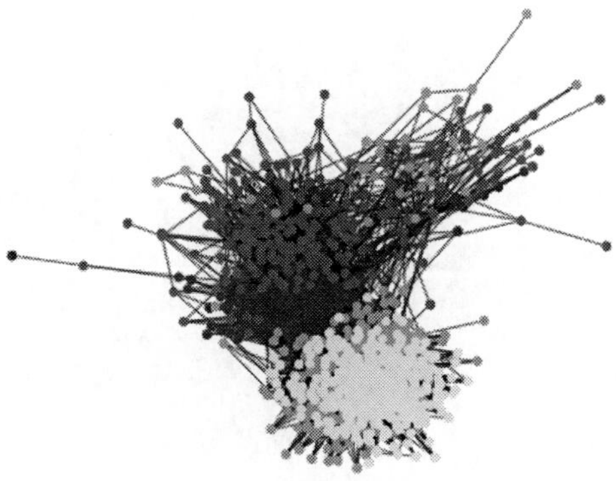

Cluster				Metrics			Sociodemographics		
	#Users	**stance**	**weighted stance**	**d(c)**	**s(c)**	**e(c)**	**Gender**	**Age**	**Ideology**
0	407	⌀: 0.333 Std: 1.247 #Users: 3.0	⌀: 0.312 Std: 1.21	0.045	2.405	3.828	M: 0.688 F: 0.312	$\leq$ 30: 0.57 $\leq$ 45: 0.204 $>$ 45: 0.226	Con: 0.386 Mod: 0.01 Lib: 0.604
1	248	⌀: 0.843 Std: 1.083 #Users: 23.0	⌀: 1.067 Std: 0.696	0.027	1.354	2.472	M: 0.573 F: 0.427	$\leq$ 30: 0.496 $\leq$ 45: 0.19 $>$ 45: 0.315	Con: 0.298 Mod: 0.056 Lib: 0.645
2	338	⌀: 1.667 Std: 0.471 #Users: 3.0	⌀: 1.667 Std: 0.471	0.051	0.737	11.577	M: 0.55 F: 0.45	$\leq$ 30: 0.503 $\leq$ 45: 0.157 $>$ 45: 0.34	Con: 0.337 Mod: 0.041 Lib: 0.621
3	471	⌀: -1.167 Std: 0.0 #Users: 1.0	⌀: -1.167 Std: 0.0	0.063	1.734	8.548	M: 0.724 F: 0.276	$\leq$ 30: 0.473 $\leq$ 45: 0.187 $>$ 45: 0.34	Con: 0.461 Mod: 0.013 Lib: 0.527

Figure 9: Sampled stance (unweighted and weighted average), *separability* s(c), *density* d(c), *expansion* e(c) and predicted socio-demographics of the detected communities in the discussion around **veganism-animalrights** on Reddit. The weighted stance is calculated based on the user's degree in the graph

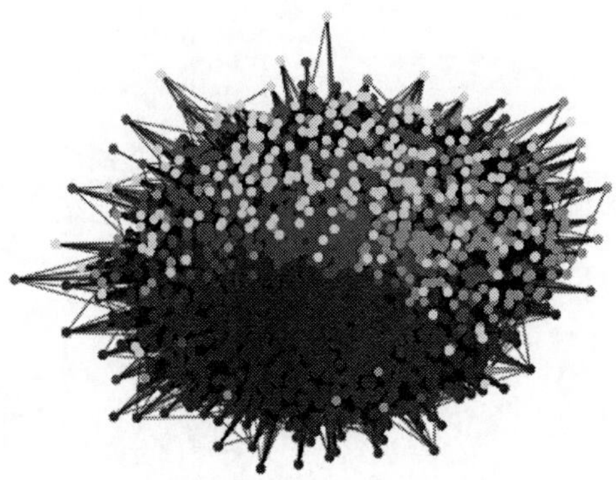

Cluster				Metrics			Sociodemographics		
	#Users	**stance**	**weighted stance**	**d(c)**	**s(c)**	**e(c)**	**Gender**	**Age**	**Ideology**
0	1460	∅: -0.73 Std: 0.754 #Users: 27.0	∅: -0.829 Std: 0.555	0.049	1.343	26.633	M: 0.942 F: 0.058	$\leq$ 30: 0.14 $\leq$ 45: 0.338 $>$ 45: 0.521	Con: 0.701 Mod: 0.023 Lib: 0.276
1	903	∅: -0.53 Std: 1.029 #Users: 35.0	∅: -0.561 Std: 1.047	0.049	0.499	44.104	M: 0.947 F: 0.053	$\leq$ 30: 0.175 $\leq$ 45: 0.368 $>$ 45: 0.457	Con: 0.714 Mod: 0.014 Lib: 0.271
2	259	∅: 0.0 Std: 0.0 #Users: 0.0	∅: 0.0 Std: 0.0	0.046	0.17	35.062	M: 0.919 F: 0.081	$\leq$ 30: 0.154 $\leq$ 45: 0.421 $>$ 45: 0.425	Con: 0.73 Mod: 0.012 Lib: 0.259
3	229	∅: -0.853 Std: 0.547 #Users: 5.0	∅: -0.977 Std: 0.212	0.028	0.102	30.825	M: 0.891 F: 0.109	$\leq$ 30: 0.288 $\leq$ 45: 0.319 $>$ 45: 0.393	Con: 0.664 Mod: 0.017 Lib: 0.319

Figure 10: Sampled stance (unweighted and weighted average), *separability* s(c), *density* d(c), *expansion* e(c) and predicted socio-demographics of the detected communities in the discussion around **brexit** on Reddit. The weighted stance is calculated based on the user's degree in the graph

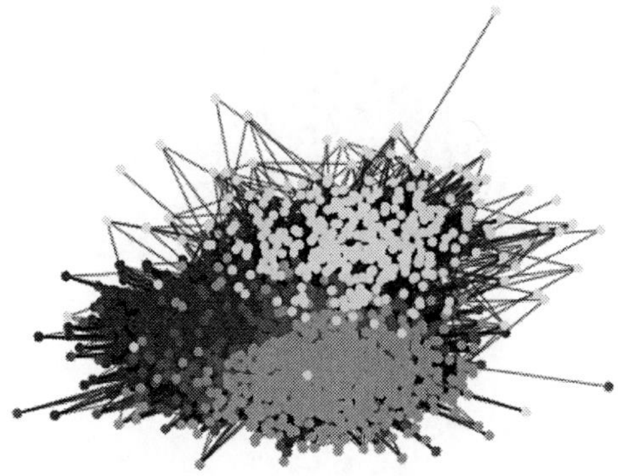

Cluster				Metrics			Sociodemographics		
	#Users	stance	weighted stance	d(c)	s(c)	e(c)	Gender	Age	Ideology
0	845	⌀: 0.0 Std: 0.816 #Users: 3.0	⌀: 0.176 Std: 0.472	0.047	0.813	24.555	M: 0.931 F: 0.069	$\leq$ 30: 0.346 $\leq$ 45: 0.452 > 45: 0.202	Con: 0.685 Mod: 0.004 Lib: 0.311
1	615	⌀: -0.295 Std: 1.212 #Users: 3.0	⌀: -1.063 Std: 1.263	0.039	0.345	35.093	M: 0.914 F: 0.086	$\leq$ 30: 0.315 $\leq$ 45: 0.506 > 45: 0.179	Con: 0.685 Mod: 0.002 Lib: 0.314
2	898	⌀: 0.14 Std: 0.648 #Users: 37.0	⌀: 0.115 Std: 0.701	0.039	0.684	25.758	M: 0.93 F: 0.07	$\leq$ 30: 0.331 $\leq$ 45: 0.453 > 45: 0.216	Con: 0.688 Mod: 0.004 Lib: 0.307
3	396	⌀: -0.688 Std: 0.872 #Users: 18.0	⌀: -0.533 Std: 0.858	0.034	0.903	7.328	M: 0.917 F: 0.083	$\leq$ 30: 0.338 $\leq$ 45: 0.359 > 45: 0.303	Con: 0.614 Mod: 0.008 Lib: 0.379

Figure 11: Sampled stance (unweighted and weighted average), *separability* s(c), *density* d(c), *expansion* e(c) and predicted socio-demographics of the detected communities in the discussion around **capitalism** on Reddit. The weighted stance is calculated based on the user's degree in the graph

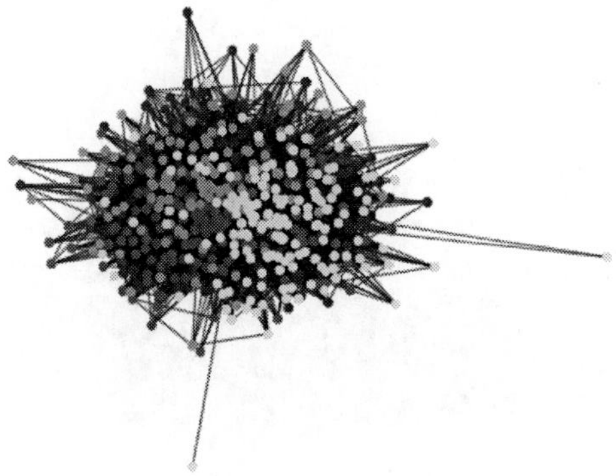

	Cluster			Metrics			Sociodemographics		
	#Users	**stance**	**weighted stance**	**d(c)**	**s(c)**	**e(c)**	**Gender**	**Age**	**Ideology**
0	105	⌀: 1.5 Std: 0.5 #Users: 2.0	⌀: 1.211 Std: 0.408	0.107	0.28	19.819	M: 0.971 F: 0.029	$\leq$ 30: 0.276 $\leq$ 45: 0.276 $>$ 45: 0.448	Con: 0.467 Mod: 0.067 Lib: 0.467
1	147	⌀: 0.533 Std: 0.972 #Users: 10.0	⌀: 0.699 Std: 0.641	0.117	0.427	19.98	M: 0.952 F: 0.048	$\leq$ 30: 0.34 $\leq$ 45: 0.299 $>$ 45: 0.361	Con: 0.49 Mod: 0.041 Lib: 0.469
2	123	⌀: 0.7 Std: 0.4 #Users: 5.0	⌀: 0.76 Std: 0.425	0.109	0.316	21.146	M: 0.927 F: 0.073	$\leq$ 30: 0.382 $\leq$ 45: 0.333 $>$ 45: 0.285	Con: 0.341 Mod: 0.057 Lib: 0.602
3	158	⌀: 1.016 Std: 0.778 #Users: 22.0	⌀: 1.146 Std: 0.443	0.11	0.446	19.373	M: 0.956 F: 0.044	$\leq$ 30: 0.31 $\leq$ 45: 0.285 $>$ 45: 0.405	Con: 0.456 Mod: 0.044 Lib: 0.5

Figure 12: Sampled stance (unweighted and weighted average), *separability* s(c), *density* d(c), *expansion* e(c) and predicted socio-demographics of the detected communities in the discussion around **nuclear-energy** on Reddit. The weighted stance is calculated based on the user's degree in the graph

Author Index

Association for Computational Linguistics
209 N. Eighth Street
Stroudsburg, Pennsylvania 18360

ISBN 978-1-7138-5640-5

CURRAN ASSOCIATES INC.
proceedings
.com